Barnes & Noble Critical Studies

General Editor: Anne Smith

The Art of Alexander Pope

THE ART OF
ALEXANDER POPE

edited by

Howard Erskine-Hill
and Anne Smith

BOOKS
10 East 53d St., New York 10022
(a division of Harper & Row Publishers, Inc.)

Barnes & Noble Books
Harper & Row, Publishers, Inc.
10 East 53rd Street
New York

ISBN 0–06–492029–4

To
MAYNARD MACK
—master of the poet, and the song

First published in the U.S.A. 1979
© 1979 by Vision Press, London

Printed and bound in Great Britain
MCMLXXIX

Contents

Introduction

by HOWARD ERSKINE-HILL

It is a mark of Pope's vitality in the minds of modern readers that he provokes such different responses. A hostile early reaction is common; more considered views are divided between those who, not denying him greatness, find stronger literary interests elsewhere, and those whose devotion to Pope increases as their knowledge of his poetic character extends.[1] This situation, in which all find Pope a formidable presence, can be explained in several ways. Pope's writings and their intricate relation with his time challenge by their difference from what our implicit assumptions tell us poetry should be. This challenge may be met by that generous effort of historical imagination and exploration which is the basis of serious criticism. The divided and troubled response to Pope in our time betokens a conflict between the Romantic movement, of which even in the late twentieth century we are the unsuspecting heirs, and the Modernism of the earlier twentieth century. No great literature is the sole possession of the academic world, and the more we discount academic views the more we are made to feel the demand that art should be warm, spontaneous, personal, and morally and spiritually uplifting. That is the legacy of Romanticism, so potent that it seems almost "natural"; we dismiss it at our peril. A superficial glance at the writing of Pope, on the other hand, discovers it to be public, largely satiric, and self-consciously formal. The Modernism of Pound and Eliot (to look no further) affords us no brief against such qualities—indeed in many ways it helps us to draw closer. The reader of Pound's Usury Cantos can find there a bridge to Pope's poetry against corruption, while *Homage to Sextus Propertius* is no bad basis for understanding the meaning of "imitation" in Pope's *Imitations of Horace*. The fragmented epic structure of *The Waste Land* is a good vantage point from which to view the formal

6

innovations of *The Dunciad*, Pope's most difficult and experimental poem.

Insight into earlier literature can be gained this way, and need not mislead providing we test it through proper historical verification. Indeed it is not only Modernism that helps us appreciate Pope. Even the Romantic assumptions to which he seems at first so inimical help us to see in him qualities not always apparent on the shock of first encounter. Without putting public concerns behind him Pope developed a most subtly inflected personal voice:

> Late as it is, I put myself to school,
> And feel some comfort, not to be a fool.
> Weak tho' I am of limb, and short of sight,
> Far from a Lynx, and not a Giant quite,
> I'll do what MEAD and CHESELDEN advise,
> To keep these limbs, and to preserve these eyes.
> Not to go back, is somewhat to advance,
> And men must walk at least before they dance.
> (*Imitations of Horace*, Ep. I. i., 47–54)

In his essay in the present volume, Frank Stack says of these lines that they are "pure Horace, touched at every point by Pope": where "Horace turns to satirize others, Pope speaks only of himself." There is delicate self-mockery and pathos in the placing of the words (". . . some comfort" . . . ". . . not a Giant quite") and in the last couplet we are shown a personal humility in the proud satirist. These lines modify their Horation original so as to allude to Pope's personal situation. Pope presents himself in many of his poems but, as Maynard Mack has shown in a seminal essay,[2] when he does so he plays many roles. Autobiographical content is shaped to a rhetorical end. In this way Pope can be personal and public at the same time. Several essays in this book discuss the presented self in the writings of Pope and his age. Ian MacKillop in "The Satirist in His Own Person" brings forward the relevant French background to Pope's practice, in showing how "a creative problem close to Pope's" was handled by Molière and Boileau. Frank Stack in "Pope's *Epistle to Bolingbroke* and *Epistle I. i*" considers Pope's self-presentation in relation to the example of Horace. They bring out the range and individuality of Pope's self-creation. And it is not only here that Pope creates himself by playing a part. He does so in his letters, yet the relation of letters with poems is a little-explored aspect of Pope's work. In his essay "Pope Plays the Rake . . ." James A. Winn makes a fascinating foray into this area, suggesting the subtle self-transformations involved in the writing of *Eloisa to Abelard*, the extraordinary Ovidian love-poem which almost every generation of Pope's readers has admired, except perhaps our own. A further aspect is suggested by Simon Varey in "Rhetoric and *An Essay on Man*". Pope does not present himself directly within the *Essay*, yet his rhetorical strategies: questionings, displays, deductions, affirmations, establish a relation of poet to reader, poet to mankind, which was offered as a retrospective and prospective justification of Pope's poetic career. Here the satiric poet brings forward his general principles, the most positive orientations which he trusts his poetic rhetoric may display in their most communal and available aspect. It is clear that the word "public", though applied to Pope with perfect truthfulness, must be qualified in the light of familiarity with his poetry. Public and personal support one another so well that they shade into one another; the voice of the virtues is there, certainly, but also the images of of the man.

The term "satiric" demands similar qualification. It is always confusing. Not in itself a literary form, satire is an attitude, a stance, a procedure. It assails by wit, ridicule, exposure and denunciation. On this definition, not even the forms most associated with satire, in the hands of authors most known for satire, are consistently satiric. Certainly Pope's satiric works are not. They can also speak in the vein of epic and the vein of comedy, with a voice of praise, devotion or affection, they are sensitive to the beautiful, fragile and ephemeral, they know moods of sadness and fear as well as of ardour and hope. It is because Pope's satire is just a part, albeit a major part, of this synthesis that it is so effective.

> In vain to Deserts thy Retreat is made;
> The Muse attends thee to the silent Shade:
> 'Tis hers, the brave Man's latest Steps to trace,
> Re-judge his Acts, and dignify Disgrace.
> When Int'rest calls off all her sneaking Train,
> And all th'obliged desert, and all the Vain;
> She waits, or to the Scaffold, or the Cell,
> When the last ling'ring Friend has bid farewel.

Ev'n now she shades thy Evening Walk with Bays,
(No Hireling she, no Prostitute to Praise)
Ev'n now, observant of the parting Ray,
Eyes the calm Sun-set of thy various Day . . .
(*Epistle to Robert Earl of Oxford*, 27–38)

Thus Pope (speaking of his friend the poet Parnell) can describe, and practise, his idea of the role of poetry in society. Robin Grove, in his exploration of *The Rape of the Lock*, "Uniting Airy Substance", may well conjure with the terms "immortality poem" and "love-poem" and conclude that in this poem, "so much revised and altered, we see Pope come to realize that amongst the things we lastingly value is mutability itself". The brilliancy of Pope's mock-epic satire, with its breathtaking diminutions and magnifications, can indeed lead to this view. Further, complexity of this kind reminds us that some of Pope's most celebrated poems are hardly satiric at all. The list is considerable, and includes the precocious *Pastorals* with their exquisite harmony of scene and sound; *Windsor Forest*, whose spatial and temporal vision of "Golden Days" is discussed here by Pat Rogers; the little-known Epistle *To Addison*;[3] the *Elegy on the Death of An Unfortunate Lady*; *Eloisa to Abelard*; *The First Ode of the Fourth Book of Horace*—and the *Iliad* translation. *That* ambitious and exacting poetic enterprise, which won Pope so much eighteenth-century fame, should, now the Twickenham Edition has brought it out, be increasingly read and discussed. Felicity Rosslyn, in "Pope on the Subject of Old Age", discusses his treatment of Homer's Nestor and Priam. Speaking of the scene in *Iliad* XXIV when Priam denounces his followers after the death of Hector, she argues that the picture of Priam deranged and unjust with grief touched a comparable depth of feeling in Pope to that of Homer's image of Priam desecrated by dogs; Pope compels the reader "to feel in all its intransigence '*the Force of Adversity on an unhappy old Man*' ". Spence recounted how Pope later read this passage of Homer, "and was interrupted by his tears". These are things that should be remembered when we speak summarily of "Pope the satirist".

The third quality that strikes the reader who opens Pope for the first time is his self-conscious formality. Trouble over the alleged "artificial regularity of the heroic couplet" is inevitable at first but soon resolved as the ear learns to catch Pope's expressive variations upon an expected norm. Close reading soon reveals his expressive counterpoint:

> *Gay* pats my shoulder, and you vanish quite;
> Streets, chairs, and coxcombs rush upon my sight;
> Vext to be still in town, I knit my brow,
> Look sow'r, and hum a tune—as you may now.
>> (*Epistle to Miss Blount, on her leaving the Town*, 47–50)

> Lo! at the Wheels of her Triumphal Car,
> Old *England*'s Genius, rough with many a Scar,
> Dragg'd in the Dust!
>> (*Epilogue to the Satires, Dialogue I*, 150–52)

> Approach: But aweful! Lo th' *Ægerian* Grott,
> Where, nobly-pensive, ST. JOHN sate and thought;
> Where British Sighs from dying WYNDHAM stole,
> And the bright Flame was shot thro' MARCHMONT's Soul.
> Let such, such only, tread this sacred Floor,
> Who dare to love their Country, and be poor.
>> (*Verses on a Grotto by the River at Twickenham*, 9–14)

Rejection of the vulgar error that Pope's couplets are monotonous sometimes brings another error in its train: that Pope lavishes such care on individual couplets that he neglects the need for a larger coherence. This is often said, but rarely shown. In the first place it is worth considering his paragraphs. Let anyone who thinks Pope's poems are no more than a loose collection of brilliant couplets read, for example, *An Essay on Man*, II. 1–18, or *To Bathurst*, 299–314, or Dialogue I of the Epilogue to the Satires, 131–70. If any doubts his capacity to shape narrative, let him look at *The Rape of the Lock*, III, 19–104 (the game of Ombre), or *To Bathurst*, 339–402 (the story of Sir Balaam). More important, and more controversial, is the question of the expressive unity of Pope's major poems as his repeated additions and revisions have left them to us. Here there is certainly room for new work, though the fact of Pope's self-conscious formality does not mean that it is formalist criticism that has necessarily most to offer. Robin Grove, without much dwelling on *The Rape of the Lock* as mock-epic, shows the imaginative maturation of the poem through revisions extending from 1711 to 1736. That is one thing we can mean by unity. Pat Rogers, starting from the formalist description of *Windsor Forest* as a "loco-descriptive poem", displays its imaginative procedure and coherence by attending to its interplay of spatial and temporal range. What gives *To Arbuthnot* its power and coherence is the way that, from the exasperated familiarity of its opening, it raises the emotions to the very pitch of the hatred of evil, in the Sporus portrait, and then lays them to rest in domestic sentiment at the end. This satiric epistle has a tragic as well as a laughing aspect, and follows the arc of Aristotelian catharsis. Again, we know that Pope was much concerned with the harmonies and symmetries of the Palladian architecture of his time. Architectural images, it seems, afforded him not only metaphors for creative civilization (as at the end of *To Burlington*) but ways of thinking about the structure of certain of his poems. In my essay, "Heirs of Vitruvius" I suggest that Pope drew on architectural pattern to achieve formal and expressive structure in his *Epistles to Several Persons*, in the individual epistles, and in the group of four in which he seems to have wanted to leave them at the end of his life.

Paradoxically, it is when we turn to the extraordinary *Dunciad* of 1743, so elusive of formal definition, that a formalist approach is most fruitful. Insufficient critical attention has been paid to the operation of the poem as a whole. The category of mock-epic has (it is true) been applied to it, and has brought into focus the creative interanimation of Pope's poem with the *Aeneid* and *Paradise Lost*, but when we think of *The Dunciad* as a mock-epic of which *creation* itself is the epic (and Virgil and Milton but interpreters of that creation) we may feel some limitation in the approach. This is suggested by Philip Brockbank's essay, "The Book of Genesis and the Genesis of Books: The Creation of Pope's *Dunciad*". By stressing all the ways in which the poem evokes and enacts creativity, Brockbank shows it to be much more than a poem about poetry. This essay, remarkable for its verve, freshness and intimacy with the allusive range of Pope's text, speaks of the poem as "phantasmagoric territory", as "a flux", but still "composed within the large metaphor which makes the creation of fiction analogous to the creation of the natural world". These terms are flexible enough to accommodate the poetic varieties of the work and yet indicate its imaginative coherence. I would only add that, as with that other great eighteenth-century work of formal innovation, Swift's *Tale of a*

Tub, Pope does not wish us to lose our awareness of forms in the flux of his poem. That would be for the reader to "roll in one vortex" only. The phantasmagoria of *The Dunciad* is, on the contrary, astonishingly aware of different forms, different ways of seeing, different worlds. Dream-poem, vision, epic, mock-epic, processional panegyric, travesty, elegy, essay, annotation, metamorphosis—*The Dunciad* touches all these, each of which can seem momentarily as distinct as an individual couplet within the larger structures of paragraph and poem. The unique form of *The Dunciad* is its precariously creative synthesis of forms. It is a work of such originality that criticism has only begun to grasp it.

Clive Probyn's essay "Pope's Bestiary", offers an approach not to a particular work but to Pope's poetry as a whole. A strength of twentieth-century criticism has been its capacity to explore poetic imagery. Probyn aptly directs this skill towards an aspect of Pope's imagery which links him with the later seventeenth century and its reiterated comparisons of man with animal, the age which produced Hobbes's *Leviathan*, Rochester's *Satire Against Reason and Mankind* and Dryden's *Hind and the Panther*. This essay also demonstrates the connection between Pope's animal imagery generally and his display of the created order in *An Essay on Man*. Thus:

> The spider's touch, how exquisitely fine!
> Feels at each thread, and lives along the line:
> (*Essay on Man*, I. 217–18)

is normative to the deviation of:

> Ye tinsel Insects! whom a Court maintains ...
> Spin all your Cobwebs o'er the Eye of Day!
> The Muse's wing shall brush you all away:
> (Epilogue to the Satires, Dialogue II, 220–23)

A final appreciation of Pope could well start with *An Essay on Man* which proves such a stumbling block to the modern reader. Persistent misunderstanding regularly tears four words, "Whatever Is, Is RIGHT" from their poetic contexts in Epistles I and IV. A reading of the whole poem does not sustain the facile charge of complacency and bland optimism. It is rather a poem of submission and affirmation: critical enough of human pretension and the human world, *An Essay* uses descriptive eloquence to generate, in the very face of these, an affirmative ardour towards the providence of God. This ardour, conveyed in poetry of astonishing density, colour and life, is then endorsed in concise and abstract sentences, so that the experience of the reader and the art of the poem is in one way a consort of particular with general, a dialogue between sensuous and abstract.

An Essay on Man shows Pope extending his range, seeking to counter-balance salient developments in his own work (the 1729 *Dunciad* was recently published) and using art to dramatise the tension created by opposing energies and perceptions in man;

> With too much knowledge for the Sceptic side,
> With too much weakness for the Stoic's pride,
> He hangs between; in doubt to act, or rest,
> In doubt to deem himself a God, or Beast . . .
>
> (II. 5–8)

Characterised by this many-eyed responsiveness, what Pope offers us is a poetry of emotion, judgement and wisdom. Why should we hesitate to go to poetry for what it may tell us about living in the world? We may read *An Essay on Criticism*, as David Morris admirably demonstrates in this book in an article which will long remain important, because the poem offers a real contribution to critical thought. We may read Pope's social poetry because it offers the first artistic critique in our literature of the interpenetration of financial corruption, government, and an ideal of civilization. We may read him because he offers a poetry of political opposition: not our first (we remember Marvell in the Restoration and, more cautious, Dryden after 1688) but the first of real eloquence, and one that penetrated the drives of political tendency which, for better or worse, made the Walpole régime crucial in the history of Britain.[5] But when we find these things in Pope, we find them in a canon of poems which also knows what Homeric heroism is, and Christian ethics, and domestic affection, and sadness, and self-doubt, and independence, and determination and attack. We find all these interrelated, not offered as an intellectual system, but, what poetry can do better, as an enactment of living in the world without ignorance and with feeling.

13

INTRODUCTION

EDITORS' NOTE: *THE ART OF ALEXANDER POPE* was originally planned *by Anne Smith, and the varied responsibilities of editing a collection such as this were at first borne by her. At a later stage Howard Erskine-Hill joined her as co-editor, and the remaining work on the volume has been done in full collaboration.*

H.E-H.
A.S.

NOTES

1 For a fuller introductory appreciation of Pope than space permits here, see G. S. Rousseau, "On Reading Pope" in Peter Dixon, ed. *Alexander Pope*, in the Writers and their Background Series (London, 1972). For a recent statement of the hostile view, see James Reeves, *The Reputation and Writings of Alexander Pope* (London, 1976).

2 Maynard Mack, "The Muse of Satire" in R. C. Boys, ed. *Studies in the Literature of the Augustan Age* (Ann Arbor, Michigan, 1952) and in Ronald Paulson, ed. *Satire: Modern Essays in Criticism* (New Jersey, 1971).

3 See Howard Erskine-Hill, "The Medal Against Time", *Journal of the Warburg and Courtauld Institutes*, vol. xxvii (1965).

4 For a synthesis of recent study on *The Dunciad*, with some new suggestions, see Howard Erskine-Hill, *Pope: The Dunciad* (London, 1972).

5 This book does not, for the most part, attempt to read Pope in his full historical context. Studies which do so are: Maynard Mack, *The Garden and the City: Retirement and Politics in the Later Poetry of Pope, 1731–43* (Toronto and London, 1969); Howard Erskine-Hill, *The Social Milieu of Alexander Pope* (New Haven and London, 1975); and Bertrand A. Goldgar, *Walpole and the Wits: The Relation of Politics to Literature, 1722–42* (Lincoln and London, 1976). Richly interesting for the historical understanding of Pope is J. P. Kenyon, *Revolution Principles: The Politics of Party 1689–1720* (Cambridge, 1977).

14

1

Civilized Reading:
The Act of Judgment in
An Essay on Criticism

by DAVID B. MORRIS

> Men must be *taught* as if you taught them *not*;
> And Things *unknown* propos'd as Things *forgot*.[1]

Alexander Pope's earliest didactic poem, *An Essay on Criticism*
(1711), has proved so successful in representing the unknown as
the forgotten that its claims to originality and importance are today automatically dismissed. One standard history of criticism
summarizes the poem with routine nonchalance: "There are
repetitions and inconsistencies, some conventional pronouncements along with injunctions of lasting value; but nowhere (and
this should be emphasized) are the principles organized into a
coherent whole, and no cut-and-dried theory therefore emerges."[2]
Readers attentive to Pope's many direct borrowings and indirect
allusions find it easy to regard the *Essay* as an urbane collection
of platitudes: "What oft was *Thought*" (298). Indeed, the poem's
ostensible subject evokes so little serious attention that it is regarded as a screen for loftier ambitions. "Pope's object in the
Essay on Criticism," we are told, "is not to say something original
about criticism, but to announce himself as a poet."[3] Almost no
one believes that the twenty-three year old prodigy capable of
composing such a learned and skillful poem could have thought
seriously or cared deeply about the nature of literary criticism.
Particularly because modern studies have focussed on its treatment of wit, the *Essay* is commonly discussed as a poem about
poetry with an unfortunately misleading title.[4] I wish to propose
a very different view: that *An Essay on Criticism* is an original
and significant document in the history of critical theory.

1 Introduction: The Historical Context

Some of Pope's distinguished contemporaries would seem to support the claim of originality and significance. Addison lauded the poem as a "Master-piece" (*Spectator* 253). Joseph Warton, adept in the labyrinth of ancient and modern critical tradition, ranked the youthful poet among "the first of critics".[5] Samuel Johnson grew even warmer in his praise, calling the poem one of Pope's "greatest" works. If Pope had written nothing else, he claimed, *An Essay on Criticism* "would have placed him among the first criticks and the first poets".[6] When we recall Johnson's stature as a critic and his contempt for versified platitudes, we might begin to suspect that Pope offered his contemporaries more than a slick cento of traditional lore. Both Johnson and Warton elevate Pope, as a critic, to the level of Horace, of Longinus, and of Aristotle. Their harsh treatment of other poems by Pope suggests that they had no reason to exaggerate the merits of an early work which one representative modern scholar dismisses simply as "a mosaic of scraps".[7] Clearly they found something in the poem of great value. What they found, I believe, is a stimulating and original (if submerged) theory of literary criticism.

The theory takes some finding—for it is one of the ironies of Pope's discourse on method to appear casually unmethodical, as if directed mainly by a loose association of ideas. "The Observations follow one another," writes Addison, "like those in *Horace's Art of Poetry*, without that Methodical Regularity which would have been requisite in a Prose Author" (*Spectator* 253). The appearance of irregularity, however, is not equivalent with actual lack of order, and we should recall (as a caution against hasty judgment) Pope's assertion that he had "digested all the matter in prose" before composing his poem.[8] Prosaic method may simply be disguised, for the purpose of instructing readers "as if you taught them not". Then, too, the unmethodical form alludes (as Addison noted) to Horace's prestigious *Ars Poetica*, and the allusion to Horace serves a useful purpose. It transfers to criticism, which many besides Swift viewed as a dwarfish parody of its ancient stature, the dignity and authority of a form previously employed for the discussion of poetry. And it also suggests Pope's intention to establish English criticism, as Horace had established Roman poetry and drama, on the foundations of an authentic art.

16

The inherent difficulty of this labor may help explain why Pope considered his *Essay* a work which "not one gentleman in three score even of a liberal education can understand".[9] They would not understand the poem because it proposed a theory of criticism unprecedented in their experience.

The originality of Pope's *Essay* grows apparent when we compare the poem to alternative theories of criticism current at the turn of the century, which Pope himself surveys. Essentially, the poem reveals his effort to create a middle way between two critical extremes prominent in his early years. These extremes, simplified, can be described as Authority and Taste. Authority in criticism, for Pope, involved an attitude of reverent adherence to a codified set of Rules derived from Renaissance interpretations of Aristotle and of Horace, which had received incrusted accumulations of doctrine from posterity, issuing in such petrified constructions as Corneille's treatment of the three dramatic Unities. With patriotic gallantry, Pope associated the principle of Authority in criticism with the political tyranny of absolutist France (711–14). While France erred at the extreme of slavish Authority, England failed by indulging the opposite extreme of anarchic Taste. Taste as a principle of criticism licensed more than the passing fashions in wit, such as the modish indecency and scepticism cultivated under Charles II and William (534–53). It also encouraged, as J. E. Spingarn has shown, the pleasanter critical dalliance with secluded "beauties" of poetry, invoked in a vague jargon of *"je-ne-sais-quoi"* or ecstatic cries, permitting the mystery of individual responsiveness to free critics from accountability to any principle beyond the self-illuminated ego.[10] The resulting criticism was a form of boneless cant which Pope branded "the perpetual Rapture of such Commentators, who are always giving us Exclamations instead of Criticisms" (Note to *Iliad* XV, 890). Taste licenses a total freedom from reasons; Authority shackles criticism to a set of iron Rules. Pope, of course, does not take the foolish position that all insights of taste are vacuous or all rules false. He objects instead to exalting either Authority or Taste as exclusive *principles* of criticism. It is only when wrongly hardened into rigid controlling principles that Taste degenerates into arid rapture and Authority creates the cookbook mechanisms which Pope parodies in "A Receit to make an Epick Poem" (*Guardian* 78). Although readers sometimes claim his accommodation with the Rules is equivocal or confused, Pope actually adheres to a clear distinction between practice and principle. In practice, critics can learn much by analyzing the insights of Taste and edicts of Authority. But, when adopted as exclusive principles of criticism, Authority and Taste become reductive, rigid, unwieldy simplifications, which is exactly how Pope depicts them. Between these cumbersome historical extremes, he sketches the outlines of his moderate and flexible alternative: the criticism of judgment.

The criticism of judgment, as Pope develops it in his *Essay*, provides both the theoretical foundations and the practical principles for a cohesive, original, and important form of literary criticism. One might complain, of course, that references to the term "judgment" are commonplace in critical discourse, especially as the word "criticism" derives from a Greek root (*krinein*) meaning "to judge". Certainly Dryden (to name Pope's most distinguished English predecessor in criticism) liberally sprinkles his prefaces and essays with mentions of judgment, which embrace at least three distinct but overlapping senses. In Dryden's usage, the main technical senses of "judgment" appropriate to neoclassical criticism are: (1) the mental faculty which discerns differences, controls the operations of wit, and comprehends the elements of poetic design; (2) discretion, reasonableness, good sense; and (3) the faculty which distinguishes excellence in literary works and, hence, an opinion of the quality of any work.[11] It is clear that Pope understands and exploits the traditional association of "judgment" with criticism. Thus he carefully guards his vocabulary, building a coherent diction which surrounds criticism with an idiom of judging not present in other poems. *An Essay on Criticism*, for example, employs the word "judgment" thirteen times, and "reason" only four. By contrast, *An Essay on Man* uses "reason" forty-four times, and "judgment" none.[12] Yet the traditional association of criticism and "judgment" does not mean that Pope uses the word in a traditional manner. Indeed, he often invests familiar words (like "dullness" in *The Dunciad*) with original significance, which must be construed by the reader through an encounter with specific contexts. In reading *An Essay on Criticism*, we should understand that Pope's references to "judgment" (and to its related forms) invoke a familiar, quasi-technical term. We should also understand, however, that

18

judgment had never defined a coherent *theory* of criticism. It is this central, defining position which judgement occupies in Pope's *Essay*. In effect, he captures a term with traditional, technical associations with criticism and transforms it into the sign of an original and coherent critical theory, an alternative to the personal mysticism of Taste and to the fiats of Authority.

2 Theoretical Foundations: The Search for Universals

Pope's new theory of criticism ran into immediate difficulties. Before he could develop its practical principles, he faced the prior task of explaining how valid judgement is possible. The question is not frivolous but fundamental. The practical criticism of judgment demands a theory capable of explaining its sources of validity. Otherwise, differing judgments about a single work (like differing tastes or conflicting rules) are simply indisputable. Thus within the first ten lines Pope confronts the fundamental dilemma which might overturn his whole system:

> 'Tis with our *Judgments* as our *Watches*, none
> Go just *alike*, yet each believes his own.
>
> (9–10)

A crucial human truth—the inconsistency and variance of our understandings—might suggest that judgment is completely relative and impossible to verify. A second truth, applying specifically to critics, compounds the problem of validity:

> *Authors* are partial to their *Wit*, 'tis true,
> But are not *Criticks* to their *Judgment* too?
>
> (17–18)

The benign egotism which inclines all mankind to trust their own judgments is especially well developed among critics, for whom the exercise of judgment is a characteristic function. These inherent flaws or weaknesses of judgment would seem enough to stop Pope cold, suggesting the need for a more reliable standard. In fact, the case *against* judgment could hardly be stronger. It is the strength of Pope's fundamental doubts about the validity of judgment which creates the energy and rationale for the entire first section of the poem. With allowance for tangential pursuits,

Part One of *An Essay on Criticism* may be read as a comprehensive, theoretical defense of the very *possibility* of valid judgment.

The possibility of valid judgment, for Pope, depends not on repairing the inherent weaknesses of human understanding but on defining fixed theoretical standards, outside the individual, which create the norms for reasoning justly about literature. The weakness and variance of human understanding are facts which, as Locke argued persuasively, do not preclude the possibility of knowledge. Although individual judgments will differ, the existence of theoretical standards outside the particular critics establishes a norm against which variance may be measured and corrected. For example, the minor differences from clock to clock do not preclude the possibility of correct timekeeping. In Pope's day, the newfangled pocket-watches which adorned the gentry could be corrected against the tolling church bells, just as a century later official clocks could be regulated by the standard of Greenwich time.[18] The possibility of correct time is thus established by the existence of a fixed standard outside the individual, so that we accept minor variations as inevitable and inconsequential. In cases of dispute—if your watch says ten and mine twelve—we can resolve our differences by appealing to the outside standard which creates the possibility that one of us is correct. Pope's attitude toward judgment is implicit in the simile of clockwork which he introduces. Minor variances prove acceptable and major differences may be adjudicated once criticism has established the *possibility* of valid judgment by articulating the fixed theoretical standards which govern literary analysis.

Pope's articulation of the fixed standards for criticism occupies two parallel passages, symmetrically placed and linked through style, which comprise the rhetorical peaks of Part One. They are far more than fragments of practical advice to critics: do this, don't do that. They define the norms which make valid judgment possible. The first standard cites the stability and universality of nature as one basis for valid judgment in criticism:

> First follow NATURE, and your Judgment frame
> By her just Standard, which is still the same:
> *Unerring Nature*, still divinely bright,
> One *clear*, *unchang'd*, and *Universal* Light,

> Life, Force, and Beauty, must to all impart,
> At once the *Source*, and *End*, and *Test* of Art.
>
> (68–73)

The passage is so familiar that readers ignore its specific purpose within the context of Pope's *Essay*. We should notice
initially that its subject is not nature but how to "frame" one's
judgment. Nature is praised specifically because it provides a
"just Standard" for the regulation of individual judgment. It is
not here (as often) a set of practical maxims but an abstraction
which creates the possibility of judging rightly. The high level of
generality in Pope's description, for which he is sometimes cen-
sured, befits the articulation of a theoretical norm. The fixity and
universality of nature provide a standard of measurement, so that
all practical exercises of individual judgment derive their validity
from its presence and power. Nor is its power owing to human
choices or arbitrary convention, like Greenwich or the metric
system. As Pope's ruling metaphor implies, the theoretical standard which nature provides for criticism is "just" because, like the
sun, its potency belongs to the inherent order of things.

The second theoretical standard validating the possibility of individual judgment shifts the locus of permanence from nature to
art. Again, because the familiarity of the passage sometimes glazes
the eye, we should notice that the latent but true subject is how
to "steer" one's judgment:

> *You* then whose Judgment the right *Course* wou'd steer,
> Know well each ANCIENT's proper *Character*,
> His *Fable, Subject, Scope* in ev'ry Page,
> *Religion, Country, Genius* of his *Age*:
> Without all these at once before your Eyes,
> *Cavil* you may, but never *Criticize*.
>
> (118–23)

If criticism is to become an art—not frivolous objections about
taste or rules—it requires a firm theoretical foundation, and
Pope's praise of the Ancients transcends conventional panegyric
to create the foundation of a coherent critical theory. True, other
writers advise reading the Ancients, just as they advise following
nature. What matters is not the source of Pope's ideas. What
matters is not their familiarity. What matters is Pope's *use* of
traditional materials. And within the context of his *Essay*, Pope

21

invokes the Ancients—just as he invoked nature—for the original purpose of defining fixed, universal standards which create the possibility of valid judgment in criticism. Knowledge of the Ancients permits critics to steer a "right Course" much as fixed stars allow mariners a confidence in the very possibility of navigation. "Before the use of the loadstone, or knowledge of the compass," wrote Dryden, reflecting upon his early efforts in criticism, "I was sailing in a vast ocean, without other help than the polestar of the Ancients, and the rules of the French stage amongst the Moderns."[14] Criticism, despite Dryden's strenuous practice, had not advanced in England to the status of a fully self-conscious art. Still the province mainly of idle aristocrats or professional hacks, it failed to establish the kind of theoretical foundation which Dryden had struggled to discover. In isolating nature and the classics as universal standards validating the possibility of individual judgment, Pope went beyond Dryden's personal quest. He offered English criticism the theoretical foundations of an authentic art. His next step, logically, was to sketch the practical principles and methods which guide the critic's day-to-day encounter with literary texts.

3 Judgment as Critical Method: The Logic of Probability

One feature which distinguishes Pope's system from earlier theories of criticism is not only its theoretical basis but also its association with a specific method of reasoning. The rejection of Authority and Taste involves for Pope the rejection of an entire way of thinking about literature. Authority and Taste deal equally in certainties: they do not invite reasoned disputation because they hold an absolute power, personal or impersonal. Pope, as we have seen, is not afraid of proclaiming certainties when he announces nature and the classics as providing just theoretical standards for validating the possibility of judgment. Part One thus treats the act of judgment within a context of universal, certain, permanent, theoretical values. In Parts Two and Three, however, Pope moves from the establishment of theoretical absolutes to the exploration of particular, variable, practical aspects of critical activity. This movement from theoretical to practical, from universal to particular, from permanent to variable is reflected in his new concern with a world of mutability and limitation. While the theoretical standards for criticism are presented as universal and unchanging and certain, the actual texts to be judged and the daily practice of judgment belong to the fluctuating realm of time and change, where customs alter, creeds lapse, and languages decay. Indeed, the tone of Parts Two and Three is set decisively by the extended comparison (219–32) which describes the potential vastness of human knowledge and the frailty of our individual understandings. The learning of a lifetime is merely prelude to the awesome discouragement which might strike the most tireless climber:

> Th' *increasing* Prospect *tires* our wandring Eyes,
> Hills peep o'er Hills, and *Alps* on *Alps* arise!
>
> (231–32)

Pope's powerful image of human limitation, which so deeply impressed Johnson, is especially appropriate at the beginning of Part Two, where certainties are left behind. It creates an implicit contrast with the hymn-like celebration of the "Immortal" (190) Ancients which had closed Part One, leading the reader artfully from the realm of timelessness to time, from past clarity to present complexities and doubt. Pope's couplets still carry a crisply authoritative tone when defining terms or giving direct advice, but their assurance flows from observation, logic, and tradition—not from indisputable Authority. Even his most confident assertions in Parts Two and Three are subtly modified by their placement within a context where certainty has vanished.

The vanishment of certainty—the central fact underlying the final two sections of Pope's *Essay*—leads to an association between criticism and a method of reasoning which becomes a distinguishing mark of the period. This is the method of probable reasoning. And probable reasoning becomes, for Pope, indistinguishable from the act of judgment which comprises his definition of criticism.

The importance of probable reasoning to the spirit and shape of eighteenth-century thought can hardly be overstated. As Hoyt Trowbridge explains, probable reasoning "was conceived during the period as the most legitimate and valid method—for Locke, in fact, the only possible method—in most of the arts and sciences and in the everyday thinking of rational people".[15] Its influence upon literary criticism proved especially decisive. In

23

1764 the young Edward Gibbon could write: "Geometry is employed only in demonstrations peculiar to itself: criticism deliberates between the different degrees of probability."[16] Criticism is thus defined for Gibbon (as for more experienced critics) by its use of a particular method of reasoning, and his distinction between geometric demonstrations and degrees of probability echoes Locke's influential *Essay Concerning Human Understanding* (1690), where the method of probable reasoning was persuasively described and developed. There Locke distinguishes between two forms of knowledge: the "clear and certain" knowledge which he imagistically associates with the broad daylight of truth; and a lesser, uncertain, tentative kind of knowing which he describes as "the twilight . . . of probability".[17] The twilight of probability is, in fact, Locke's metaphor for the normal state of human intelligence, for he believed (as Pope stated in "The Design" prefixed to *An Essay on Man*) that there "are not *many certain truths* in this world". Probable reasoning, in Locke's view, is divine recompense for the absence of certainty. Limited and fallible, it nonetheless guides us through the doubtful twilight realms where demonstrations, proofs, and certainties are chimerical.

Nowhere in *An Essay on Criticism* does Pope claim, directly and explicitly, that English criticism must henceforth be characterized by the method of probable reasoning. His indirections are sufficient. The final two sections suffuse an awareness of human limits and temporal change which defy certainties, encouraging the development of a probabilistic spirit of inquiry. Further, his practical principles of criticism (as we will see) require for their application a spirit and method of probable reasoning. Pope's practicing critic constantly assesses degrees of probability and constructs hypotheses about intention or design, and these activities demand the exercise of probabilistic thought, however informal its character. But Pope's association between criticism and probable reasoning needed no direct and explicit statement because it was also implicit in his choice of terms. Locke's famous distinction between certain and probable knowledge occurs in the chapter entitled "Of Judgment". And there Locke clearly states that the mental power of judgment holds full sway over the operations of probable reasoning. As he declares unequivocally, "the faculty which God has given man to supply the want of clear and certain knowledge, in cases where that cannot be had, is *judgment*: whereby the mind takes its ideas to agree or disagree; or, which is the same, any proposition to be true or false, without perceiving a demonstrative evidence in the proofs."[18] In capturing the traditional, technical term "judgment" as the sign for his new theory of criticism, Pope gained more than the sum of its traditional meanings. The prestige of Locke's *Essay* had endowed "judgment" with the connotations of an entire method of thought —probabilistic reasoning—which conforms exactly with the spirit and demands of Pope's critical system. It is always possible to assume, of course, that Pope's choice of terms was a happy accident. Nevertheless probable reasoning—whether Pope derived its tenets from Locke or from his own thought and reading—underlies his entire approach to the practice of criticism. For Pope, the act of judgment is synonymous with the method and spirit of probabilistic thought.

The important association between criticism and probable reasoning helps considerably to explain the extravagant praise by eighteenth-century critics such as Johnson, for whom (like Gibbon) the methods of probabilistic thought were inseparable from the methods of criticism. The substitution of probability for the dogmatic certainties of Authority and of Taste had a profoundly liberating effect. Old doctrines, like the critical Unities, could be shed. "To judge therefore of Shakespeare by Aristotle's rules," Pope was to write in the spirit of independent, probable inquiry, "is like trying a man by the laws of one country who acted under those of another."[19] Pope's legal metaphor of judging—always present, if indistinct, in his vocabulary of judgment —suggests another important benefit of substituting probability for truth. Far from inducing a resigned relativism, as if loss of certainty meant that all judgments were equally doubtful, the exercise of probable reasoning exalts rather than diminishes the critic's role. As his metaphor of judging implies, the end of criticism, for Pope, is evaluation. Eventually the critic reveals himself as a literary arbiter, even as the concluding portraits of exemplary critics reveal Longinus gowned in legality as an "ardent *Judge*" (677). The *act* of judgment, involving the method of probabilistic thought, issues eventually in the *pronouncement* of judgment: the "Sentence" (678) handed down by Longinus. Evaluation, as the final purpose of criticism, gives the critic an important social role, rather than a purely personal function. The rigorous separation of good from bad writing serves the world of letters in the same way that a wise judge serves a social community, with the added boon that wise critics reward as well as punish. It is precisely *because* criticism ends in judgments of value that Pope cares deeply about the methods by which just evaluaations proceed. As a native of twilight uncertainties, his ideal critic endows the act of judgment with a spirit of probable reasoning, judiciously weighing the various degrees of probability, which characterizes the best English criticism for the remainder of the century.

4 *Practical Principles of Judgment: Propriety*

The association between criticism and probable reasoning exerts a powerful influence over the practical principles of judgment which Pope sparingly defines. In fact, despite the swirl of specific maxims, sententious learning, examples, portraits, and anecdotes which pack the final two sections, Pope restricts himself to two subsuming principles: propriety and generosity. Almost every precept or fragmentary insight after Part One pertains to these comprehensive practical principles. Like most of the important concepts in *An Essay on Criticism*—nature, judgment, wit, the ancients—propriety and generosity assemble, under deceptively simple terms, a complex series of related ideas. Propriety, for example, evokes for most modern readers a simple limiting notion of shallow correctness, the counterpart of etiquette in manners. But for Pope the term evoked connotations almost exactly opposite to the inflexible codes which we associate with propriety. Not a set of rules but an abstraction whose content constantly shifts, propriety exists only in the harmonious relationship between two or more elements. Its nature is fluid and indefinite because harmonious relationships may assume many different shapes. There is, however, one concept upon which Pope's complex idea of propriety entirely depends. This concept, crucial to understanding *An Essay on Criticism*, is the idea of poetic wholeness.

Pope's idea of poetic wholeness, especially when compared to earlier treatments of unity in drama and epic, achieves a flexibility and comprehensiveness which free criticism from narrow, rigid obsession with the details of "correct" composition. Poetic wholeness, for Pope, involves the harmonious relationship between two major elements of composition which he calls (although not with absolute consistency) Conception and Execution. Conception denotes the essential mental work of the poet which governs the underlying form and purposes of a work: authorial intention, choice of genre, establishment of a basic moral pattern, and disposition of the structural design. Execution, on the other hand, involves the actual process of writing. It compasses what Pope calls "the Thoughts, the Expression, and the Numbers".[20] The poet's movement from Conception to Execution is a descent from ideas into the materials of poetry: meter, style, and statement. Both, of course, are essential to a finished work. And the actual history of composition may not follow a clear sequence from Conception to Execution, as if the poet were a builder working from blueprints. But despite a discontinuous or experimental process of composition, the finished poem is always, for Pope, a work in which the harmonious relation between Conception and Execution creates a form of imaginative wholeness. No matter how skillful the verse, no matter how polished the style, no matter how witty the texture of poetic statement, a work which lacks the guidance of a primary Conception fails to attain wholeness. It is this lofty ideal of poetic wholeness which Pope contrasts with the trifling of mere gentleman-wits, who divert themselves with isolated felicities of Execution: "pretty conceptions [i.e., witty thoughts], fine metaphors, glitt'-ring expressions, and something of a neat cast of Verse".[21] His own professional career is a long protest against the aristocratic tradition of gentleman-poets who dally with verse in their spare time. And *An Essay on Criticism* protests vigorously against their doubles in criticism: mere critical triflers, who ignore the primacy of Conception and cavil at minor infelicities of Execution. Hence his harsh censure of critics who distort their judgment through a *"Love to Parts"* (288). True criticism, for Pope, requires a vision of poetic wholeness. Only through a knowledge of poetic wholeness, as compounded of Execution and Conception, can criticism render the valid judgments of propriety which are its ultimate business.

The principle of propriety applies not only to the relation between Conception and Execution. It extends also to judgments

27

concerning the specific parts of Execution: the thoughts, words, and meters which must be judged also in relation to lesser, local harmonies of their own. In discussing wit or conceits, for example, Pope argues that true wit exists in the harmonious relationship among idea, image, and expression, thus effectively imposing upon the rebellious faculty of wit a local standard of propriety and justness. In judging diction the same principle applies: a propriety of words to subject and to occasion. As for versification, where Pope illustrates his ideal with vivid imitations, propriety reveals itself in the echoing relationship between sound and sense. Pope is not diffident, of course, about expressing his opinions forcefully on these matters. But, especially in the context of Parts Two and Three, readers surely can distinguish between advice and laws. The crucial point is that Pope applies to the judgment of particular parts the same subsuming principle of propriety which he applies to judgment of the whole. The value of propriety, for Pope, lies in its freedom from the absolute, universal, fixed laws of criticism which limit both poets and critics alike. It opens access to the *varieties* of justness not comprehended solely within "Aristotle's rules".

Pope used to claim, according to Joseph Spence, that "all the beauties of gardening might be comprehended in one word, variety".[22] The power of variety as an aesthetic principle is now somewhat difficult to imagine; mixed literary forms and cultural pluralism are today wholly acceptable. But in Pope's time the pressures of critical tradition stressed generic purity, artificial symmetries, and unity through uniformity. Thus it is important to notice the metaphors of dress (318) and of fashion (333) which Pope associates with poetic diction because, like his extended elegiac lament for the mutability of language (476–93), they emphasize the facts of time and change and variety which are intrinsic to literature. Diction which appeared just and natural in one age, Pope knew, might sound outlandish in another. And poems inevitably assume the specific proprieties influenced by a particular age, country, and poetic character: "*Homer* hurries and transports us with a commanding Impetuosity, *Virgil* leads us with an attractive Majesty: *Homer* scatters with a generous Profusion, *Virgil* bestows with a careful Magnificence: *Homer* like the *Nile*, pours out his Riches with a sudden Overflow; *Virgil* like a River in its Banks, with a gentle and constant Stream."[23] Each writer, in other words, creates a different form of propriety. The variety implicit in Pope's practical principle means that, unlike some of his contemporaries and predecessors, he does not feel forced to choose between different forms of literary merit: Homer *or* Virgil, Pindar *or* Horace, Shakespeare *or* Jonson. Propriety admits diverse individual possibilities of justness. And only such an elastic, inclusive principle would itself be appropriate, in Pope's view, to a criticism locked within the world of change, uncertainty, and human limitation. Against such inevitable confinements, it offers an unprecedented freedom to discover the unique proprieties of even the wildest works.

5 *Practical Principles of Judgment: Generosity*

The undogmatic flexibility implicit in Pope's critical principles not only extends to his treatment of generosity but also finds its clearest expression there. Persons are the ultimate source of literary judgment, and thus no critical theory would be complete for Pope which did not account for the personal, ethical aspect of criticism. Knowledge of propriety must be complemented by equal achievements of character, as the opening couplet of Part Three proclaims:

> LEARN then what MORALS Critics ought to show,
> For 'tis but *half* a *Judge's Task*, to *Know*.
> (560–61)

Even in an age of moralists, Pope's stress upon the ethics of criticism is extraordinary. Moral character comprises fully *"half"* of the critic's equipment and identity. This fact alone would argue for the prominence of Pope's *Essay* in the history of critical theory. And it also suggests a strong personal relevance to the work, considering his later emphasis upon moral poetry and his lifelong combat with duncical critics whose characters as well as writings were open to attack. Criticism for Pope is always an expression of moral character. Character, however, can express many different kinds of virtue. Thus, in order to understand Pope's concentration upon the ethics of generosity, we need to see how generosity was a virtue particularly relevant to the problems he confronted in *An Essay on Criticism*.

One reason for Pope's stress upon generosity is historical. At the turn of the century, two stereotypes dominated the portraits of critics: the coffeehouse witling and the ill-tempered crank. Witlings, fops, and callow socialites exposed the shallowness and ignorance of contemporary criticism, as satirized in the parade of Ned Softleys and Dick Minims who mumbled platitudes or flaunted banalities. But probably the main satiric image was the carping, ill-natured critic, irascible, cantankerous, proud—an outlaw from polite society. Thus Swift was merely perpetuating a stock image when he described criticism in *A Tale of a Tub* (1704) as the allegorical offspring of Ridicule and Pride. For Pope, a surly disposition was the necessary cause of all bad criticism. "Sure upon the whole," he wrote in 1717, "a bad Author deserves better usage than a bad Critic; a man may be the former merely thro' the misfortune of an ill judgment, but he cannot be the latter without both that [i.e. ill judgment] and an ill temper."[24] While a knowledge of propriety rescued criticism from the ignorance of witlings and fops, the principle of generosity promised to cure the splenetic distemper which Pope believed inherent in all bad criticism. The generous critic, for Pope, has resources of character which assure that judgment will operate with temperance and humanity, isolating the much satirized crank as a relic from primitive times.

A second reason for Pope's emphasis on generosity of character is epistemological. Generosity is for Pope indispensable to the conduct of criticism because personal judgment, in literary matters, requires the encounter with uncertainties and imperfect knowledge. In addition, it implicitly recognizes the human limitations and tendency to error which critics and poets both share. As a poet as well as a critic, Pope understood that no poem completely satisfies its author: "We grasp some more beautifull Idea in our Brain, than our Endeavors to express it can set to the view of others; & still do but labour to fall short of our first Imagination. The gay Colouring which Fancy gave to our Design at the first transient glance we had of it, goes off in the Execution; like those various Figures in the gilded Clouds, which while we gaze long upon, to seperate the Parts of each imaginary Image, the whole faints before the Eye, & decays into Confusion."[25] Pope's language of transience here parallels his perception, in the *Essay*, of how time damages the poem, blurring its diction and effacing its design. And because the actual poem is inevitably for Pope a betrayal (492) of the imagination, some residue of flaw must accompany even the most polished work. His urgent call for critics to "befriend" (474) true merit—in the face of time's hostility—is not only based on the acceptance of imperfections. It also links generosity to the social virtue of friendship, almost a deified concept in Pope's estimation. And as a social force friendship and generosity permit the possible recreation of the genuine community of discourse which characterized the ancients:

> The gen'rous Critick *fann'd* the *Poet's Fire*,
> And taught the World, *with Reason* to *Admire*.
> (100–1)

As friendly intermediaries rather than rigid inquisitors, critics both instruct readers and encourage poets, resuming their lapsed social function as a civilizing force. Generosity, in humanizing knowledge and in tempering intellectual judgment with ethical awareness, elevates criticism to a moral art capable of improving the quality of English literary life. Acknowledging inherent limitations in the work, in the critic, and in the very possibilities of human knowledge, it meets error with the spirit of forgiveness which is for Pope one mark of a *"Divine"* (525) nature.

Generosity in *An Essay on Criticism* achieves the exalted status finally of an ethical opposite to pride, which Pope cites as the source of most errors in critical judgment. The effect of pride, within Pope's *Essay*, is always a pressure toward partiality and fragmentation, blocking comprehensiveness of vision. In its pressure against wholeness, pride radically constricts understanding by attaching us to personal opinions and to favored parts of composition. Because the principle of propriety required an understanding of poetic wholeness, it offered one means of counteracting the fragmentations of pride expressed in bad critics as a *"Love to Parts"*. But partiality takes another threatening form in *An Essay on Criticism*. This form of partiality, rooted in pride, is the narrow intolerance of prejudice. Prejudice expressed itself in many ways: in the curse of party which divided Augustan writers along political lines; in favoritism for Ancients or Moderns; for English writers or French; or for opposing schools of wit. Such hardened prejudice, which transformed the poet's life (as Pope complained) into a form of warfare upon earth, made fair judgment completely impossible. Thus, while the *Essay* heaps

31

extensive censure on obsessive scrutiny of mere "parts" of Execution (289–383), it also attacks at almost equal length partiality expressed as prejudice favoring writers from one historical period, one political party, one country, or a single school of wit (384–473). The cure for this divisive spirit of prejudice is generosity. Generosity extends the broad tolerance of propriety to the quarrelsome realm of social, political, and literary prejudice. Generosity permits the critic an approach toward wholeness. It seeks to move criticism from a warfare of factions to a civilized catholic form of discourse among persons too large-spirited for parties or partiality or prejudice of any kind.

It should be clear that generosity is not for Pope a simple or obvious virtue, like thrift. But its most important function has yet to be mentioned. Stated briefly, generosity solves one major problem inherent in Pope's critical theory. He insists, as we have seen, that judgment considers the *"Whole"* (235) work. And wholeness requires us to understand the poet's mental processes which constitute Conception. Thus Pope insists that criticism must always regard the writer's purposes (255), judging performance in the light of intentions. But there is an old problem lurking in this good advice. How can the critic achieve a vision of the whole without access to the poet's mind? Not all intentions and purposes can be reconstructed from a faithful study of the text. How, then, can the critic presume to understand mental processes and latent purposes which are required for an understanding of the *"Whole"* work? Pope's answer to this difficult question is the power of sympathy. Like candor and forgiveness, sympathy helps to make up the comprehensive virtue of generosity. In effect, critical sympathy is for Pope the achievement of an intuitive emotional and intellectual unity with the author. Through long study and generous feeling, the critic gradually begins to feel and think exactly like the writer: "No Longer his *Interpreter*, but *He*."[26] This virtual identification of author and critic in a oneness of spirit allows presumptive reconstructions of plans and purposes and processes which complement a study of the text. And in such a complementary understanding of outer text and inner process lies, for Pope, the entire perfection of judgment:

> A perfect Judge will *read* each Work of Wit
> With the same Spirit that its Author *writ*,

32

Survey the *Whole*, nor seek slight Faults to find,
Where *Nature moves*, and *Rapture warms* the Mind.
(233–36)

It is generosity in this largest sense—an intuitive, emotional sympathy with the author—which licenses the lesser forms of generous criticism which overlook slight faults. The "perfect Judge" whom Pope depicts is no ordinary critic. The act of judgment is redefined ultimately as fusing knowledge with passion. And passion, rather than spending itself in the idle ecstasies of taste, leads us firmly back to the work, helping to recreate a vision of "the *Whole*" by recreating the "same Spirit" which moved the writer. Such a critic is impartial in a special sense. Not, clearly, through cold disinterest. But through engagement of emotion and knowledge in a comprehensive expression of character, such as we see in Longinus:

An ardent *Judge*, who Zealous in his Trust,
With *Warmth* gives Sentence, yet is always *Just*;
Whose *own Example* strengthens all his Laws,
And *Is himself* that great *Sublime* he draws.
(677–80)

Sublimity, Longinus had said, is the echo of a great soul. And generosity, for Pope, always retains its etymological link with nobility of character, urging that good criticism is inseparable from moral goodness and magnanimity in the critic.

6 Conclusion: Pope as Metacritic

"Criticism," wrote Samuel Johnson in 1751, "reduces those regions of literature under the dominion of science, which have hitherto known only the anarchy of ignorance, the caprices of fancy, and the tyranny of prescription."[27] Johnson's mid-century statement is a history as well as a definition of criticism. It charts the progress from the "prescriptions" of Authority and the "caprices" of Taste which Pope's *Essay* helped to initiate and secure. Johnson's important phrase "dominion of science" does not imply that criticism now belonged to the disciplines of natural philosophy, like chemistry or physics, but that it had attained coherence as a branch of useful knowledge. It was Dryden, in Johnson's view, who deserved credit as "the father of English criticism": "the writer who first taught us to determine *upon principles* the merit of composition".[28] Dryden's primacy is indisputable, for he did more than any writer of his age to free criticism from the confusions and ignorance in which he found it. But Dryden was most successful as a practising critic, not as a theorist of criticism. Modern scholars still have trouble reducing his principles to consistency and clarity, while his practice reveals a variety of different approaches and subjects, from occasional pronouncements to speculative dialogues. With the death of Dryden in 1700, there was a need to consolidate his advances and to consider the nature of criticism as a coherent discipline conscious of its own aims and methods. John Dennis, with his meaty tracts *The Advancement and Reformation of Modern Poetry* (1701) and *The Grounds of Criticism in Poetry* (1704), had already begun the task of establishing theoretical foundations for modern criticism, in what Pope could only regard as a dogmatic and misguided effort to flood England with swollen imitations of *Paradise Lost. An Essay on Criticism* in effect reclaims the legacy of Dryden for English critics, endorsing his main principles, backing his often speculative and exploratory spirit of inquiry, and providing a secure, compact, flexible *theory* of criticism to stabilize the practice of his English successors.

Historians of criticism and of critical theory should take a fresh look at *An Essay on Criticism*, for it possesses a coherence (despite its unmethodical form) and originality (despite its use of traditional materials) which deserve reappraisal. Some of the apparent familiarity of Pope's ideas derives, like the "clichés" of *An Essay on Man*, from their subsequent absorption into the language of English thought, where they proved powerfully influential. The strength of his poem, contrary to general opinion, is not in free-floating couplets of specific advice but in consolidating the fragmentary wisdom of tradition and shards of native common sense within the structure of a comprehensive theory of criticism. The specific couplets, which sometimes *sound* completely self-contained, refer to a system which surrounds them with additional meaning:

> In ev'ry Work regard the *Writer's End*,
> Since none can compass more than they *Intend*;
> And if the *Means* be just, the *Conduct* true,
> Applause, in spite of trivial Faults, is due.
>
> (255–58)

In this resounding self-contained unit, the idea of poetic whole-ness—achieved by understanding the relation between Conception (*"End"*) and Execution (*"Means"* and *"Conduct"*)—entails, as we have seen, a sequence of theoretical and practical steps. It is embedded in a theory which defines criticism as the act of judgment; which places this definition within an historical context as an alternative to criticism based on Authority or Taste; which isolates and links, in nature and the ancients, fixed standards which create the possibility of valid judgment; which associates criticism with the method and spirit of probable reasoning appropriate to a realm of limitation and uncertainty; which articulates, in propriety and in generosity, comprehensive practical principles of criticism embracing both knowledge and ethics; which directs practical criticism toward the final end of just evaluation; and which justified evaluative verdicts in the possibility of reviving a true community of discourse, with critics as the intermediaries between writers and readers, in a model of ancient civility. Pope's theory may not be "cut-and-dried" (if that is a virtue). But it certainly possesses the rigor and coherence which a useful theory of criticism requires. Where in the previous history of English criticism does one find a more fully integrated model for theory and practice?

It is true that readers must perceive the organization of Pope's critical system without the aid of prose crutches: statements of purpose, chapter headings, mathematical subdivisions, detailed logical argument, plain abc order, and utilitarian language. John Dennis specialized in such pedestrian devices, instructing mankind as if they belonged in a schoolroom. Pope, as Johnson observed truly, "had great delight in artifice, and endeavoured to attain all his purposes by indirect and unsuspected methods".[29] Believing that "Men must be *taught* as if you taught them not", Pope might well choose the subtler didacticism of apparent indirection as the best means for overcoming the normal human resistances to instruction. Providing readers with the security of familiar terms and traditional lore, he might well conceal the originality of his integrated system in an aura of "Things *forgot*", permitting memory to cushion the shock of strangeness, as well as to deflect charges of presumption. (Pope must be one of England's youngest reformers, and charges of youthful presumption, hurled like weapons by the wounded Dennis, came anyway.) But finally we should not miss the obvious point. Pope chooses to write a poem, not a treatise. The poem does possess a rudimentary order consistent with a logic of exposition. Part One treats the universal standards validating the possibility of judgment. Part Two treats the practical principle of propriety. And Part Three stresses the practical principle of generosity. Within this primitive framework, however, Pope allows himself numerous excursions, like the connected "episodes" in an epic. Further, he often approaches his subject obliquely—discussing propriety, for example, mainly through a study of specific errors of judgment. The errors, it turns out, stem from ignoring or misunderstanding the nature of propriety. Such indirections might be misplaced in a prose treatise but hardly seem grounds for censure in a poem. *An Essay on Criticism* is a supple, allusive, complex, sometimes dazzling work which need not demonstrate the sledge-hammer obviousness of a tract by Le Bossu. The coherence of Pope's theory is present for discovery and reconstruction by every reader, which increases the likelihood that we will remember and value a system which we have helped to assemble. Rhymed instruction which simply told the reader what to think Pope himself compared to jingling padlocks which imprison the mind. True didactic poems for Pope are always potential satires waiting for a victim. *An Essay on Criticism* is, as well as a coherent theory, a test of the very critical power it recommends. We must read in the constant exercise of personal judgment—or find merely a heap of fragments.

Pope, I believe, both cared deeply and thought seriously about the nature of literary criticism. He was himself a skillful practicing critic, as his essays, notes, and prefaces amply demonstrate. He was a connoisseur of critical responses to his own poems—and even reviewed his own Pastorals (favorably) when he thought critics had failed to understand their merit. Before the age of twenty, with no formal schooling, he threaded the learned tradition of classical, Renaissance, and contemporary criticism, in at least three languages. His interest in criticism runs deep, and he knew the subject thoroughly. There are no grounds for considering him a shallow opportunist looking for an untried, easy field in which to demonstrate his knack of rhyme. *An Essay on Criticism* is a major attempt to place English literary analysis on the foundation of a coherent theory. Like all his works, it is less a response to tradition than an original engagement with his own time, in the light of traditional knowledge. In his own time Pope viewed the history of English criticism as a period of general barbarity, punctuated by the ineffectual efforts of a "few" (719) sound minds. The names Sheffield, Roscommon, and Walsh— Pope's "sounder few"—hardly define a flourishing native criticism. And no one would propose to discover in their writings a coherent or effective theory of literary analysis. While France derived a certain benefit from the rules its writers slavishly copied and obeyed, England in asserting its independence from French and Roman influence also unfortunately decreed its isolation from the improvements of polite learning:

> But *we*, brave *Britons*, *Foreign Laws* despis'd,
> And kept *unconquer'd*, and *unciviliz'd*.
>
> (715–16)

The phrase "brave *Britons*" contains both a touch of irony and a trace of pride. Pope's task in *An Essay on Criticism* was to civilize the study of literature. Retaining still the spirit of independence which preserves British liberty, he wished to discover the native principles which would advance criticism from ignorance and incivility to the dominion of polite knowledge. Pope wished to move Britons, from ignorantly despising all foreign laws, toward an acceptance of principles of literary merit which English writers shared with various nations and times. The ideal, for Pope, is to be both unconquered *and* civilized. The criticism of judgment represents his first explicit effort, which continues indirectly through the writing of a lifetime, to civilize the act of reading. Not coincidentally, it provided England with a coherent native theory of criticism befitting an era which began to imagine emulating the achievements of ancient Greek and Roman civilization.

NOTES

1 *An Essay on Criticism*, ll. 574–75. All quotations from Pope's verse refer to the eleven-volume Twickenham edition of *The Poems of Alexander Pope* (New Haven, 1939–69), under the general editorship of John Butt.

2 J. W. H. Atkins, *English Literary Criticism: 17th and 18th Centuries* (1951; rpt. London, 1966), p. 167.

3 Ripley Hotch, "Pope Surveys His Kingdom: *An Essay on Criticism*", *SEL*, 13 (1973), 474.

4 See, for example, William Empson, "Wit in the *Essay on Criticism*", *Hudson Review*, 2 (1950), 559–77; Edward Niles Hooker, "Pope on Wit: The *Essay on Criticism*", in *The Seventeenth Century: Studies in the History of English Thought and Literature from Bacon to Pope, by Richard Foster Jones and Others Writing in His Honor* (Stanford, 1951), pp. 225–46; and Patricia Meyer Spacks, "Imagery and Method in *An Essay on Criticism*", *PMLA*, 85 (1970), 97–106.

5 Ed., *The Works of Alexander Pope*, 9 vols. (London, 1797), I, 173.

6 *The Lives of the English Poets* (1779–81), ed. George Birkbeck Hill, 3 vols. (Oxford, 1905), III, 228.

7 J. M. Cameron, "Mr. Tillotson and Mr. Pope", *Dublin Review*, 233 (1959), 158.

8 See Joseph Spence, *Observations, Anecdotes, and Characters of Books and Men* (1820), ed. James M. Osborn, 2 vols. (Oxford, 1966), I, 45.

9 *The Correspondence of Alexander Pope*, ed. George Sherburn, 5 vols. (Oxford, 1956), I, 128 (19 July 1711).

10 Ed., *Critical Essays of the Seventeenth Century*, 3 vols. (1908–09; rpt. Bloomington, 1957), I, lxxxviii–cvi.

11 See John M. Aden, *The Critical Opinions of John Dryden: A Dictionary* (Nashville, Tenn., 1963), p. 145; and H. James Jensen, *A Glossary of John Dryden's Critical Terms* (Minneapolis, 1969), pp. 68–70.

12 See *A Concordance to the Poems of Alexander Pope*, ed. Emmett G. Bedford and Robert J. Dilligan (Detroit, Michigan, 1974).

13 Additional "outside" standards existed as well: "apparent solar time" (the interval between two successive passages of the sun across a fixed meridian), "mean solar time" (a measure of the rotation of the earth), and "siderial time" (the interval between two successive passages of a star). "Mean solar time" was introduced in the seventeenth century.

14 In *Of Dramatic Poesy and Other Critical Essays*, ed. George Watson, 2 vols. (London, 1962), II, 73–4.

15 "Scattered Atoms of Probability", *ECS*, 5 (1971–72), 37. Trowbridge demonstrates persuasively the influence of probabilistic thought in the language and methods of Johnson's "Preface to Shakespeare".

16 *An Essay on the Study of Literature* (London, 1764), p. 51.

17 *An Essay Concerning Human Understanding* (1690), ed. Alexander Campbell Fraser, 2 vols. (1894; rpt. New York, 1959), II, 360.

18 Ed. Fraser, II, 361.

19 "The Preface of the Editor" to *The Works of Shakespeare* (1725), in *Eighteenth-Century Critical Essays*, ed. Scott Elledge, 2 vols. (Ithaca, N.Y., 1961), I, 281.

20 *Correspondence*, ed. Sherburn, I, 110 (17 December 1710). My treatment here supplements the observations of Emerson R. Marks, "Pope on Poetry and the Poet", *Criticism*, 12 (1970), 271–80.

21 *Correspondence*, ed. Sherburn, I, 110 (17 December 1710).

22 Spence, *Anecdotes*, ed. Osborn, II, 251.
23 "Preface" to *The Iliad* (1715), in *The Prose Works of Alexander Pope*, ed. Norman Ault (Oxford, 1936), p. 237.
24 "Preface" to *The Works* (1717), in *Prose Works*, ed. Ault, p. 290.
25 *Correspondence*, ed. Sherburn, I, 135 (12 November 1711).
26 Wentworth Dillon, Earl of Roscommon, *An Essay on Translated Verse* (1684), in *Critical Essays of the Seventeenth Century*, ed. Spingarn, II, 300. Pope cites Roscommon among the exemplary modern critics at the end of the poem (725–28). The idea of critical sympathy was also implicit in Longinus' theory of "emulation".
27 *The Rambler* (92), ed. W. J. Bate and Albrecht B. Strauss, The Yale Edition of *The Works of Samuel Johnson*, IV (New Haven, 1969), 122.
28 *Lives of the English Poets*, ed. Hill, I, 410–11, italics added.
29 *Lives of the English Poets*, ed. Hill, III, 200.

2

Time and Space in
Windsor Forest

by PAT ROGERS

A common device of eighteenth-century poets is what might be called the shift in dimension. Samuel Johnson begins his most famous poem with a grandiose verbal gesture: the expansiveness of his theme is rendered in spatial terms—

> Let Observation with extensive View,
> Survey Mankind from *China* to *Peru* . . .

However, *The Vanity of Human Wishes* proves to be an historical rather than a geographical survey; in the event Johnson ranges more freely over the past than the present world. Similarly James Thomson's *Liberty* proceeds from an evocation of the physical ruins of Rome to contemplation of the changes wrought by time. The opening section, "Ancient and Modern Italy Compared", is described in the argument as being "thrown into the form of a Poetical Vision. Its scene the ruins of ancient Rome." Throughout this section we are invited first to *look* (at "fractured arches" and the like), and then to *think back*. In another extended "prospect" poem, Oliver Goldsmith's *The Traveller*, there is the same geographical placing in the first few lines, and thereafter a similar interplay between description of the present state of Europe and recital of historical developments—though the history is less prominent and explicit than in Johnson or Thomson. Similarly "hill-top" poems like Richard Jago's *Edge-Hill* commonly move from a visual panorama to a review of local history and mythology.

Windsor Forest is rightly seen as a loco-descriptive poem, in which (to follow Johnson's celebrated formula) "some particular landscape is poetically described, with the addition of such embel-

40

lishments as may be supplied by historical retrospection, or incidental meditation." What I wish to argue is not that the ingredients of *Windsor Forest* have been wrongly identified, but that the way these are blended has not been fully appreciated. That is, I wish to explore the chemistry as it serves poetic ends; my aim will be to suggest the imaginative effects made possible by a constant alternation, in larger or smaller units, of time and place. Landscape and retrospection are not simply interspersed one with another; Pope uses the device of displacement to achieve a richer and more resonant statement. The Twickenham editors observe that the poem "celebrates not only the destiny of a nation, but also that of a world": [1] we might add that its prophecy extends beyond an immediately topical subject (the Treaty of Utrecht) to a wider mythical span of "golden years". The meaning expands in two related but separate dimensions.

Again, we are familiar with the idea of binary effects in Augustan poetry. A form such as mock-heroic will force two scales of value or two ways of looking at a subject into close proximity. Even at the level of syntax there is a similar process: the favoured rhetorical figures lay one element against another in contrast or comparison. And, taking the matter down to an individual word, William Empson has argued that we can detect components within the term "wit" in the *Essay on Criticism*, and see how Pope plays one off against another. "On my theory," Empson writes, "a double meaning 'A.B.' in a word often forms a covert assertion 'A=B', called an equation; it is read 'A is B' and can be interpreted in various ways, such as 'A is like B', 'A is part of B', and 'A entails B'." [2] I shall not here be exploring ambiguities within a single word as Empson does. But my account of *Windsor Forest* rests on an allied notion. In the larger units of organization, such as verse paragraphs, and in the smaller units (couplets, lines, clauses), I perceive collisions of meaning rather as Empson does. There are certain differences, however; I shall confine myself to the interplay of two specific terms—that is, my A and B will always be expressions of space and time respectively—and I shall be dealing with *difference* as much as identity. The easiest way of asserting a negative equation $A \neq B$ within Augustan idiom is to use antithesis: first A, *but* on the other hand B. However, simple parallelism can sometimes achieve the same end —this is how zeugma works. The threats posed to Belinda in

The Rape of the Lock, "Or stain her Honour, or her new Brocade . . ." are presented as straighforward alternatives, not (formally) as contrasts; the shared verb resists the implicit antithesis. There are more complex effects, for example with chiasmus: in the *Epistle to a Lady*, the face of old women, "A Fop for their Passion, but their Prize a Sot", takes the form of an inverse proportion sum—as A:B, so (all the more certainly) B:A. In *Windsor Forest*, as I see it, what happens is that the binary terms are set in varying relationships—time passes but the scene remains the same; or the scene changes but the golden age is renewed, and so on. Sometimes the dimensions vary together, a mode of parallelism; sometimes they do not, a mode of antithesis or paradox. The full import of the poetry derives from this shifting pattern of like and unlike features.

1

If we consider first the broad design, the invocation of six lines opens with a straightforward locative construction, "Thy Forests, *Windsor*! and thy green Retreats", and concludes with a tribute to the dedicatee, Granville. There follows the crucial verse-paragraph in which the beauties of the forest are described, initially by means of comparison with "the Groves of *Eden*, vanish'd now so long" and then by contrast with exotic and mythical settings. This section (7–42) contains some of the most explicit spatial writing found in the poem:

> Here in full Light the russet Plains extend;
> There wrapt in Clouds the blueish Hills ascend.
>
> (23–4)

As well as the verbs, emphasised by their rhyme, Pope employs direct situational words (*here/there*) to enhance the sense of moving in an ordered progression around a well-charted landscape. Next comes a recollection of the forest under the Norman yoke (43–92), transferred imaginatively from the New Forest to the region of Windsor and (perhaps as a consequence) couched in generalized terms (*cities, wilds, woods, dens, caves*)—the plural forms indicate a lack of topographical specificity. There *is* a vague sense of place, but it is overpowered by the strong evocation of historic processes. After this occur five verse paragraphs (93–164)

42

evoking the pursuits of the countryside through each season in turn, beginning with autumn; an extended present-tense episode contrasting with what goes before and after. From line 165 to 218 we are back in the past, with a mythological setpiece narrating the metamorphosis of the nymph Lodona. In the next section (219–34) the Thames is compared with other waters, real or legendary; then there is a section in praise of retirement (235–58), leading into a celebration of the historic associations of the area—first literary and then royal and national (259–328). The appearance of Father Thames heralds the most obvious topographical section of *Windsor Forest* (329–48), with a catalogue on Renaissance lines of the various tributaries. This issues into the prophetic vision of peace and prosperity, involving comparison with great rivers of the world and a glimpse of a magnificently renewed city of London (349–84); and finally into the picture of a harmonious world united in trade and humanity alike (385–422). There remains a brief peroration (423–34), recalling the opening and turning once again towards pastoral idiom.

Schematically the design can be set out in a simple form, which serves to illustrate the predominance in turn of temporal and spatial viewpoints.

lines	paragraphs	content	space/time	tense
1–6	1	Invocation	S	
7–42	2	description of forest	S (T)	
43–92	3	Norman yoke	T	past
93–164	4–8	seasonal sports	S (T)	present
165–218	9–10	Lodona	T	past
219–34	11	Thames	S	
235–58	12	retirement		
259–328	13–19	literary/historic links	T	past
329–48	20	catalogue of rivers	S	
349–422	21–23	prophecy	S (T)	future
423–34	24	peroration	(S)	

Crude as this layout must be, it shows the main shifts of poetic focus. Moreover, the turning-points are marked by appeals to a patriotic or party-political witness. At the end of paragraphs 1, 12, 14 and 16 as well as the beginning of 24, Pope makes direct allusion to an individual, Granville or Trumbull; at the end of paragraphs 2, 8, 19 and 22 the reference is to the Queen herself. Paragraph 3 concludes with a less open piece of Stuart propaganda, though "fair Liberty" is unquestionably a surrogate for Anne. Such firm articulation allows Pope to take in a large imaginative compass, without any fear that his readers will lose track of his ultimate purposes. At the junctures I have indicated as forming hinges of the argument, he changes direction with easy assurance, confident that the sequence of tenses and the perceptual logic of his poem will both be clear. There are no fussy bridge passages. A brisk verbal semaphore ("Not thus the Land appear'd in Ages past") and the transition from place to time is affected. A simple narrative statement ("In that blest Moment, from his Oozy Bed / Old Father *Thames* advanc'd his rev'rend Head") and we make the opposite change. Where many nineteenth-century novelists agonized over the disjunction between narrative and description, Pope without any coyness sharply alters the angle of our attention. It is not, of course, primarily a matter of his personal merits as a writer. Rather it is that the Augustan poet somehow is standing far enough away from his material to be able to make this control possible. From the start we are never quite *in* the forest, and there is no literalism offended when we are required to pull away in order to redirect our gaze to Arcadia or to envisage London as a celestial city in some imagined golden days to come.[3]

These broad effects are relatively straightforward. What happens within the verse paragraphs is at once more profound and harder to describe. The general physical movement is from the forest proper, down the Thames and its up-stream tributaries to the town and castle of Windsor, and thence to London and the open sea. Counterpointed against this is a progression from Eden and mythological antiquity through Norman tyranny, medieval wars, Renaissance poets and the Civil War down to Anne's propitious reign and the glorious future foretold. In very broad terms something like a set of equivalences can be drawn up—this is not to be taken too literally, but it does suggest an underlying thread in the imaginative design.

Provided we do not lay too much stress on any individual correspondence (which it will certainly not stand), the diagram opposite gives some clue of the way in which the poem works subliminally. Pope's immediate purposes were to endorse the peace treaty, to

S	T
Forest groves	Garden of Eden
Upper Thames and confluent stream	Classical antiquity
Hunting park	Norman reigns
Windsor	Medieval and chivalric associations (e.g. Garter)
Cooper's Hill	Seventeenth-century poets
London & Westminster	Anne's reign
Ocean beyond	Future Golden Age ensured by Utrecht settlement

congratulate his patron Granville for his diplomacy (and to welcome him to the nobility) and to locate future prosperity in a Stuart and Tory dispensation. His strategies involved a number of spatial metaphors. The forest itself stands for Edenic perfection, and also the true peace brought about by Tory diplomacy—as against the warmongering City-based Whigs and their hero Marlborough. Windsor is the fount of honour, the home of royalty, the embodiment of that national virtue which the aristocracy—now joined by Granville—incorporates. London is the centre of the court, of religious life, and of noble civilization symbolized by Anne's wise government. All these places exist in the present, linked by the Thames; they have a past and a future, but these are incorporated selectively—there is no sense within the poem of London as a medieval city.

The flexibility of poetic viewpoint can be illustrated from paragraph 2. We begin with a broad gesture outwards, to "The Groves of *Eden*, vanish'd now so long", that is a subject remote in time and space. The next line tells us that the groves yet "live" and "look green" by reason of Milton's recreation in *Paradise Lost*; the second expression renders in visual terms a fact about the moral survival of paradise. The Miltonic recollection may be active again in line 13, "Not *Chaos*-like together crush'd and bruis'd": certainly the phrase invokes a suprahistorical time-scale and asks us to think almost along physico-theological lines about beauty in the world. After this we move into more orthodox spatial terms, until presently a classical comparison is offered:

> Not proud *Olympus* yields a nobler Sight,
> Tho' God assembled grace his tow'ring Height,

45

> Than what more humble Mountains offer here,
> Where, in their Blessings, all those Gods appear.
>
> (33–6)

By a common rhetorical trick things are shown to be alike because they aren't quite alike; Olympus, and by implication the ancient world of the gods, is *not* more impressive though scenically more grand; the gods are not missed because their gifts to humanity are present in abundance. Then the concluding couplet:

> Rich Industry sits smiling on the Plains,
> And Peace and Plenty tell, a STUART reigns.

This is a dynastic claim, an assertion regarding a particular temporal state brought about by particular historical contingencies. But it is formulated as a description of the appearance of the landscape.

The technique is allegoric, very well, but not all allegory operates in precisely this way. Typically in *Windsor Forest* statements ostensibly about place (here the look of the countryside) turn out to be really statements about time (here the providential occurrence of Stuart rule). Or vice versa. At the next hinge-point, line 92, the assertion that liberty "leads in the golden Years" has a punning quality, following description of "yellow Harvests" and "unusual Grain". Locked into the phrase is a vision of ripe cornfields stretching out over the landscape. No doubt all metaphoric language has this capacity to combine perspectives in a single phrase, but *Windsor Forest* makes especially telling use of this capacity. In every crucial passage some words ask us to regard the data as something existing in space, others to apprehend them as something occurring in time. A dual perception is built into the language: the beauties of the forest are there but they are "raised" or "revived", as a distinct act, by poetry.

2

The mode of conjunction varies. Sometimes the pattern is one of simple aggregation: in Empson's algebra, ST resolves itself into "S+T".

> Here arm'd with Silver Bows, in early Dawn,
> Her buskin' Virgins trac'd the Dewy Lawn.
>
> (169–70)

Almost as classically pure is the construction of alternatives, "S or T", which we read as a kind of equivalence. The happy man secure in his Horatian retirement, occupies himself with worlds distant in one dimension or the other.

> Now marks the Course of rolling Orbs on high;
> O'er figur'd Worlds now travels with his Eye.
> Of ancient Writ unlocks the learned Store,
> Consults the Dead, and lives past Ages o'er.
>
> (245–48)

On other occasions the two elements are fused into something like oxymoron; the underlying sense is "though S, yet T". This is especially important where Pope is concerned with the eternising power of art, a theme common to much of his early work— as at the end of *The Rape of the Lock*, the lines *To Mr. Addison* and *The Temple of Fame*.

> (On *Cooper*'s Hill eternal Wreaths shall grow,
> While lasts the Mountain, or while *Thames* shall flow).
>
> (265–66)

The order in which ideas are called up here is STST/TSST, with the near paradoxical "eternal Wreaths" surrounded by other notions of topography or of duration. This is carried through at greater length a few lines further on:

> 'Tis yours, my Lord, to bless our soft Retreats,
> And call the Muses to their ancient Seats,
> To paint anew the flow'ry Sylvan Scenes,
> To crown the Forests with Immortal Greens,
> Make *Windsor* Hills in lofty Numbers rise,
> And lift her Turrets nearer to the Skies;
> To sing those Honours you deserve to wear,
> And add new Lustre to her Silver Star.
>
> (283–90)

In its original version the poem moved at this point to a conclusion similar to the one we actually have (but deferred for 150 lines). In the final paragraph, as printed in 1713, there is a dense cluster of phrases linking temporal and spatial concepts ("the Scenes of opening Fate"). The ideas mesh with one another to form a rhythm or reticulation:

47

> Ev'n I more sweetly pass my careless Days,
> Pleas'd in the silent Shade with empty Praise.
>
> (431–32)

The two lines convey closely allied notions—pleasure, vacancy, slight inutility—and yet the experience is viewed from a different standpoint in each case.

More important for the total imaginative design than this deliberately muted coda is the resonant prophecy of Father Thames which immediately precedes it. It is at this culminating moment that Pope exploits the richest resources of his displacement technique. The grand style is aptly enlisted to body forth both geographical extent and a wide sweep of history.

> Hail Sacred *Peace*! hail long-expected Days,
> That *Thames*'s Glory to the Stars shall raise!
> Tho' *Tyber*'s Streams immortal *Rome* behold,
> Tho' foaming *Hermes* swells with Tydes of Gold,
> From Heav'n it self tho' sev'nfold *Nilus* flows,
> And Harvests on a hundred Realms bestows;
> These now no more shall be the Muse's Themes,
> Lost in my Fame, as in the Sea their Streams.
>
> (355–62)

The surging movement of this verse is appropriate to the natural pulse it conveys (tides, harvests, the course of rivers). Throughout this prophetic section Pope uses connectives drawn from each dimension: there are visual signals which invite our attention to the scale of physical events (*Behold!* / *I see, I see* / *Hail!*) and also temporal links (*No more* / *Now* / *Once more* / *Then* / *Till*). The picture of the Thames at London is simultaneously a view of a splendid landscape and an account of a process—both geographical scene and historic juncture:

> Behold! th'ascending *Villa*'s on my Side
> Project long Shadows o'er the Chrystal Tide.
> Behold! *Augusta*'s glitt'ring Spires increase,
> And Temples rise, the beauteous Works of Peace,
> I see, I see where two fair Cities bend
> Their ample Bow, a new *White-Hall* ascend!
>
> (375–80)

It is writing of this order, drawing on the accumulated funds of poetic implication built up earlier, which defines the special quality of *Windsor Forest*. The great city imagined is a new place but also a new time, a stage in national revolution ushered in by the Tory peace.

As the prophecy mounts to its climax, Pope offers his vision of futurity in terms of a figurative expansion of the forest, as ships made from its timber ply great oceans:

> Thy Trees, fair *Windsor*! now shall leave their Woods,
> And half thy Forests rush into my Floods,
> Bear *Britain*'s Thunder, and her Cross display,
> To the bright Regions of the rising Day.
>
> (385–88)

The course of empire "in Times to come" is presented as a collaboration between the forest and the river, whose symbolic identities have been fully established earlier on in the poem. Then follows a characteristic flight of rhetoric, just as characteristically (for the age) expressing a pious commercial hope "that London may be made a FREE PORT" (Pope's note).

> The Time shall come, when free as Seas or Wind
> Unbounded *Thames* shall flow for all Mankind,
> Whole Nations enter with each swelling Tyde,
> And Seas but join the Regions they divide;
> Earth's distant Ends our Glory shall behold,
> And the new World launch forth to seek the Old.
>
> (397–402)

At such a juncture we require, in reading, a double focus, which allows us to respond both to the spread of concord through trade and to the sense of large historical purposes fulfilled— "distant Ends" would fit either.[4] Since this is a poem taking its origin from the Utrecht negotiations, and since these involved a marked curtailment of Spanish power in the lucrative American sector (a major, though covert, reason for the entire war), Pope's version of liberty understandably means the freeing of Spanish America. It was a process not to get fully under way for a hundred years more, and arguably by then British colonialism had supplanted Spain's over a large portion of the earth. Nevertheless the poetic intensity is genuine enough:

> Oh stretch thy Reign, fair *Peace*! from Shore to Shore,
> Till Conquest cease, and Slav'ry be no more:

49

Till the freed *Indians* in their native Groves
Reap their own Fruits, and woo their Sable Loves,
Peru once more a Race of Kings behold,
And other *Mexico's* be roof'd with Gold.

(407–12)

Just as the forest had renewed Edenic perfection (the link is made
with *groves* and *fruit*) and London had restored Augustan splendour (*kings* and *gold* refer back), so a liberated America will
fulfil ultimate and divine purposes. The Twickenham editors speak
of the conclusion as suggesting "at least half-seriously, the trans-
formation which the earth, in the fulness of time, shall under-
go".[5] I do not think there can be any doubt about the seriousness
of Pope's poetic assertions; they have the full workings of the
poem behind them, for *Windsor Forest* has been from the start
a vision of "Golden Days". Viewed synchronically, this is expressed through the symbols of forest, river, and city; viewed
diachronically, through the millennial triumph of the Stuart cause.
The art of *Windsor Forest* is built around the interanimation of
these two modes of perceiving; and the poem lives on, though the
historical prophecy has been rebutted by events and the setting
invaded by motorways, airports and suburban pollution.

NOTES

1 *Pastoral Poetry and An Essay on Criticism,* ed. E. Audra and A.
   Williams (London, 1961), p. 144. (All quotations follow this edition.)
   The introduction, pp. 131–44, supplies the best general survey of the
   poem.
2 William Empson, "Wit in the *Essay on Criticism*", reprinted in *Essential Articles for the Study of Alexander Pope*, ed. M. Mack (Hamden,
   Conn., rev. edn. 1968), p. 208. This is a more concise statement of
   Empson's theory than its elaboration in *The Structure of Complex Words*
   (London, 1951): see pp. 40–1.
3 Ralph Cohen has spoken of "the development of a comparative, historical consciousness" in poems such as *Cooper's Hill* or *Upon Apple-
   ton House*, which "tied the idea of vision to that of history". This
   "discovered relation between observations of nature and historical
   retrospection" applies even more directly to *Windsor Forest* in my
   view, though Cohen does not mention it. See Cohen, "On the Interre-

lations of Eighteenth-Century Literary Forms", (*New Approaches to Eighteenth-Century Literature*, ed. P. Harth (New York, 1974), pp. 33–78.

4 I have discussed these "large purposes" more fully in "Trade and Empire: *Annus Mirabilis and Windsor-Forest*", *Durham University Journal*, LXIX (1976), pp. 14–20.

5 *Pastoral Poetry*, p. 144.

3

Uniting Airy Substance:
The Rape of the Lock 1712-1736

by ROBIN GROVE

The critical engines have not proved fatal yet: Pope is a great deal more agile than his commentators. But then, he knew he needed to be so. He took their measure early, issuing them with Discourses on Pastoral, "Keys" to his works, or parodies of their own apparatus. ("The *Machinery*, Madam, is a Term invented by the Criticks . . .") Yet despite his efforts the Aristarchs marched on until he must have wondered if any power could stop them, the triumph of the mighty academic Dunces seeming to ensure all poets are to be laid low:

> Turn what they will to Verse, their toil is vain,
> Critics like me shall make it Prose again
> (*Dunciad*, IV, 213–14)

—except that Bentley's proud threat in its moment of utterance is turned *back* into wit, by Pope.

It is this wit, able to catch and transform pedantry itself, which makes one hope critics need not abdicate entirely, uncomfortable though we must feel under such a writer's eye. Instead we might take our cue from the criticism Pope practised on his own productions. For there we have the chance to grasp, not in theory but in living practice, the nature of his creative enterprise. It is something more fallible than he may have thought. In fact his verse turns out to be surprisingly uneven, once the high finish of its couplets has ceased to dazzle us. On the other hand, Pope's habit of "revising and re-revising", as F. W. Bateson has called it,[1] is evidence not so much of failure narrowly avoided ("an erratic stylistic sense") as of the unusual closeness of the critic in him to the creative writer. Much the most interesting revisions are those where creativity, as we watch, renews itself by repossessing and reshaping what it has already made. To call this activity "criticism" hardly seems generous enough; yet that is what it is; and it is so impressive in Pope that, far from his being over-rated now, he seems almost unrecognized as the extraordinarily flexible poet-critic he is.

Nowhere more active than in *The Rape of the Lock*, which not only provides, like *The Dunciad*, shorter and longer versions for comparison but, being his first sustainedly great work, shows his genius seized by the opportunity growing in confidence and power. In humanity too, and self-understanding. So the methodizing orator of the *Essay on Criticism* gives place to a poet whose good nature, as well as his moral sense, appears in what he made of the commission to laugh two families together again. What may have begun as a *jeu d'esprit* to be tossed aside once their breach was healed, assumed unexpected significance under his hand. Already he had transformed the quarrel itself; now, over the next years, he transformed the poem too, extending, revising, omitting—turning whatever was left of original pain into greater beauty and laughter.

Thus its history is as follows. The poem was probably begun during August 1711, and the author later said it took him less than a fortnight to compose. But no publication occurred until 20 May 1712, and Pope's rueful complaint (it "has been so long coming out, that the Ladies Charms might have been half decay'd, while the Poet was celebrating them, and the Printer publishing them") suggests he could revise at leisure what he had composed in such dextrous haste. Whether or not he did re-work the poem at this point however he was certainly re-thinking it soon after it appeared. His burlesque *Receit to make an Epick Poem*, in the *Guardian* of 10 June 1713, is one clue to that, and by 8 December of the same year he is writing to Swift that the revisions to the *Locke* are complete. This second version, in five Cantos not two, was released in March 1714, and within four days had sold "to the number of three thousand, and is already reprinted". A third edition—in effect, another reprinting—followed in July; a fourth which did introduce minor changes, mainly of punctuation, came just over a year later, in September 1715, by which date Pope was claiming sales in excess of six thousand copies. Public interest in the poem clearly kept pace with the author's own. The last substantial revision to it was made for his collected *Works*, 1717, an edition which not only intensified the effect of earlier re-writings but added Clarissa's thirty lines in Canto V, "to open more clearly the MORAL of the Poem". With that, Pope's revisions were virtually complete. His few later emendations, with one exception perhaps, promote ease rather than increased richness of reading. We are left therefore with three significant texts: *The Rape of the Locke* (hereafter *Locke*, or 1712); the version of 1714 which introduces the Sylphs; and (1717) the poem more or less as we have it today. The overlappings and metamorphoses show us Pope's imagination re-imagining a piece already so finished that, in one critic's judgment, he could not hope to better it, and so should leave well alone.

1

Addison's advice, though it irritated Pope, was obviously sincere. The *Locke* is a beautifully accomplished poem which makes so much of its slight material that no one would predict its author could make more. And as it happens, a modern reader taking up the standard text might scan its first dozen lines without realizing how new a poem this version, post-1717, is. But whereas ll. 13–14 originally read:

> *Sol* thro' white Curtains did his Beams display,
> And op'd those Eyes which brighter shine than they
> (1712)[2]

—and that was how things stayed in 1714—now, in the latest version of the poem, a different action is commenced:

> *Sol* thro' white curtains shot a tim'rous ray,
> And op'd those eyes that must eclipse the day
> (1717)

The changes are not extensive. Both couplets gallantly flatter Belinda, and the first has if anything a more forthright energy. But only in the later version does the Sun himself offer the masculine compliment of "shooting" his Ray through her Curtains, to turn tentative as he touches them and gently enters in. He has *cause* to be timorous this time, when her eyes eclipse Nature's

own light: day itself—with which we reach astronomical gran-
deurs hardly realized in the sunrise of version I. Trope here, in
1717, approaches Metaphysical conceit; but Pope's decorum creates
something unlike any earlier good morrow. For the outside universe, like the sexual awareness of writer and reader, graciously
keeps its place: sunlight trembles to enter Belinda's room; its
fierceness hesitates, then quietens, crossing the line-break to "ope"
her eyes so gravely; and Pope's amusement tenderly encompasses
it all. He has, re-writing, strengthened both the ardour of the sun
and the power of Belinda's beauty, while the harmonic consciousness of the Augustan couplet, composing things into so luminous
a whole, enables him to distribute through the phrasing more
mockery and more praise both at once. Nor does he choose between them. Rather, delight and irony intensify each other, and the
couplet-form itself shines brighter in his mind the more daring
the range of innuendo it contains.

So it will be my argument that what opened before Pope as he
strove with his poem was a new sense of the aesthetic (which in
this case is to say, the human) issues entailed in his mock-heroic
world. In fact, mock-heroic itself, the superior irony it implies, is
questioned and explored: as in the present couplet. For the
Belinda of 1712 is the possessor of eyes so conventionally marvel-
lous that they are, merely, "brighter" than the sun. It took Pope
some time to see that simple increase or diminution, the trick of
mock-heroic, would never be enough. The ironies it yields are
telling, but too easy. Hence the quite different order of metaphoric
play in the revision of 1717, where in place of quantification comes
active, sexual beauty—Belinda's of course, but surely the sun-
god's as well: each inviting the other's advance, although to accept
would be to be mastered or eclipsed. At one stroke now, the
ambiguous drama of the poem is ready to waken into life, leaving
mock-heroic for the sake of pleasures of a subtler, more poignant
kind. To achieve that certainly took more than local smoothing
of the verse. Nor do we appreciate the revisions if we stress only
Pope's large reforms, such as the insertion of the Sylphs, and
the card-game, and Clarissa's "good Humour" speech. Pope was
proud of his new Machinery, as Warburton reports, but pleased
most of all that he had prepared the poem to receive it and was
able to make it work. So his first re-writings prepare us also to
receive his imagination's most audacious creatures.

No doubt it's for this reason that he worked so minutely over the opening sequences themselves.

> What dire Offence from Am'rous Causes springs,
> What mighty Quarrels rise from Trivial Things,
> I sing—This Verse to C—l, Muse! is due;
> This, ev'n *Belinda* may vouchsafe to view:
> Slight is the Subject, but not so the Praise,
> If she inspire, and He approve my Lays.
>
> (I, 1–6; 1712)

Read one way, the lines have truly epic sonority and syntax; for a moment they bring what the age had been taught to recognize as Homeric passions into sight. Next moment, though, the mighty subject just proposed is mocked, its "dire" threat emerging from trivial things and offset by the twangling music of a modern bard endeavouring to pluck impressive noises from an instrument inadequate to the task (*springs/Things/sing*). It makes such a good joke that the author is willing to bear the cacophony. ("Amrus cauzis . . . Horrible!" Tennyson wailed, "I would sooner die than write such a line.") But while critics as fine-eared as he and Bateson regret the dissonance, Pope more wittily retains it through all his emendations—if only because a reader accustomed to Grand Style needs to be kept on guard. Otherwise, he will din himself into accepting anything, even the next couplet, so long as it's pitched high enough.

> Slight is the Subject, but not so the Praise,
> If she inspire, and He approve my Lays.

A compliment certainly to Belinda and Caryll: between them they make whatever a poet does worthwhile; but this gallantry contains an insolence that dares them to notice it—so slight a subject for the verse as she is, and he so undiscriminating that he'll approve effusions regardless of merit or fault. If a final compliment survives, it does so by winning its way through audacities like this.

In all, it would be wrong to call this first opening to the poem less than brilliant. The only doubt might be as to its equilibrium: whether the manner isn't too heavily loaded against the matter, the shuttling from Epic to Commonplace too briskly demeaning? So it is interesting to gather Pope's own sense of justice hadn't been satisfied either. In 1714 he removes some of the heavy emphasis compelled on the reader by over-frequent capitals. 1717 brings a more inward-reaching change; for now the poem opens not with "Quarrels"—"What mighty Quarrels rise from Trivial Things" (I, 2; 1712)—but with a more questioning line: "What mighty contests rise from trivial things" (1717). The alteration is slight: one word; but where the original had the ring of contempt about it (merely, what happened between the Petre and Fermor families), the later noun is hoveringly suggestive: more resonant, because more abstract. For "Contest" takes many shapes, from heroic *agon* to petty squabble, and the new word leaves the ironies open, where the earlier had witheringly closed them off.

Couplet by couplet, then, Pope strives beyond his "history" into the larger significance that history contained. And as the poem increases in power, so do we as readers, its demands extending our capacities too, until in the quarrels over Arabella Fermor's hair we glimpse those graver conflicts in which virginity indeed is rent, and, simultaneously, fulfilled. Of course such innuendo was always present; the phrasing is *very* explicit, from the title, daring the reader to take it seriously, down to the "softest bosoms" and the play on Belle Fermor's name:

> Say what strange Motive, Goddess! cou'd compel
> A well-bred *Lord* t'assault a gentle *Belle?*
> (I, 7–8; 1712)

The poet's problem is to keep the implications of his language active but at bay—and in this the knowingness of mock-heroic was a positive liability, edging couplets towards the very cynicism decorum would suppress. Pope took years arriving at any solution. Even now, his apostrophe to the Goddess is one point where the poem slightly grates. Yet the irony he finally achieved turns mock-heroic back against itself, which was what he needed to do. For what produced indecorousness in the first place was this inflated style's refusal to be kept down: it *will* call the spoiling of a hair-style an "assault", a "rape", and the only way for 1712 to dismiss the shadow of reality thus roused was to make the actors seem incapable of sexual feats of the kind. Hence the sarcastic reduction:

> And dwells such Rage in *softest Bosoms* then?
> And lodge such daring Souls in *Little Men?*
> (I, 11–12; 1712)

57

Warton and others say Pope refers to short Lord Petre here; and certainly mock-heroic is keen to measure discrepancies, setting mighty Souls against their lack of inches. So this particular sneer survives in all the editions looked at so far. Not till 1736 when the last telling change to the Canto was made does Pope escape the superior "heartless" manner mock-heroic had imposed. He does escape however, by taking on himself the force of the jibe directed, till then, *away* from the clever poet. Now, that critical sense which is morality-in-practice involves him also in the irony, and syntax is re-worked to include not just Belinda, the Baron, and the poetic Muse, but the poet's own vulnerable self. Just for a moment the verse admits that "lively little creature, with long Arms and Legs: a Spider is no ill Emblem of him": the tiny poet *"Dick Distick by Name"* whose caricature Pope had drawn in *The Guardian* No. 92, and the self-image of the homunculus, painful and absurd, is gathered into the suavity of the lines. A quarter of a century after they were first laid down, the couplets are made to run as follows (and a footnote inserted to draw attention to the change):

> Say what strange motive, Goddess! could compel
> A well-bred Lord t'assault a gentle *Belle*?
> Oh say what stranger cause, yet unexplor'd,
> Cou'd make a gentle *Belle* reject a Lord?
> In tasks so bold, can little men engage,
> And in soft bosoms dwells such mighty Rage?
>
> (1736)

The "tasks" include those laid on the poet himself, whose most adventurous powers are needed if he is, thus engaged, to proclaim what the Goddess will reveal. Pope too becomes one of the little men who rise to bold undertakings, but on his own creative terms.

2

The revisions one on another of these opening lines show a poet fighting free of mock-heroic in order to establish the manner *appropriate* for an incident which, realistically viewed, makes any concern about it seeem absurd. "Slight is the subject," Pope admits. But then, realism itself is one of the attitudes the poem calls in question. It always did. Even the original *Locke* mocks naturalism with great *brio*; the trouble is, it still retains a quasi-

naturalistic form. Thus the ordinary world is not so much transformed as derided by the "epic" beauties superimposed on it. And
the discrepancy between the two is pointed up by the brisk transi-
tions propelling the story forward.

> *Sol* thro' white Curtains did his Beams display,
> And op'd those Eyes which brighter shine than they;
> *Shock* just had giv'n himself the rowzing Shake,
> And Nymphs prepar'd their *Chocolate* to take;
> Thrice the wrought Slipper knock'd against the Ground,
> And striking Watches the tenth Hour resound.
> *Belinda* rose, and 'midst attending Dames
> Launch'd on the Bosom of the silver *Thames*
>
> (I, 13–20; 1712)

Sun-rise to embarkation takes only three couplets. Pope's instinct
was right when he postponed the voyage, transferring it to what
became Canto II. But even with this prolongation of poetic time
the new poem, 1714, fails to make the most of the world he is
venturing upon. Like 1712, it spends its skill edging the narrative
forward, happy with the neat *appearance* of making points.

> *Sol* thro' white Curtains did his Beams display,
> And op'd those Eyes which brighter shine than they;
> Now *Shock* had giv'n himself the rowzing Shake,
> And Nymphs prepar'd their *Chocolate* to take;
> Thrice the wrought Slipper knock'd against the Ground,
> And striking Watches the tenth Hour resound.
> *Belinda* still her downy Pillow prest,
> Her Guardian *Sylph* prolong'd the balmy Rest.
>
> (I, 13–20; 1714)

As yet, nothing much is generated by the bringing together of
Belinda and Sol, Nymphs and lapdog. If anything, a smoother
rhythm—"Now *Shock* . . ."—weakens the briskness with which
the little creature first started into life. And for most of the
passage the halves of each couplet adhere in demure ironies with
nowhere significant to go. Pope is too concerned with getting his
new actors, Ariel and the others, onto stage to be fully alert to the
beauty and ridiculousness of the world awakening inside his verse.
Only when his expansion of the poem was complete, and Belinda
and the Sylphs secure, did his imagination, re-inspired by them,
return to play over opportunities missed before. Not till 1717 do
the Nymphs disappear (called to a far better joke at their entry

in I, 62) and little dog Shock become one of a *class* of pampered creatures, all knowing what fashion demands of them and ready to meets its ordinances on the stroke of the clock. It is a breathtaking metamorphosis.

> *Sol* thro' white curtains shot a tim'rous ray,
> And op'd those eyes that must eclipse the day;
> Now lapdogs give themselves the rowsing shake,
> And sleepless lovers, just at twelve, awake:
> Thrice rung the bell, the slipper knock'd the ground,
> And the press'd watch return'd a silver sound.
>
> (I, 13–18; 1717)

The watches of earlier versions simply told the time. Now, their very mechanism's delicacy is felt, returning its "silver" sound to the finger's pressure. All sensuous response is heightened, to make the beauties of the passage tender, intense and ample in quite new ways. Here the sun-god himself parts curtains and eyelids timorously, only to deepen the luxury of balmy rest. No longer hurried through the jokes, we are allowed to catch lovers and lapdogs waking absurdly on time, yet to feel also the innocence of Belinda's sleep, untouched in its perfection, shaded by pure curtains, and not quite broken as the faint chimes measure the end of her virginal repose. Even as the world around her stirs, the one soft pressure, to awake, is reciprocated by the pressure of her dream and her head on its downy pillow. And this moment suspended between worlds makes way for the entry of her Sylph. "Thrice rung the bell, the slipper knock'd the ground"—those fragile dotted-rhythms are an overture to the airy substance, the thin glittering textures of the sylphic vision.

Pope's changes in short[3] ensure that the Sylphs are introduced to a poem, a reader, prepared for the miraculous to happen. Already, before Ariel appears, the sights and sounds of normality are being transfigured, which was necessary if the poem were to move beyond mock-epic. For inherent in the structure of a world "naturalistically" portrayed are assumptions which make any quarrel over a lock of hair look ridiculously small. Whereas what Pope came to see in his poem as he re-made it over and over again was something beyond a jest. Even naturalism with its disturbing appetites and touching inadequacies is left behind as satire opens into ambiguous celebration.

To be sure, the Belinda of 1712 had been captivating ("Love in these Labyrinths his Slaves detains"), but she was something of a pantomime virago too. By contrast, the Belinda of 1714 is exquisite, pitiable, and threatened. Yet so long as the poem remained story-bound the realisms of time and place, discrepancies between inflated statement and all-too-trivial deed, were liable to re-emerge and dispatch her. Therefore Pope creates a world whose *every* aspect is transformed. Inside Belinda's bedroom (itself raised to new beauty) he evokes her sleep, and within the interior time of that, her dream. The Sylphs who now enter the poem exist in their own element, hardly subject to mortal pains.

3

From here on Pope's revisions are less a matter of re-writing lines and couplets than of his bringing into the poem such unforeseen vivacities that its proportions are quite changed. Almost nothing of 1712 is actually discarded, so we see the more clearly the effect of its new environment, where the carried-over poetry feels so very different. What has happened is a shift in gravity, so to speak. Its centre is placed, not in mock-epic, but in Sylphs (of all creatures) who do their utmost to control events even as events take Belinda away from them, into the social world. Of course, seen from one angle Society is the very arena in which the Sylphs desire her to shine: on their terms only, though. Thus, as she wakes from her Morning-dream, to pass to the dressing-table, thence to the barge and card-party, rape and final battle —five stages of progressive engagement in the dangerous world of the sexes—so her progress is mapped out yet at the same time shielded by five insertions of sylphic matter, one to each new Canto. But the importance of these diminishes as the poem goes on. Occupying most of the foreground in Canto I, the Sylphs are little by little displaced until, in Canto V, they attract only a glance or two before the battle ends. So we watch them give way to cards, lovers, spleen and even speeches. Yet even so, the extent of their jurisdiction isn't easily defined. Maybe they *are* limited to standing-by, as Dr. Johnson thought: powerless to affect action in any way that counts. On the other hand, their power over the vanity of the human heart increases as events go on. And as for the poem's climax, if the Lock must be lost (as it must) its translation to the sky beyond the reach of any Ravisher is just the compromise which would please them most. For although the Sylphs withdraw in the closing sequences, neither the Lords *nor* the Ladies who are left have won.

Such equivocation is typical. Even Pope's original *Locke* makes "realism" about the fops and belles of modern society no very simple thing. Measured against Homeric heroes, these contemporaries of ours appear preposterously small: we must be realistic about them. But then, doesn't the light of common day show up past grandeur too, making us wonder if we are realistic about *it*? For whatever anyone did at great Anna's Hampton Court, some divinity or hero in Homer, Vergil, Milton, had done it before— a comparison which necessarily works both ways. So far, so complex. In 1714 these ironies redouble. They endure no breach but an expansion, into something more luminous and airy still. For the new poem sets a parallel below the human scale, as well as one above. We move not just among divinities now, but sylphids who, so much smaller, more delicate than humanity, provide their own commentary on it, and on its Homeric counterparts. The "humbler province" of these spirits is to tend the Fair, waging campaigns, not to avenge an epic wrong but to protect brocade. At the same time, though, we should not underestimate these battles. Just because of their tiny size they hold a kind of terror, as sylphic consciousness receives the brunt of happenings which to human sight hardly signify at all. "To save the Powder from too rude a Gale" takes courage if the lightest zephyr *is* a gale, not in poetic hyperbole (our gross point of view), but as experienced by translucent fluttering Sylphs. And so with the most delicately miniature events. The intensity with which delight, pain, danger, are felt by these filmy bodies makes the Sylphs' world momentarily vast, like wilds *inside* the "crystal" of the air.

> Some in the Fields of purest *Æther* play,
> And bask and whiten in the Blaze of Day.
> (II, 79–80; 1714)

An exquisite vulnerability (the condition of the creatures' freedom) is registered as they "whiten" in the Blaze of Day, sensitive even to the point of extinction.

To call such beings the "Machinery" of the poem is engagingly sly, but Pope's witticism reminds us how fine and mutltiple are the ways by which he mingled their insubstantial presence into the human drama. Had we not had the *Locke* of 1712 for comparison, we might never have been alerted to the Sylphs' seductions of tempo itself. But as against the briskness with which the heroine was first sent on her way the moment the clocks struck ten—

> *Belinda* rose, and 'midst attending Dames
> Launch'd on the Bosom of the silver *Thames*
> (I, 19–20; 1712)

—the revised poem allows her morning-rituals all the time in the world. In fact sylphic episodes in general are marked by suspension or tremulous pause. It is when the necessities of bodily life are allayed—when people do not *have* to wake, or get themselves somewhere, or eat from sheer hunger—that the Sylphs' opportunity appears. In spite of which it is above all these fastidious spirits who manifest the body's power. To them, all physicality may be threatening, but not even fine-dressed fops and ladies concern themselves more with the preciousness of bodily life. With the Sylphs' arrival in 1714 Belinda's living beauty is realized to the full as, surrounded by them at her dressing-table, laying artifice upon artifice, she grows lovelier while we watch. Nor is that loveliness mere daubing, as Dennis protested in his badtempered *Remarks on Mr. Pope's Rape of the Lock*, 1728. Belinda assisted by these Celestials in painting a "purer" blush on her cheeks is practising no fraud on nature, but bringing forth what nature is capable of, in an ideal world.

> Repairs her Smiles, awakens ev'ry Grace,
> And calls forth all the Wonders of her Face
> (I, 141–42; 1714)

Unaided realism could not see those wonders though, or make us respect her, if it were not for the Sylphs. In Canto I we have just begun to feel their presence, hardly accustomed as yet to the diminutive intensities of experience as proved on sylphic pulses. Tactfully, Pope reserves some of his best jokes in that style for episodes still to come. Yet already he is preparing us to realize what the world to Sylph-consciousness might be like.

> This Casket *India*'s glowing Gems unlocks,
> And all *Arabia* breaths from yonder Box.

The Tortoise here and Elephant unite,
Transform'd to *Combs*, the speckled and the white.
Here Files of Pins extend their shining Rows,
Puffs, Powders, Patches, Bibles, Billet-doux.
(I, 133–38; 1714)

Two perspectives are present here. By one, the world's spaciousness is ludicrously reduced: continents only aids to vanity; Arabia itself distilled to a perfume, and even that put away in a box. From another angle, though, closer to the "essence" of things, the dressing-table is a wonder of sensuous life. What fragrance is released by that tender verb, "And all *Arabia* breaths . . ."; the very pins allure the eye, drawing up in miniature formation to "extend their shining Rows"; while as for the purpose behind the boudoir's array, the verse is alert to the merest hint—as when it catches Tortoise and Elephant coupled in love-play, before the prudent explanation ("*Combs*") returns the stage to rights. We may not be ready to view the scene as Sylphs do, but the episode foreshadows something of what such visions might be like.

Yet even so, our delight in the Sylphs and what they make of feminine beauty is carefully restrained. Pope is aware of Belinda with an admiration fuller, more delicate than theirs, though it permits him to be critical with a gravity her aerial flatterers never approach at all.

And now, unveil'd, the *Toilet* stands display'd,
Each Silver Vase in mystic Order laid.
First, rob'd in White, the Nymph intent adores
With Head uncover'd the *Cosmetic* Pow'rs.
A heav'nly Image in the Glass appears,
To that she bends, to that her Eyes she rears
(I, 121–26; 1714)

The Sylphs encourage this strange separation of self from appearance, and to their blandishments Belinda is only too ready to succumb. Succumb she does, moreover; but not entirely. For Pope genuinely does allow her freedom. Compared to the verse the Sylphs attract, the ampler quieter movements of the writing here open a silence around Belinda, even amid her self-regard. The emphasis falls less on the vanity of her devotions than on the slow ritual movements by which living figure and mirror-image answer one another. Her reflection itself "appears" as if of its own voli-

64

tion, and there is a self-forgetfulness in the posture of the girl, rapt before this beautiful Other who is distanced as well as disclosed by her glass. In all, she is touchingly innocent, as though fashionable Society really were a *pastorale* where fine ladies appear as Nymphs, not in spite of their cosmetic arts but because of them indeed.

All the same, as this triumph of modishness shows, there is a dismaying side to the obligatory "innocence" of a belle. She must attract men—to be irresistible is her *raison d'être*; and yet no whisper of notoriety must blow on her, since reputation is a tissue so fine it is easily spoilt forever, and Appearances (if nothing else) must be kept intact. Even should she "yield" to a lover, therefore, that must be made a victory too. The successful beauty never gives herself away. So we begin to see the perilous balance a Belinda must maintain. The perfection of her virginity *is* something to be treasured. Whether as the Sylphs would cherish and adorn it, though, is another matter. For they teach armed frigidity.

> Favours to none, to all she Smiles extends,
> Oft she rejects, but never once offends.
> Bright as the Sun, her Eyes the Gazers strike,
> And, like the Sun, they shine on all alike.
> (II, 11–14; 1714)

Brilliance and poise are what the Sylphs admire: a femininity able to excite but endlessly refuse; and its quality is well suggested by that hard verb, "strike". At this point however it needs to be said that precisely this was the nature of Belinda's triumph in the first, pre-sylphic poem too. 1712; I, 27–30: her dazzling appearance on the barge occurs in just these terms—a fact which helps us grasp what happened to material Pope carried over from earlier to later version.

It is rather like the situation described in Eliot's famous essay.

> The existing order is complete before the new work arrives; for order to persist after the supervention of novelty, the *whole* existing order must be, if ever so slightly, altered . . .[4]

When Pope revised the *Locke* of 1712, something new was made not only in re-written or added verse, but also out of poetry left untouched. That is, the changed context changed our reading even of lines which remained the same. And indeed Pope's own sense

of what he'd created in 1712 altered as his understanding of
Belinda grew. She had always been accorded a suitably double-
edged praise; he now saw how much *more* troubling those ironies
became, once drawn into the orbit of the Sylphs. Who better than
they to applaud the frigidity of the coquette, armed for conquest
and victorious in her disdain of every suitor? On the other hand,
who better than Sylphs to reflect the transience of beauty, touchingly ephemeral no matter how exploited or misused? In a poem
alive with such creatures, Belinda's own beauty is refracted and
heightened again by "thousand bright Inhabitants of Air". We have
not exactly left the world of Fashion and current cliché; rather,
we are enabled to *see* its hyperboles, and feel the implications of
their sensuous force, as if for the first time. So it is with the compliment to Belinda's dazzling eyes. In the poem of 1712 such
praise was *de rigueur*: "lively Looks", radiant non-committal smiles,
all part of the conventional armoury of the belle. By 1714 however
the ironies of that language are persuaded into the narrative
drama itself. Compliment and metaphor are so far mythologized
that they become presences in their own right, imaginary landscapes (almost) which Sylphs at least might inhabit. Thus the
Thames-voyage in the newly-conceived Canto II opens with a
passage of operatic splendour.

> Not with more Glories, in th'Etherial Plain,
> The Sun first rises o'er the purpled Main,
> Than issuing forth, the Rival of his Beams
> Lanch'd on the Bosom of the Silver *Thames*.
> (II, 1–4; 1714)

Restoration gallantry, with its "Goddesses" and "Nymphs", now
finds itself put to the test. Belinda, to eyes adjusting themselves
to sylphic vision, seems "divine" indeed. Of course, the poetry is
careful to suggest what is dubious about such glories: the florid
Drydenesque of the lines is, by Pope's own standards, in poor
taste, the Sylphs being conservative-vulgar in literary matters as
in others, I suspect. Yet what living metaphors are released.
Through the eulogy, Homeric amplitude is gained by common
day ("th'Etherial Plain"), while Belinda, seen to be heavenly as is
a belle's prerogative, gives light to all the world, even her satellites
("Fair Nymphs, and well-drest Youths around her shone") gleam-
ing not with the light of their own finery, as they did in 1712, but

with that of *her* beams, received and given back to add to her proper glory. It is as though the very tropes acclimatize themselves to a poem containing Sylphs and, in doing so, reveal intensities we never knew they held.

No such coherence governs action in the poem of 1712. There, Belinda rises, embarks, and after the (inset) Baron's sacrifice, her arrival at Hampton Court is simply announced: "Close by those Meads for ever crown'd with Flow'rs" (I, 65; 1712). Tempo is a matter of moving the story forward. Whereas by 1714 each "soft transition" helps to create new meaning. Hidden metaphors are released; the Baron performs his sacrifice to Love, and this time the object of his prayers comes in view: a moment of pause not thought of when Belinda made her original journey.

> But now secure the painted Vessel glides,
> The Sun-beams trembling on the floating Tydes,
> While melting Musick steals upon the Sky,
> And soften'd Sounds along the Waters die.
> Smooth flow the Waves, the Zephyrs gently play[,]
> *Belinda* smil'd, and all the World was gay.
> (II, 47–54; 1714)

Floating, poised, the "painted Vessel" is as much Belinda as the barge she rides in, and we feel the precarious balance of them both as, "secure" on trembling sunbeams, they bear their precious freight. Nothing more beautifully embodies the values upheld by so much Augustan art: the smoothness of surface, the "social" aplomb, the yielding sentiment exquisitely restrained by decorum. We might almost call Belinda herself, like the poetry in which she is created, a Metaphor for the politeness of high eighteenth-century civilization.

But that *is* too abstract. Pope's verse is content to assemble a fine variety of poetical Device, all the way from Heroic to lyrical-popular, and then at the proper moment divert attention from itself, in honour of Belinda. Neither the poetry nor she need be treated as "metaphor" for anything else, since they are both so alive themselves. With Belinda, however, the question remains, what will she make of that life? For seemingly she holds herself aloof. "Favours to none, to all she Smiles extends": that is the Goddess who is carried on the barge, indifferently smiling on all alike. Being a Goddess, the imperturbable ease which Fashion decrees and well-bred Literature seeks (the *Tatler*, No. 5) is already hers, and it protects her from any discomforting approach. Yet the verse throbs on every side with contrary undermeanings: "trembling", "melting", "soften'd"—the language of sentimental romance, climaxing in its favoured euphemism, "die". The Belinda who outwardly is all uncommitted elegance now seems, should her weakness be discovered, only too ready to succumb: an estimate which again applies to the Augustan art the lines ironically represent (the chiasmus of 1.51, 'Smooth flow the Waves . . ." is noticeably elegant-sentimental). With either party, however, Pope is too polite to insist. He provides something more fascinating than mockery: a transition to the region of the Sylphs through, of all things, the clichés which betray the belle's secret romantic heart.

We might have supposed the Sylphs would have nothing to do with worldly amours. "Reject Mankind" is after all the doctrine they have preached. But what leads to *sylphic* chastity, it turns out, is the very language of flirtation, "playing" on the scene to heighten it as no other hyperbole could. Meltingly tender attitudes are struck; sunbeams tremble, senses interchange till music steals upon the Sky and sound expires in Water. And these ardours prelude the reappearance of the Sylphs who alone are refined enough to possess the scene, although more evanescent even than it.

> Soft o'er the Shrouds Aerial Whispers breath,
> That seem'd but *Zephyrs* to the Train beneath.
> Some to the Sun their Insect-Wings unfold,
> Waft on the Breeze, or sink in Clouds of Gold.
> Transparent Forms, too fine for mortal Sight,
> Their fluid Bodies half dissolv'd in Light.
> Loose to the Wind their airy Garments flew,
> Thin glitt'ring Textures of the filmy Dew;
> Dipt in the richest Tincture of the Skies,
> Where Light disports in ever-mingling Dies,
> While ev'ry Beam new transient Colours flings,
> Colours that change when'er they wave their Wings.
> (II, 59–70; 1714)

The vision is more than enchanting: it is weirdly seductive too— partly *because* it cannot bear the lightest touch of grosser things. As the Sylphs half-reveal their fluid bodies, whisper overhead, "loose" their garments, or sink in pleasures where no mortal can follow, they eerily, fastidiously tantalize human sense. For, like the language of the barge-scene, they palpitate with "romantic" feelings. Of a highly specialized sort. From their vantage-point where they sport and flutter they watch over the purity of melting Maids; but purity as they value it is no very virginal state.

> Know further yet; Whoever fair and chaste
> Rejects Mankind, is by some *Sylph* embrac'd:
> For Spirits, freed from mortal Laws, with ease
> Assume what Sexes and what Shapes they please.
> (I, 67–70; 1714)

Ariel's phrasing already hints at the unearthly perversions of sylphic love. Soon he takes open pleasure in the corruptions practised on womankind by his cousin Gnomes.

> 'Tis these that early taint the Female Soul,
> Instruct the Eyes of young *Coquettes* to roll,
> Teach Infants Cheeks a bidden Blush to know,
> And little Hearts to flutter at a *Beau*.
> (I, 87–90; 1714)

Yet the full force of his offer to Belinda is not felt until we have discovered the alarming fact that the language of ardour and that of false-romantic frigidity are, or can be, the same. It is like the dilemma Empson summarizes in his chapter on double-plots: "Everything spiritual and valuable has a . . . revolting parody, very similar to it, with the same name. Only unremitting judgement can distinguish between them."[5] With Belinda, secure in her painted Vessel and smiling on all to the accompaniment of "melting", "dying" sounds, the problem is not just, Will she be gained by the Baron? but the more complex issue, Will she yield to any earthly lover, or is her heart reserved for a simulacrum of love: the sterile coquetries of Sylphs?

4

That the Sylphs have already won far-reaching victories is evident from the stylizations of fashionable life itself. Passages which in 1712 read as entertaining mock-heroic assume a more sinister fascination in the later versions with virtually no word changed. So whereas the following had been an easy jest at would-be epic's exaggerations—

> For lo! the Board with Cups and Spoons is crown'd,
> The Berries crackle, and the Mill turns round.
> On shining Altars of *Japan* they raise
> The silver Lamp, and fiery Spirits blaze,
> From silver Spouts the grateful Liquors glide,
> And *China's* Earth receives the smoking Tyde.
> (III, 105–10; 1714. cf. I, 89–94; 1712)

—arriving at the passage in its new context it makes sense to ask (as it hardly did before), What consciousness is registering the physicalities of social life in so acute a way? In 1712 to speak of a cup as "*China's* Earth" was a joke relished for its own sake. But now the shift of scale is full of purpose. For sylphic delicacy is amazed at the grossness of porcelain, endangered (comically) by coffee-floods, and aware that those "fiery Spirits" which promote new stratagems in the Baron's brain may, on inspection, turn out to be sister Termagants after all. The verse quivers with this sylphic sense of things. Yet the Sylphs are not the only ones abnormally responsive to the physical world, and thus over-ready to idolize or fear it. Rather, *their* sensibility blends into the fine textures of fashionable life, and into the consciousness of its inhabitants—as in the next lines, added of course when the poem was re-composed:

> Strait hover round the Fair her Airy Band;
> Some, as she sip'd, the fuming Liquor fann'd,
> Some o'er her Lap their careful Plumes display'd,
> Trembling, and conscious of the rich Brocade.
> (III, 113–16; 1714)

The "careful" gestures—hovering, sipping, fanning—are divided between belle and Sylphs, each mimicking the other, as it were. The graces of civilization, which make it so rich and beautiful a thing, have as their parody a conscious simpering niceness. Unregenerate fact is not good enough for these refined creatures—the cultivated beauties *or* the disembodied Sylphs.

Yet even that does not put it strongly enough. The more we register the physical world through the aerial consciousness of Sylphs, the more tantalizingly desirable fineness of beauty seems. But to maintain the exquisite purity which Sylphs admire is a torment to nature; and we feel the strain in the Sylphs' own

70

characteristic motion, "trembling" and "flutt'ring" in restless ecstasies of care. Like the belle, they guard painfully ephemeral beauties: frail china jars, honour, the flirt of a fan or down of powder on a cheek. One does not need to threaten such creatures; the very refinement they value is perilous enough—liable to look like nature racked to a nicety of form. For how can such beauty last? Is it even endurable, when it depends on perfection being kept intact? so that the Sylphs' commission is to ensure the Fair as frivolously uncommitted as themselves.

> Whatever Spirit, careless of his Charge,
> His Post neglects, or leaves the Fair at large,
> Shall feel sharp Vengeance soon o'ertake his Sins,
> Be stopt in *Vials*, or transfixt with *Pins*;
> Or plung'd in Lakes of bitter *Washes* lie,
> Or wedg'd whole Ages in a *Bodkin's* Eye:
> *Gums* and *Pomatums* shall his Flight restrain,
> While clog'd he beats his silken Wings in vain;
> Or Alom-*Stypticks* with contracting Power
> Shrink his thin Essence like a rivel'd Flower.
>   (II, 125–34; 1714)

Cosmetics as a brutal menace are funny in their way, but there is a strange sexual foreboding here as, on behalf of the human beauties as well as the Sylphs, the wit feels out the sensitive points of spirit-body where ruin can enter it. Transfixed with pain, stopped up, over-flooded, its softness shrunk and damaged: real dangers lie in wait if sylphids sin by leaving humanity "at large". Therefore propriety is revenged when all the artifices which should aid frivolity are used to disable flightiness, natural expression of coquettes, even after death. What anguished imprisonment of body and fluttering spirit together is rendered by those verbs, "plung'd", "clog'd", "wedg'd". Whether we look from the human viewpoint or the Sylphs', the freedom of each form of life to be itself is tyranny over the other.

Yet each in a way needs its tyrant. Without the Sylphs, Belinda would be less magical than she is—that much is clear from the *Locke* of 1712. Without *her* living frailty on the other hand, the Sylphs would have nothing so precious to exercise upon. The deeper we move into the work, the more poignant these inter-relations become, and the richer the irony Pope commands. His attention broadens masterfully; wherever he turns in the completed

71

poem, he perceives the contradictions of its social world with a sympathy increasingly sharp, and wittily humane.

Even as originally conceived, Hampton Court demanded more than lightness from him. It lets a glimpse of a larger, more disturbing world into the poem.

> Hither our Nymphs and Heroes did resort,
> To taste awhile the Pleasures of a Court;
> In various Talk the chearful hours they past,
> Of, who was *Bitt*, or who *Capotted* last:
> This speaks the Glory of the *British Queen*,
> And that describes a charming *Indian Screen*;
> A third interprets Motions, Looks, and Eyes;
> At ev'ry Word a Reputation dies.
> *Snuff*, or the *Fan*, supply each Pause of Chatt,
> With singing, laughing, ogling, and all that.
>   Now, when declining from the Noon of Day,
> The Sun obliquely shoots his burning Ray;
> When hungry Judges soon the Sentence sign,
> And Wretches hang that Jury-men may Dine;
> When Merchants from th'Exchange return in Peace,
> And the long Labours of the *Toilette* cease—
> The Board's with Cups and Spoons, alternate, crown'd;
> The Berries crackle, and the Mill turns round.
>
>   (I, 73–90; 1712)

The passage is a striking one; all the more so for the bitterly simple irony it yields. Admittedly the lines contrast the gossips and the gallows (aristocrats are safely remote from the violence outside) while simultaneously yoking them together (Nymphs brutally indifferent as hanging Judges). But by placing the passage neatly between great Anna's tea-taking just before, and the Statesman's coffee just after, Pope reduces this to a manageable pattern of shock. Each appetite, it turns out, can be measured against another: hungry Judges' against starvelings', and both of them against the thirst fine gentlemen have to "taste awhile" the pleasures of a Court. Intense as it may be, the satiric gaze travels evenly all the way from the Queen to the Wretches over whom she rules.

But when Pope re-imagined his poem in 1714 simple ironies were transformed to complex ones. The first sign is the splendid deepening of tone, as easy jokes ("Of, who was *Bitt* or who

Capotted") disappear, and a new rhythm announces a rich inexorable change of key.

> Mean while declining from the Noon of Day,
> The Sun obliquely shoots his burning Ray;
> The hungry Judges soon the Sentence sign,
> And wretches hang that Jury-men may Dine;
> The Merchant from th'*Exchange* returns in Peace,
> And the long Labours of the *Toilette* cease
>
> (III, 19–24; 1714)

Instead of relying on a "When" to suspend four clauses in turn, heavy with anticipation, the sentence now moves inevitable and calm. Authorial knowingness gives way to a feeling that time surrounds all actions with an equal pressure: "Mean while": an impersonal authority extended over all things, to give dignity to belles and wretches alike. For death may seize one sooner than another, but finally in this long perspective the facts of nature are equidistant from all men, like the sun. Hunger and vanity, selfishness, desperate need, each has its place in the rhythmic procession, as light declines, the felons hang, and the Merchant and the Beauty, freed at last from their labours, can remain at peace. The scale on which we are invited to feel, and the undisturbed spaciousness in which the most incongruous things are set, allows us to realize that even frivolity need not be satirically dismissed. All human facts are capable of grandeur of a kind.

Of course there is no chance we can hold such a vision steady. Ordinary feeling cannot support it, nor indeed can Pope's art, since the same quick searching powers of mind which opened the perspective to us necessarily relinquish it again. But we could hardly wish this otherwise. For the poetry seems to gain strength from recognizing just how elusive the moral order it creates from moment to moment is. No solidified morality could do justice to Belinda's world; and strict justice anyway is the last thing Sylphs would want. *Their* indifference, however, is not freedom so much as a parody of it: a parody of the value Pope can see even in frailty, frivolity, confusion.

> Whether the Nymph shall break *Diana's* Law,
> Or some frail *China* Jar receive a Flaw,
> Or stain her Honour, or her new Brocade,
> Forget her Pray'rs, or miss a Masquerade,

Or lose her Heart, or Necklace, at a Ball;
Or whether Heav'n has doom'd that Shock must fall.
(II, 107–12; 1714)

Trivial disasters and real ones are no sooner opposed than their boundaries disappear, leaving a poignancy at this flickering and fading, this merging of values which ought to be distinct. The Sylphs are the shimmering, helpless, half-dissolved guardians of a moral order as flimsy as their own aerial forms. Once such creatures entered the verse, no fixed morality *could* remain. The human viewpoint, the sylphic, the epic sense of things, all play into and out of one another, the limitations of each suggested by the presence alongside it of these contrary possible worlds.

5

It isn't easy to keep all this in balance. The poem is beautiful enough to distract us from the necessary judgments, at the same time as its beauty must be part of whatever judgment we make. But try to formulate the relations of Sylphs to fashionable world, and the choices by which we are faced are disturbing—as the earliest critique of the poem showed. For when the revised *Lock* first appeared (March, 1714), six copper-engravings accompanied its text, giving visible shape to the impression made on one contemporary at least. And to Du Guernier the engraver the spirits appear as quasi-diabolic imps. In Umbriel's case that is not surprising (*illus.* Canto IV); but fondling Belinda on her bed (*illus.* Canto I) is an incubus-Ariel, surely; while elsewhere too the spirits have a mocking predatory look. Never more so than when, in the guise of *putti* (Frontis.), they surround the girl with their own large baby-forms: one trying on her shoes, another tasting her scent-bottle, while some shower her with playing-cards, hold the glass to focus her difficult cosmetic art, or hover wonderingly beside her funeral-urn. In the shadows a belial-cherub lurks; in the foreground another whose legs have openly taken satyr's shape experiments with a mask to cover his horns.

So far as Pope's letters show, he did not commission these engravings himself. On the other hand, his letter of 2 November 1716 sends "inclosed Directions" to the new artist, Gribelin, whose decorative panel for the poem in the large-paper edition of 1717 clearly derives from Du Guernier's old Frontispiece (and

Pope's life-long interest in the Sister-art of painting suggests how ready he would have been to concern himself with illustrations to his works). Cards, urns, cosmetics, satyrs, and a belle at her looking-glass all reappear in a "Hampton Court" setting filled with busy Sylphs. The point is not that the illustrations in every case are so much cruder than the verse; inevitably, they are; but that to conceive, even momentarily, the Sylphs outside the quick light fascinations of that verse brings up decisions of the very kind the Celestials try to keep in abeyance. Having said that, though, the engravings can be allowed to lapse, as Pope allowed them to. Anything they have to offer is already more finely achieved in his verse—and achieved, as the *Rape* moves towards its climax, through a variety of episodes and forms.

Like other readers, Johnson felt some of Pope's means of conveyance could be spared. The second half of the poem might be thought to duplicate effects already obtained. But it seems to me a rather different world is entered with Canto III. After glittering Sylph-induced visions, we come to the weighty matter of cards, and, weightier still, the game which cards enable the characters to play out and, simultaneously, disguise.

> *Belinda* now, whom Thirst of Fame invites,
> Burns to encounter two adventrous Knights,
> At *Ombre* singly to decide their Doom;
> And swells her Breast with Conquests yet to come.
> (III, 25–9; 1714)

"Thirst", "Burns", "swells": urgent, if formalized, sexual suggestions initiate the culminating movement of the work.

At first everything is ceremonious, tableau-like; but the game's formality itself overthrows such elegant manners. Within minutes Belinda is set about by warriors and swarthy Moors; Giant Limbs are spread around; bawdy intimations peep from unexpected places ("Puts forth one manly Leg, to sight reveal'd; / The rest his many-colour'd Robe conceal'd"), for the decorum of normal perspective is unsettled: the very care with which the card-game is elaborated (never Lilliputian, yet minutely exact—editors explain how you play it) sees to that. So by the time "The Nymph exulting fills with Shouts the Sky", these global reactions have overridden the difference between moral triumph and a game of cards. In Belinda's world anyway the difference is hard to maintain, when Sylphs show an airily equal concern for chastity and for china jars. Thanks to the best efforts of polite society and its perfect "essence" the Sylphs, the very words by which we designate moral choice have been emptied of meaning, until what guards the purity of melting Maids is vanity (if the truth were spoken), "Tho' *Honour* is the Word with Men below". In such a world it is no use appealing to principle, or natural feeling either. Only through feints and rules, as in Ombre, society's game, is honest emotion brought into play; but the formality of the game *can* touch it off. Belinda's paleness and excitement, though properly concealed by "Heaps on Heaps" of cards, infuse a live, unsylphic passion into Hampton Court. Committed now, as she never was in the barge-scene, her moment of spontaneity frees her, only to expose her to real danger straight away.

Not that the Baron in himself has serious sexual force. That much was plain when his altar to Love was built out of paper Romances. But as Pope's understanding of his poem grew, so did his power to realize deeper wrongs. In 1714 he still laughed at the sentimental clutter of the sacrifice-pile (unchanged since the original *Locke*), and jibed at the Baron's corsets.

> There lay the Sword-knot *Sylvia*'s Hands had sown,
> With *Flavia*'s Busk that oft had rapp'd his own . . .
> (II, 39–40; 1714)

But by 1717 Pope is less indulgent. Sardonically he now picks out the evidence of promiscuities and broken trusts, oddments in odd numbers, whose pathetic incompleteness testifies to the lover's "ardent" Heart:

> There lay three garters, half a pair of gloves;
> And all the trophies of his former loves.
> With tender Billet-doux he lights the pyre,
> And breathes three am'rous sighs to raise the fire.
> (II, 37–43; 1717)

Adult sexuality always remains beyond him. Even to start with it was coffee that inflamed him to the rape, by sending its modish Vapours to his brain. The Pope of 1712 is startlingly clear about the Baron's action: what it means to him, and to the inhabitants of his society.

He first expands the glitt'ring *Forfex* wide
T'inclose the Lock; then joins it, to divide;
One fatal stroke the sacred Hair does sever
From the fair Head, for ever, and for ever!
　　The living Fires come flashing from her Eyes,
And Screams of Horrow rend th'affrighted Skies.
Not louder Shrieks by Dames to Heav'n are cast,
When Husbands die, or *Lap-dogs* breath their last,
Or when rich *China* Vessels fal'n from high,
In glittring Dust and painted Fragments lie!
　　　　　　　　　　(I, 115–24; 1712)

In its fashion, masterly. At no point do we reach an easy climax, but register each transition, as the noble sonority of one paragraph ("for ever, and for ever") turns into cheap shrill shriekings in the next. Nor is deflation Pope's only tactic. Rather, satiric reversals are themselves reversed, as the flippancy about Husband-lapdogs modulates into a graver tone: "Or when rich *China* Vessels . . .": perhaps beauty's painted fragments have a sadness after all.

One might have hesitated to suppose Pope could better the passage. But in 1714 he did so, by inserting the Sylphs. They help us feel the cutting of the Lock as real violation—both of Belinda's beauty, and of the code of manners which holds this civilization by fine threads. Graceful and ceremonious, the perfection Belindas achieve is easily lost—which indeed is part of their charm.

Swift to the Lock a thousand Sprights repair,
A thousand Wings, by turns, blow back the Hair,
And thrice they twitch'd the Diamond in her Ear,
Thrice she look'd back, and thrice the Foe drew near.
Just in that instant, anxious *Ariel* sought
The close Recesses of the Virgin's Thought;
As on the Nosegay in her Breast reclin'd,
He watch'd th'Ideas rising in her Mind,
Sudden he view'd, in spite of all her Art,
An Earthly Lover lurking at her Heart.
Amaz'd, confus'd, he found his Pow'r expir'd,
Resign'd to Fate, and with a Sigh retir'd.

The Peer now spreads the glitt'ring *Forfex* wide,
T'inclose the Lock; now joins it, to divide.

77

> Ev'n then, before the Fatal Engine clos'd,
> A wretched *Sylph* too fondly interpos'd;
> Fate urg'd the Sheers, and cut the *Sylph* in twain,
> (But Airy Substance soon unites again)
> The meeting Points the sacred Hair dissever
> From the fair Head, for ever and for ever!
>   Then flash'd the living Lightnings from her Eyes,
> And Screams of Horror rend th'affrighted Skies.
> Not louder Shrieks by Dames to Heav'n are cast,
> When Husband's or when Monkeys breath their last
>   (III, 135–58, 1714)

The deed is magnified to its most heroical size; but that is appropriate, and not mock-epic indulgence, since this time the doom-filled language really belongs to some of the participants. A deed of these dimensions certainly can disable Sylphs, whose light militia succumbs to punctilio itself (a parallel here to the card-game), when a thousand wings "take turns" to disarrange the hair, and even Ariel for all his captaincy is too graceful not to "recline" on the nosegay and capitulate at first glimpse of the Enemy, with a resigning "Sigh". At the catastrophe therefore we shake free of ineffectual Sylphs and return to human actors instead.

But Sylph-consciousness is not so easily laid aside. The longer Pope contemplated his poem, the less it seemed possible to disengage polite behaviour from those exquisite perversions of good-breeding the Sylphs offer. The two are dismayingly alike. So much so that by 1717 he felt he must add Clarissa's speech, "to open more clearly the MORAL", and coming back to the climactic rape saw nicer distinctions called for there as well. Increase of wit now means increased humanity too.

> Not louder shrieks to pitying heav'n are cast,
> When husbands, or when lapdogs breathe their last;
> Or when rich *China* vessels, fal'n from high,
> In glittering dust, and painted fragments lie!
>   (III, 156–59; 1717)

The burlesqued "Dames" of 1712 and 1714 vanish, though their shrieks continue to be heard: by a "pitying" Heaven which does not mock in any simple way but listens, tenderly receptive, to the cries mounting up from foolish human kind. And the tightened zeugmatic syntax points where the folly came from: "When husbands, or when lapdogs", the women are practising sylphic equations of things which ought to be kept apart. By identifying the malaise, we resist it; and once we do, the helplessness which mourns dogs, husbands, porcelain, all at once or else in nicely calibrated sequence can be granted its proper pathos. Such detachment, in Sylphs *or* their followers, is pitiable, though very nearly indestructible as well. So the couplets rouse finenesses of sympathy from everything they touch, down to the "glittering" dust of l.159 over which, with its vowel restored, the voice is allowed to hesitate lamentingly. Neither sympathy nor dismissal is good enough. Even the phrase "wretched Sylph" stands midway from petulance ("the wretched thing, it will get in the way") and Miltonic sadness ("what futile suffering presumption brings on itself"). As the Baron's scissors close on Belinda and her guardians, we value what is destroyed as highly as we may; then all at once see the loss as laughably minute. For how much *is* destroyed? The scissors themselves, opening "T'inclose" and joining "to divide", interpret their own action two ways.

One can see with what care Pope worked over the scene, and why such care was needed. His language, its blend of familiarity, grandeur and fastidiousness all sharpened to a tiny point, enables him to draw up meanings which otherwise lie out of sight, too imponderable, or else too gross, for delicate verse to handle. As it is, however, the solemn latinisms are absurd, yet they outline the Baron's every gesture as his "fatal Engine" mimes a sexual act and at the same time substitutes for one. I mean, his rape of course is nothing more than imitation. The irony is that in fashionable life a substitute-rape may be *worse* indeed than a real one: for the Baron violates exactly what can't be secret—the way Belinda looks; whereas sexual acts can be (in every sense) "unknown".

We might call it Thalestris-morality: a code of Appearances, where nothing counts unless seen, and every truth is reduced to the nice (or horrid) "things they say": "And all your Honour in a Whisper lost". It didn't take the final versions of the poem for Pope to uncover this; he had dramatized such pseudo-morality in the *Locke* of 1712.

> Oh had the Youth but been content to seize
> Hairs less in sight—or any Hairs but these!
> Gods! shall the Ravisher display this Hair,
> While the Fops envy, and the Ladies stare!

Honour forbid! at whose unrival'd Shrine
Ease, Pleasure, Virtue, All, our Sex resign.
(II, 19–24; 1712)

The shameful ease of the declension can tempt the prude (shaking her head to hear of Pleasure's name) as well as the libertine. For to this idol *Honour* women sacrifice the honour they really have, chaste Virtue, until by a series of self-undoing puns the language of "purity" is turned inside out to reveal a morality antisexual indeed, being frigid and promiscuous both at once. All this is already present in the *Locke*. What Pope did in 1714 was to body it forth in a new drama, not of Lovers and Ladies only, but of Sylphs, as his wittily exact Dedication declares:

> For they say, any Mortals may enjoy the most intimate Familiarities with these gentle Spirits, upon a Condition very easie to all true *Adepts*, an inviolate preservation of Chastity

—"the most intimate Familiarities", with the sole proviso that real sexuality is foresworn. That indeed is the libidinous "Chastity" you embrace in embracing Sylphs: a mock-virginity from which the spirits of "Honour" can never break themselves. All is Appearance, maintained by flawless ego in a travesty of authentic self-venturing and self-possession. Hence Ariel's command, "Thy own Importance know". Yet narcissistic, titillating, though the Sylphs may be, they turn the falsity to magic of a kind. Aloft in the poem's own crystal wilds of air, they give a new dimension to human lives, and new comedy by which those lives are beautified and judged.

To say that a sexual drama runs through the poem is true enough, then, in an abstract summary way. Pope does examine genteel society and Belinda's development (or failure to develop) as a woman. But where we conceptualize, he makes real the shimmering sensuous fragility of the Sylphs: not as a covering myth which adroit readers must prize off to get to the "real" concerns, but as *itself* the other side to darker forces. Almost literally so. For Belinda's world through Cantos I to III is registered as surfaces: looking-glass, silver Thames, flat playing-cards, light sparkling on objects, reflected as sheen or lustre, or glittering in films of air. Not until Canto IV does its underside appear. In the Cave of Spleen, however, is summoned up a darkened, hollowed world, thick with vapours, dreams, conscious forms of voluble aching emptiness. Here are windy bags, sighing Jars and calling Bottles. Obviously (too obviously, perhaps, for all the elegance of wit) this is the realm of Uterus, and of what etymology proclaims is its "hysteric" power.

> Hail wayward Queen;
> Who rule the Sex to Fifty from Fifteen,
> Parent of Vapors and of Female Wit,
> Who give th'*Hysteric* or *Poetic* Fit
> (IV, 57–60; 1714)

But the uterus rules not only women; sexual nature in them, satisfied or distorted, affects us all. And Pope's wit goes deeper; to associate these distortions with the very refinements (poetry, etc.) civilized living applauds. That, and not a simpler point about "frustration", is what the Cave reveals. For in one creative act the valuable and degrading are fused: art, religion, manners, all momentarily sink back to baseness as though by some entropic law. Poetic and hysteric fit are equally available, *each* one a parody of the other; "Men prove with Child, as pow'rful Fancy works"; while as for the godly, pettishness and prayer are indistinguishable.

The implications of all this have been teased out often enough. Art and Neurosis, civilization and its discontents—such interpretations of the Cave are unavoidable this century, I suppose. Yet they don't suggest how imaginative Pope is in his audacities, how un-programmatic in short. Nor do they remind us that the ironies of Spleen continue to the end. For the Goddess fills her wondrous bag with a full supply of current affectations, sighs, sobs, Passions, and the rest; yet up from this nether realm comes the one thing— outrage—by which perverted nature might after all be healed.

To bring release out of affectation took Pope some time. His first presentation of Belinda's grief was inclined to burlesque her.

> But see! the *Nymph* in Sorrow's Pomp appears,
> Her eyes half languishing, half drown'd in Tears;
> Now livid pale her Cheeks, now glowing red . . .
> (II, 59–61; 1712)

By 1714, however, she contrives to be touching just because she is (thanks to the spirits) so stylish. Hers is sorrow in the modern way, the only way she knows; for Umbriel breaks his vial, and

81

> see! the *Nymph* in beauteous Grief appears,
> Her Eyes half languishing, half drown'd in Tears;
> On her heav'd Bosom hung her drooping Head,
> Which, with a Sigh, she rais'd; and thus she said.
>
> (IV, 143–46; 1714)

The performance does not cease to be affected; gracefulness in Belinda's world is always liable to be that; but all Pope's re-writings so far prepare us for the appeal of her (ridiculous) grief. Indeed, the newly tender cadence of the lines prompts us to realize that, just as there is a sense in which she awaits the Baron, tempting him to rape (the conscious smoothness of that bended neck exposing the delicious curls), so likewise when he's accomplished the deed her dismay is not that he's done so much, but that he has not done more. Aided by graces Umbriel supplies, her indignation invites a further, more genuine assault.

> See the poor remnants of these slighted hairs!
> My hands shall rend what ev'n thy rapine spares:
> These, in two sable ringlets taught to break,
> Once gave new beauties to the snowy neck;
> This sister-lock now sits uncouth, alone,
> And in its fellow's fate foresees its own;
> Uncurl'd it hangs, the fatal sheers demands;
> And tempts once more thy sacrilegious hands.
> Oh hadst thou, cruel! been content to seize
> Hairs less in sight, or any hairs but these!
>
> (IV, 167–76; 1717)

The lines, originally given to Thalestris, are only *just* polite enough to lie within Belinda's range; and that she speaks them shows how little she pretends to smiling indifference now. She draws all eyes, as by a verbal blush, to the tempting other Hairs. But that is because her indignation has, only, worldly knowing forms to take. So her half-innocent heroics shade into *double-entendre* (1717 actually introduces the word "rapine"). Thus sylphic values have not exactly been discarded; rather, they *contribute* to Belinda's finally un-sylphic appeal. And that, with all its implications, is central to the poem I think. For to the end we never know how far she is actually set free. To be sure, she is no mere coquette. Even at her dressing-table she is a living beauty. And at the moment of climax Ariel finds an earthly lover lurking at her heart, where pure sylphic frigidity should be. So the Sylphs are obliged to retire, leaving the mortals to battle for themselves. But ("see how oft Ambitious Aims are cross'd") the outcome of the battle is unclear. The Lock is lost, yet gained by no earthly lover; Belinda's marred beauty is not repaired by beauty of a deeper kind, since to take up her role as Woman she must lose that of Virgin first, and this in Pope's poem we never see her do. For one thing, it wouldn't be proper. Instead, we see her enlist more firmly in the Amazonian values of her world, and thus earn Clarissa's famous warning against "Flights and Screams and Scolding". It is a timely rebuke; for Belinda retreats from womanliness, it seems, to defend the injured vanity of the unmaturing belle; and compared with those airs, Clarissa's speech does sound like "the MORAL" of the poem.

> Oh! if to dance all night, and dress all day,
> Charm'd the small-pox, or chas'd old age away;
> Who would not scorn what huswife's cares produce,
> Or who would learn one earthly thing of use?
> To patch, nay ogle, might become a Saint,
> Nor could it sure be such a sin to paint.
> But since, alas! frail beauty must decay,
> Curl'd or uncurl'd, since Locks will turn to grey,
> Since painted, or not painted, all shall fade,
> And she who scorns a man, must die a maid;
> What then remains, but well our Pow'r to use,
> And keep good Humour still whate'er we lose?
>   (V, 19–30, 1717)

After such a speech is it not a mark of Belinda's shallowness that she frowns, and, worse still, takes arms with Thalestris?

Though I would once have said so, Pope's discrimination is I now think more subtle. For he detects the taint of high-minded insincerity in Clarissa's over-conscious speech: the cosy touches ("to patch, nay ogle"), the unctuous advice, to "trust me, Dear! good Humour can prevail". If Belinda must accept the alternatives, of scorning a man or dying a maid, it is not on these self-satisfied terms. They bring us close to poignant realizations, then substitute new falsity in place of old. So as against Clarissa's campaign of smiling well-used "Pow'r", the termagant anger to which Belinda gives way turns out to be honest, life-engaging after all.

> See fierce *Belinda* on the Baron flies,
> With more than usual lightning in her eyes:
> Nor fear'd the Chief th'unequal flight to try,
> Who sought no more than on his foe to die.
> (V, 75–8; 1717)

No doubt a Belinda freed from "social" values altogether would satisfy us more. Pope doesn't allow that, though. Too intelligent to imagine that liberation ever comes except on terms that sociey itself provides, he sees Belinda's selfhood to some extent set free, but always as the selfhood of one society rather than another. Yet here the poem's finest paradoxes appear. The way into freedom is for Belinda to act upon the forms and frivolities, even the bad-humoured ones, her society provides. And in doing so, a kind of reality is achieved. It isn't perfect; it involves silliness, temper, vanity, and so on; and the ultimate fate of the belle—fulfilment, or bitter old age—still remains unknown. But not even the sylphic Essences of society ever achieve much more. Like Belinda's, their beauty is would-be perfect, but actually tremulous and troubled—which, far from being a defect, increases beauty the more. Indeed, their fluttering anxious guardianship heightens the vulnerability, hence preciousness, of whatever they guard.[6]

> Some o'er her Lap their careful Plumes display'd,
> Trembling, and conscious of the rich Brocade.

Such protection invites disaster; so too the outrage of the belle; but in either case that is almost the highest compliment Pope can pay. For it enables him to show his heroine a woman after all, and there is a triumphant sadness in his apotheosis-tribute to her mortal frailty.

> When those fair suns shall set, as set they must,
> And all those tresses shall be laid in dust;
> This Lock, the Muse shall consecrate to fame,
> And midst the stars inscribe *Belinda*'s name!
> (V, 147–50; 1717)

Only if the hair is ravished can Belinda gain "new glory", and only if she is laid in dust can Pope immortalize her in the "shining sphere", the civilization, of his verse.

6

Immortality-poems are not what we think of as his province, but he strove to give his verses at least such permanence as art may have. Unlike the quick-fading effusions of scribblers and critics, they last, with a lastingness secured by every scrupulosity of rewriting. Indeed, Pope's genius is strong enough to delight in the very things which resist immortalizing: nonsense precipitate like running lead, momentary monsters that rise and fall—it is a positive pleasure to bring them, too, into the couplet's order. The more highly finished his art, in fact, the readier it seems to catch things which have no permanence at all: transitory, unfinalized things. The ephemeral always fascinated him, and his interest in the women of fashionable life is surely part of this. For the beauty of the Belle, by its nature, cannot endure. All such beauty, and hers especially, becomes a ghost of what it was, at the end of Moral Essay II still desolatingly in motion. The very graces by which she heightens her appeal, and the artifice which would camouflage decline, show how precariously she reigns. So it is not surprising such figures attract a curious play of feeling as Pope contemplates their careers: indignation, shocked disgust, a darting tender fondness. They occasion some of his greatest poetry, from the *Locke* of 1712 to the great anti-type of the belle, Queen Dulness herself, gross, grave, laborious, busy, bold and blind, and gauzily be-fogged or tinselled o'er in varying fool's colours. But *The Dunciad* claims attention on its own. More to the point are the women of the "social" poems: the two Epistles to Miss Blount, or (still more) the Moral Essays, work of an older poet prepared to admit a violence his earlier celebrations hardly show. For there *is* an idealizing strain in *The Rape of the Lock*: to incorporate it was necessary to Pope's critique of that world; whereas the Moral Essays tackle not just society as it might wish to appear, but sprawling energies of a far more savage kind. Even the death-bed scenes of Epistle I, or Pope's vision of a femaleness in, of all things, money itself (Epistle III), cannot match the portraits of the second Essay: Narcissa, Flavia, Atossa and the rest, not shielded by pathos like earlier Unfortunate Ladies ("Life's idle business at one gasp be o'er"); on the contrary, the unpathetic now becomes a positive Popean strength as he contemplates their appetites and habits, coupling

... Sappho at her toilet's greazy task,
With Sappho fragrant at an ev'ning Mask:
So morning Insects that in muck begun,
Shine, buzz, and fly-blow in the setting-sun.
(*Epistle II, To a Lady, Of the Characters of Women*, II. 25–8)

Disgust and revulsion are strong; but so too is the sheer vitality of these insects whose inhuman processes are not just to be shuddered from. If anything, their life-cycle, from its start in muck to its self-regenerating end, prompts wonder at its being so rapid and complete—prompts delight indeed (witness that attractive "Shine"), and this ambivalence transfers itself back to Sappho, so that the first couplet's cruel antithesis is turned by the second into a metamorphosis natural as insects' under a setting sun.

Yet, characteristic of the Moral Essays, these transformations are caught in a single sentence and the arc of a single day. Belinda at *her* dressing-table is not summed up in any such vignette or left like Sappho in two dire couplets finished and transfixed. Of course, considering the appetites with which the second Epistle deals, one can see why its episodes detach themselves into a row of portraits. The rebellious warring energies of these women, the ferocity of their demands on life, defeat all attempts to set them in a poetic-moral order—particularly the attempts of a little, laughed-at gallant like Pope. It is a more confident impulse that carries Belinda out into her world, to surround her with Sylphs and launch her on the silver Thames. Now, in the midst of polite society, Pope's landscapes, Nymphs, Swains, elementals, evoke a pastoral freedom. We glimpse (if only glimpse) an innocence older than Christianity, in the vision of Arcadia and "*Diana*'s Law". Unlike the Moral Essays, and like no other poem he wrote, this has the shape of myth. But in the end it is clear that no myth was capable of holding Augustan idealism and reality together. By the time of *The Dunciad* there was no epic unity eighteenth-century England could sustain in the imagination of its greatest writer; and if *The Rape of the Lock* suggests there might have been, it can do so only because it encloses itself in its own world perfectly. It does not require the praise of modern criticism, that it is or that it sustains a poetic myth.

Rather, if we follow where the poetry itself is at its most vital and engaged, we come almost always to Belinda and her Sylphs.

In imagining them, Pope's touch is exquisitely fine. Nowhere else I know of does he so movingly evoke the promise, and vulnerability, of woman's nature. So this, more than his Epistles to Miss Blount, is a love-poem I want to say, though of a strange and beautiful remoteness. "Strange", because it is addressed only to a Belinda, who lives (only) in the art of the poet himself. Nevertheless a love-poem is one of the things it is. But then, resemblances, echoes of all kinds, live fleetingly in the verse, and to feel their momentary pressure is enough. For in this poem, so much revised and altered, we see Pope come to realize that amongst the things we value lastingly is mutability itself.

NOTES

1 In F. W. Bateson and N. A. Joukovsky, eds., *Alexander Pope: A Critical Anthology* (Harmondsworth, 1971), p. 288; and see pp. 238–95 generally.

2 I quote the poem as printed in the following sources:

For 1712: the text of "the first and only edition" of the two-Canto *Locke*, in *Miscellaneous Poems and Translations. By Several Hands* (pub. Lintott), which is carried over *literatim* as *The Rape of the Locke* in the Twickenham Edition of *The Poems of Alexander Pope*, vol. II (ed. Tillotson).

For 1714: *The Rape of the Lock. An Heroi-comical Poem*. In Five Canto's. (Pub. Lintott.) First impression, 4 March 1714, with Frontispiece and five illustrations. (Scolar Press facsimile, 1970.)

For 1717: the poem as it appeared in Pope's *Works* (pub. Lintott); large folio, with Frontispiece and decorations; 1717.

For 1736: the poem as it appeared in vol. 1 of Pope's *Works . . . with explanatory Notes and additions never before printed* (pub. Lintott); octavo; 1736.

3 Following the stages of the text, so minutely worked over from 1712 to 1717, makes it appear unlikely that Pope simply failed to notice the repetition he was committing when he bought two forms of one word together in consecutive lines: "And the press'd watch return'd a silver sound. / *Belinda* still her downy pillow prest . . ." (1717). An "oversight", writes Bateson; "regrettable clumsiness". I would say the problem is not that Pope overlooks the duplication, but that he insists on it too much. Delicate yet automatic mechanisms guide the belle in her dreams as much as in her daily round: that I think is the suggestion of the carried-over word. But Pope's insight, as the poem grows, frees itself from any such regularized satire. The Sylphs are more volatile and surprising than "Machinery" could be: their invisible life (being

the essence of vanished coquettes) is indeed a way of society infusing its values secretly into each new generation.

4 "Tradition and the Individual Talent", in *Selected Essays*, 1953, p. 15.
5 *Some Versions of Pastoral*, 1935; Chapter 2, p. 68.
6 On this aspect of the poem, see Irène Simon, "Pope and the Fragility of Beauty", *Revue des Langues Vivantes*, vol. 24 (1958), pp. 377–94; and Bliss Carnochan in *Explicator* (1964).

4

Pope Plays the Rake: His Letters to Ladies and the Making of the *Eloisa*

by JAMES A. WINN

The notion of a special style for writing to ladies was a cultural norm when Pope began writing letters. The great French letter-writers Jean Louis Guez de Balzac and Vincent Voiture cannot claim exclusive credit for creating such a style, but their letters to and about women are particularly skillful examples of the mixture of compliment, raillery, and fantasy which was the accepted posture; they were evidently useful examples for the young Pope. From Balzac, he learned the trick of referring to mistresses by Latin names, thus not only hiding the identity of any real mistress, but also blurring the distinction between real and imaginary mistresses. Here is Balzac, writing to a political friend:

> Whilst you employ your houres in gayning hearts and Votes, and happily lay the foundation of some eminent enterprize; I here enjoy a reposednesse not unlike that of the dead, and which is neuer rouzed but by *Clorinda*'s kisses.[1]

And here is Pope, writing to his early town friend Henry Cromwell:

> I made no question but the News of *Sappho*'s staying behind me in the Towne wou'd surprize you. But she is since come into the Country, and to surprize you more, I will inform you, that the first Person she nam'd when I waited on her, was one Mr. *Cromwell*.
> (25 April 1708; I, 47)[2]

From Voiture, Pope learned even more, as a number of well-known specific borrowings indicate.[3] More important than those borrowings are some basic strategies for writing to women. Behind these strategies, for Voiture, lies the assumption that *all* ladies, whatever their age or marital status, are to be addressed as if they were available for romance. For Voiture, if we believe his boasting, that assumption may have had a measure of validity; he claimed that "he had made Love from the Scepter to the Sheep-Hook, and from the Coronet to the round-ear'd Cap."[4] For Pope, making such an assumption involved more imagination and less performance. In the letters of both men, the resulting style uses raillery, compliment, and *double-entendre* to insinuate the writer's fundamentally sexual response to the woman being addressed. The writer usually portrays himself as languishing; exaggeration is fundamental. Both writers find a fine phrase too tempting to use just once; both send similar love-letters to different ladies. Voiture even writes an all-purpose love-letter "to his Unknown Mistress".[5]

In approaching Voiture's letters, and Pope's imitations of them, modern readers must forget modern preoccupations with "sincerity".[6] When Voiture, thanking Madame de Rambouillet for a thank-you note, tells her that Alexander the Great "would have set more Value upon this Honour, than he did on the *Persian* diadem", he does not expect belief; he does expect her to be charmed by his comic extravagance. And this extravagance extends beyond compliment to declarations of romantic infatuation. Here is Voiture, describing a woman's letter to him as an act of magic:

> Even tho' I were utterly ignorant of your being a great Magician, and having the Art of commanding Spirits, the Power you have over my Affections, and the Charms I find in all you write to me, would be sufficient to inform me, that there is something supernatural in you. By the Help of your Characters, I beheld, upon a little Bit of Paper, both Temples and Goddesses; and you shew'd me all the Persons I love in your Letter, as in a Conjurer's Glass.[7]

Pope's imagination, the producer of the sylphs of the *Rape of the Lock*, responded to and imitated this fanciful strain in Voiture. A passage in a letter to Lady Mary Wortley Montagu is quite similar:

> The poetical manner in which you paint some of the Scenes about you, makes me despise my native country and sets me on fire to fall into the Dance about your Fountain in Belgrade-village. I fancy myself, in my romantic thoughts & distant admiration

of you, not unlike the man in the Alchymist that has a passion
for the Queen of the Faeries. I lye dreaming of you in Moon-
shiny Nights exactly in the posture of Endymion gaping for
Cynthia in a Picture.

([Autumn 1717]; I, 439)

In both letters, a fanciful context makes possible such phrases as
Voiture's "the Power you have over my Affections" and Pope's
"my romantic thoughts & distant admiration of you". In both
cases, there is reason to suspect the writer of making admissions
in such a context that he would not or could not make in more
straightforward prose. A recent study argues that "the life and
letters of Voiture betray a 'malaise', due to the tension provoked
by the flights of fantasy struggling against stark realism."[8] Pope's
letters to ladies betray a similar struggle.

Pope had less elegant models among English translators and
imitators of these French letters. Tom Brown, indefatigable translator of Pliny, Voiture, and an obscure but smutty sixth-century
Greek named Aristaenetus, produced innumerable letter-collec-
tions, which included his own efforts, some translations, and letters
attributed to such genuine rakes as Rochester. These letters
employ coarser tactics than Voiture's; *double-entendre* is a basic
technique, as it is in Restoration stage comedy, and the ranting
of Restoration tragedy also spills over into such passages as this
exaggerated outburst in a letter Brown attributed to Otway:

My TYRANT!
I Endure too much Torment to be silent, and have endur'd it too
long not to make the severest Complaint. I love You, I dote on
You; *Desire* makes me mad, when I am near You; and *Despair*,
when I am from You. Sure, of all Miseries, *Love* is to me the
most intolerable: it haunts me in my *Sleep*, perplexes me when
waking; every melancholy Thought makes my *Fears* more powerful; and every delightful one makes my *Wishes* more unruly.[9]

In Pope's early letters to Wycherley and Cromwell, he uses the
methods of these letters to affect the *persona* of the rake. One of
the most interesting examples is this set-piece to Cromwell:

The Morning after I parted with you, I found my self (as I had
prophesied) all alone, in an uneasy Stage-Coach; a doleful Change
from that agreable Company I enjoyed the Night before! without
the least hope of Entertainment, but from my last recourse in

such cases, a Book. I then began to enter into acquaintance with the Moralists, and had just receivd from them some cold Consolation for the Inconveniences of this life, & the Incertainty of human Affairs: when I perceivd my Vehicle to stop, & heard from the side of it the dreadful News of a Sick Woman preparing to enter it. 'Tis not very easy to guess at my Mortification, but being so well fortifyd with Philosophy, I stood resign'd with a Stoical Constancy to endure ye worst of Evils, a Sick Woman! I was indeed a little comforted to find by her Voice & Dress, that she was young & a Gentlewoman; but no sooner was her Hood remov'd, but I saw one of the finest Faces I ever beheld, & to increase my Surprize, heard her salute me by my Name. I had never more reason to accuse Nature for making me Shortsighted than now, when I cou'd not recollect I had ever seen those fair Eyes which knew me so well; & was utterly at a loss how to address myself, till with a great deal of Simplicity and Innocence she let me know (even before I discover'd my Ignorance) that she was the Daughter of one in our Neighborhood, lately marry'd, who having been consulting her Physicians in Towne, was returning into the Country, to try what good Air and a new Husband cou'd do to recover her. My Father, you must know, has sometimes recommended the Study of Physick to me, but *the Dev'l take me* if ever I had any Ambition to be a Doctor till this Instant. I ventur'd to prescribe her some Fruit (which I happen'd to have in the Coach) which being forbidden her by Her damn'd Doctors, she had the more Inclination to. In short, I tempted, and she Eat; nor was I more like the Devil, than she like Eve. Having the good Success of the foresaid Gentleman before my eyes, I put on the Gallantry of the old Serpent, & in spite of my Evil Forme, accosted her with all the Gayety I was master of; which had so good Effect, that in less than an hour she grew pleasant, her Colour return'd & she was pleas'd to say, my Prescription had wrought an Immediate Cure. In a Word, I had the pleasantest Journey imaginable, so that now, as once of yore, by means of the *forbidden Fruit*, the *Devil* got into *Paradise*—I shou'd not have us'd this last Phrase but that I know your civill Apprehension will not put any ill Construction upon it, & you will firmly believe that we were as modest—even as Sapho & Mr. C.

(11 July 1709; I, 66–7)

Pope assumes here the diction and attitudes of the Restoration rake. It is easy to imagine the casual swearing ("Her damn'd Doctors"), the cavalier dismissal of the "Moralists" as providing "cold Consolation", and even the well-worked-out Miltonic simile in the mouth of one of Wycherley's heroes. However, the way the simile of the serpent is introduced and handled, especially the phrase "in spite of my Evil Forme", shows Pope's awareness of his failure to meet one of the qualifications of the Restoration rake—physical beauty.

It is a reasonable guess that this early and fashionable *persona* of the rake had a rather limited basis in fact. Pope may have tried to keep up with Cromwell, Cheek, Wycherley, and his other town friends in whoring, as we know he foolishly tried to hold his own in eating and drinking. Still, George Sherburn's assertion that "Pope, conscious of his physical inferiority, put up a brave front at being a rake" seems much the wisest explanation for Pope's frequent early suggestions that he knew well the ways of the prostitutes of Drury Lane.[10] No doubt there was more talk than action, but Pope's later urinary difficulties, for which he was operated upon in 1740, may have resulted from indiscretions in his youth. "Such urethral stricture as he experienced," according to Nicolson and Rousseau, "was probably the result of gonorrhea, contracted in youth."[11] Cheselden, Pope's surgeon, told Spence:

> I could give a more particular account of his [Pope's] health than perhaps any man. Cibber's slander of a carnosity [is] false. [He] had been gay, but left it on his acquaintance with Mrs. Blount.[12]

But all this is speculation, and it does seem likely that Pope's frequent illnesses and the constant frailty of his tiny frame rendered frequent expeditions to bawdy houses impossible. Cheselden's statement, presumably based on Pope's own remarks, seems reasonable too: Pope had good reason to abandon even the pretence of active raking upon meeting the lovely, eligible, and Roman Catholic Blount sisters.

Just when this meeting took place remains obscure,[13] but by 1711 he knew them well enough to feel the force of their considerable charms, and to report his feelings to Cromwell:

> . . . I am at this instant placd betwixt Two such Ladies that in good faith 'tis all I'm able to do, to keep my self in my Skin. . . . Let me but have the Reputation of these in my keeping, & as for my own, let the Devil, or let Dennis, take it for ever! How gladly wou'd I give all I am worth, that is to say, my *Pastorals*

for one of their *Maidenheads*, & my *Essay* for the other? I wou'd
lay out all my *Poetry* in *Love*; an *Original* for a *Lady*, & a *Translation* for a *Waiting Maid*!

(I, 137–38)

The insinuation about maidenheads (suppressed, incidentally, in
Pope's published versions of the letter, but not in Curll's) is en-
demic to the rakish style, but his suggestion that he would barter
his poetical works for the favors of the sisters implies that he felt
himself genuinely smitten. His description of his works as "all I
am worth" is not to be taken lightly, and despite the playful suggestion that a lady is worth an original, and a waiting maid only
worth a translation, one doubts that he would really have traded a
poem for any of the nameless (and perhaps imaginary) "*Saphos*"
about whom he joked with Cromwell and Wycherley.

The Blounts were different. As respectable Catholic young ladies
who happened to be Pope's age and were blessed with fine eyes,
they must have struck Pope as ideal, and surely they found him,
at the very least, an interesting visitor. He was witty, and sophisticated to a degree, and becoming rather famous. But even his
earliest letters to them show a tendency to keep his wit under
control, as he told them in 1713:

> You see Ladies, I can write Seriously when I am truly myself,
> tho' I only Railly when I am displeasd with others. The most
> that any one shall get from me who would cause misunder-
> standings, is Contempt & Laughter; Those who Detest that evil
> way can have nothing less than an Entire Esteem such as will
> make me always Ladies, Your most obliged obedient humble
> Servant, A. Pope.

(I, 183)

Just two years later, in a letter to Martha alone, Pope rejects wit
even more pointedly:

> Madam,—I am not at all concern'd to think that this letter may
> be less entertaining than some I have sent: I know you are a
> friend that will think a kind letter as good as a diverting one.
> He that gives you his mirth makes a much less present than he
> that gives you his heart; and true friends wou'd rather see such
> thoughts as they communicate only to one another, than what
> they squander about to all the world . . .
> I wou'd cut off my own head, if it had nothing better than wit

94

in it; and tear out my own heart, if it had no better dispositions
than to love only myself, and laugh at all my neighbours.

[February 1715?]; I, 280)

Pope's awareness that this kind of language was a break with
the gallant tradition shows in another letter of the same year, in
which he sends Martha a dense, serious opening paragraph about
temporality, city life, and death, and continues:

> This is an odd way of writing to a lady, and I'm sensible
> would throw me under a great deal of ridicule, were you to
> show this letter among your acquaintance.
>
> ([1715]; I, 319)

It *is* an odd way of writing to a lady, and doubtless Pope was
correct in suggesting that his style might be ridiculed by Martha's
acquaintances. But there was a more serious kind of ridicule for
him to fear: laughter based on the ludicrous spectacle of a four
foot-six inch poet, however witty, courting the elegant and stately
Martha and Teresa. The Blounts lacked substantial dowries, but
they were young enough and pretty enough to be flattered and
flirted with by men much more attractive than Pope, who had told
Caryll as early as 1711 that he was "that little Alexander the
women laugh at" (I, 144). As George Sherburn astutely points
out, "he does not mean 'ladies' ",[14] but there was always the
possibility that the Blounts, who were "ladies", would laugh at
him as well. Pope's way of protecting himself from such ridicule
is delicate self-ridicule. He writes to Martha:

> May you have all possible success both at your Devotions this
> week, & your Masquerade the next: Whether you repent or Sin,
> may you do all you wish; and when you think of me, either laugh
> at me or pray for me, which you please.
>
> ([March 1716?]; I, 339)

And, with a wit that does not quite hide the pain, he tells Teresa:

> Madam,—I have so much Esteem for you, and so much of the
> other thing, that were I a handsome fellow I should do you a
> vast deal of good: but as it is, all I am good for is to write a
> civil letter, or to make a fine Speech. The truth is, that consider-
> ing how often & how openly I have declared Love to you, I am
> astonished (and a little affronted) that you have not forbid my
> correspondence, & directly said, *See my face no more.* It is not

enough, Madam, for your reputation, that you keep your hands pure, from the Stain of Such Ink as might be shed to gratify a male Correspondent; Alas! while your heart consents to encourage him in this lewd liberty of writing, you are not (indeed you are not) what you would so fain have me think you, a Prude! I am vain enough to conclude (like most young fellows) that a fine Lady's Silence is Consent, and so I write on.

(7 August [1716]; I, 349–50)

The psychological situation here is truly complex: Pope's only real attraction, his way of competing with the Blount's handsomer beaux, is his wit; but as he confesses, he would like to dispense with wit and confess his increasingly serious feelings about them; however, the danger that they may laugh at a declaration of love requires that that declaration be couched in terms which are self-protective; and the mode of self-protection which works best is—wit. So what amount to confessions of love are disguised by such comical strategies as these comparisons of the ladies to food-stuffs:

I love no meat but Ortolans [rich game birds], and no women but you. Though indeed that's no proper comparison but for fatt Dutchesses; For to love you, is as if one should wish to Eat Angels, or drink Cherubim-Broth.

(13 September 1717; I, 428)

For in very deed Ladies, I love you both, very sincerely and passionately, tho not so romantically (perhaps) as such as you may expect who have been us'd to receive more Complimental Letters and High flights from your own Sex, than ever I am like to reach to. In earnest, I know no Two Things I would change you for, this hot Weather, except Two good Melons.

([June 1717]; I, 409)

However, sometime after Pope's father's death on 23 October 1717, an occasion on which the Blounts were very kind to him, a severe misunderstanding occurred, or perhaps it was a series of misunderstandings. The letters from Pope to the sisters about this situation are openly, painfully emotional—unlike any previous letters. Gone are the rakish and self-protective effusions of wit. Pope writes in unmistakable pain, forced by that pain to acknowledge his real need for the Blounts, recognizing with excruciating

clarity that his physical form makes impossible a satisfactory fulfillment of that need. The longest and most moving of the letters
is this one:

Dear Ladies,—I think myself obligd to desire, you would not put
off any Diversion you may find, in the prospect of seeing me on
Saturday, which is very uncertain. I Take this occasion to tell you
once for all, that I design no longer to be a constant Companion
when I have ceas'd to be an agreable one. You only have had, as
my friends, the priviledge of knowing my Unhappiness; and are
therefore the only people whom my Company must necessarily
make melancholy. I will not bring myself to you at all hours, like
a Skeleton, to come across your diversions, and dash your pleasures: Nothing can be more shocking than to be perpetually
meeting the Ghost of an old acquaintance, which is all you can
ever see of me.

You must not imagine this to proceed from any Coldness, or
the least decrease of Friendship to you. If You had any Love for
me, I should be always glad to gratify you with an Object that
you thought agreable. But as your regard is Friendship & Esteem;
those are things that are as well, perhaps better, preservd
Absent than Present. A Man that you love is a joy to your eyes
at all times; a Man that you Esteem is a solemn kind of thing,
like a Priest, only wanted at a certain hour to do his Office:
'Tis like Oyl in a Sallet, necessary, but of no manner of Taste.
And you may depend upon it, I will wait upon you on every real
occasion, at the first summons, as long as I live.

Let me open my whole heart to you: I have some times found
myself inclined to be in love with you: and as I have reason to
know from your Temper & Conduct how miserably I should be
used in that circumstance, it is worth my while to avoid it: It is
enough to be Disagreable, without adding Fool to it, by constant
Slavery. I have heard indeed of Women that have had a kindness
for Men of my Make; but it has been after Enjoyment, never
before; and I know to my Cost you have had no Taste of that
Talent in me, which most Ladies would not only Like better, but
Understand better, than any other I have.

I love you so well that I tell you the truth, & that has made
me write this Letter. I will see you less frequently this winter,
as you'll less want company: When the Gay Part of the world
is gone, I'll be ready to stop the Gap of a vacant hour whenever
you please. Till then I'll converse with those who are more Indifferent to me, as You will with those who are more Entertaining. I wish you every pleasure God and Man can pour upon ye;

and I faithfully promise you all the good I can do you, which is, the Service of a Friend, who will ever be Ladies, Entirely Yours.

(I, 455–56)

Even in this painful context, Pope mentions the disparities between his poetical talent, which the ladies presumably enjoy, and his sexual "talent", which he now realizes they will never taste. Earlier in the same year, in a slightly happier context, he had made a metaphor combining the two talents, telling the sisters that he "past . . . the day in those Woods where I have so often enjoyd— an Author & a Book; and begot such Sons upon the Muses, as I hope will live to see their father what he never was yet, an old and a good Man". This seems jovial enough, although certainly self-protective. The real pathos comes as the letter continues, with verses in which it is suddenly clear that, in poetry at least, Pope thinks of the Blounts as the Muses:

I made a Hymn as I past thro' these Groves; it ended with a deep Sigh, which I will not tell you the meaning of.

All hail! once pleasing, once inspiring Shade,
  Scene of my youthful Loves, and happier hours!
Where the kind Muses met me as I stray'd,
  And gently pressd my hand, and said, Be Ours.
Take all thou e're shalt have, a constant Muse:
  At Court thou may'st be lik'd, but nothing gain;
Stocks thou may'st buy & sell, but always lose;
  And love the brightest eyes, but love in vain!

(13 September 1717; I, 428–29)

Pope's realization that he was to love the Blounts in vain was no doubt building up for some time, but clearly the painful incidents recorded in the letters of late 1717 and early 1718 represent a climax of a sort. The immediate results included Pope's settling an annuity of forty pounds a year on Teresa (10 March 1717–18), with the condition that she not marry during the six years for which it was drawn up. These conditions have been called "curious" and "inexplicable", but as Pope explained to Teresa in a letter which seems to relate to the subject, she had "exprest [her] self desirous of increasing [her] present income" (I, 468). Pope's gift to her was certainly generous, and no doubt made it possible for her to keep up, in dress and style, with the court ladies whose friendship evidently meant so much to her. As to the provision about her marrying, it hardly seems unreasonable: if,

98

as was far from impossible, some eligible man had decided to marry Teresa, it would have been embarrassing for him as well as for Pope for the annuity to be continued. In any case, the long-range result of the misunderstanding was a permanent break with Teresa; Pope last wrote to her in 1720, but Martha, by contrast, "remained to the end of his life, through slanders and imbroglios, the faithful center of Pope's affections".[15]

The pain his courtship of the Blounts cost Pope was real, but we ought to remember, in reading these letters, Pope's flair for self-dramatization. Even those strange words, "I have heard indeed of Women that have had a kindness for Men of my Make," probably reflect Pope's knowledge of a legend about a queen in love with her dwarf—a legend recounted in an anonymous quasi-Chaucerian poem in Tonson's 1709 *Miscellany*.[16] Pope alludes more explicitly to that legend in a letter to Lady Mary Wortley Montagu, in which he promises, playfully, to "meet you in Lombardy, the Scene of those celebrated Amours between the fair Princess and her Dwarf" ([October 1716]; I, 365). The simple fact that Pope was actively corresponding with Lady Mary all during the climactic years of his relationship with the Blount sisters suggests the extent to which letters to all those ladies involve imaginative role-playing; in June 1717, for example, he wrote to Lady Mary, "I have left off all correspondence except with yourself" (I, 405–6), but within a matter of days he was sending his *Works* to the Blounts, with a gallant letter (see I, 409). Norman Ault's description of the letters to Lady Mary as "both ardent and tinged with a playful extravagance which suggests that his gallantry was not meant to be taken too seriously"[17] is sensible, and clearly applies to many of the letters to the Blounts as well. Pope himself, however, often suggests the opposite: he claims that his wit and fancy are disguises for genuine and serious feelings. In any case, however playful or extravagant, the fantasies in which Pope could imagine that his physical deformity was overlooked or altered or reversed deserve careful attention. The tale of the queen and the dwarf was one such fantasy; a more complicated one, about nakedness, occurs repeatedly in letters to both Lady Mary and the Blounts. Here is its first appearance:

I think I love you as well as King Herod could Herodias, (tho I never had so much as one Dance with you) and would as freely give you my heart in a Dish, as he did another's head. But since Jupiter will not have it so, I must be content to show my taste in Life as I do my taste in Painting, by loving to have as little Drapery as possible. Not that I think every body naked, altogether so fine a sight as yourself and a few more would be: but because 'tis good to use people to what they must be acquainted with; and there will certainly come some Day of Judgment to uncover every Soul of us. We shall then see how the Prudes of this world owed all their fine Figure only to their being a little straiter-lac'd, and that they were naturally as arrant Squabs as those that went more loose, nay as those that never girded their loyns at all.

(18 August [1716]; I, 353)

These rich and striking metaphors are connected as brilliantly as we expect such metaphors to be connected in Pope's poems, but it is the last one which is most important. Even Pope's choice of words is telling: when he suggests that "Prudes" will be exposed on the Day of Judgment as "arrant Squabs", he is using one of the cruel epithets John Dennis had hurled at him in his attack on the *Essay on Criticism*—an attack which was only the first of many pamphlets shamelessly exploiting Pope's deformities. Dennis had written:

And now if you have a mind to enquire between *Sunning-Hill* and *Ockingham*, for a young, squab, short Gentleman, with the forementioned Qualification, an eternal Writer of Amorous Pastoral Madrigals, and the very bow of the God of Love, you will soon be directed to him.[18]

Ruefully viewing his own twisted body, constantly reminded of its flaws by Dennis and others, Pope devised this expressive fantasy of the Last Judgment, in which people whose earthly bodies had been normal, but whose souls were twisted, would be exposed. Laughed at by women for whom his appearance was his most important quality, he took understandable refuge in his poet's pride, as he explained to the Blounts in a darker version of the same image:

How can a poor Translator and Harehunter hope for a Minute's memory? Yet He comforts himself to reflect that He shall be remembered when people have forgot what colours you wore, and when those at whom you dress, shall be Dust! This is the Pride of a Poet, let me see if you dare owne what is the Pride of

100

a Woman, perhaps one article of it may be, to despise those who think themselves of some value, and to show your friends you can live without thinking of 'em at all. Do, keep your own secrets, that such fellows as I may laugh at ye in the valley of Jehosaphat, where Cunning will be the foolishest thing in nature, & those white Bums which I dye to see, will be shown to all the world.

(8 October [1718]; I, 515–16)

That there is a certain violence in this fantasy cannot be denied, but it also cannot be denied that Teresa Blount cared mightily about dress and appearance. It was that care which caused her cruelty to Pope, who had recognized it as early as the autumn of 1716, when he wrote to Martha, who was at home in the country while Teresa went to the birth-night party for the Prince of Wales:

> Let your faithless Sister triumph in her ill-gotten Treasures; let her put on New Gowns to be the Gaze of Fools, and Pageant of a Birth-night! While you with all your innocence enjoy a Shadey Grove without any leaves on, & dwell with a virtuous Aunt in a Country Paradise.
>
> (I, 375)

The phrase "without any leaves on" may be read as a bit of pastoral whimsy, since a leafless grove is hardly shady, but the overtones of "innocence" and "Paradise" make another reading possible. The phrase may modify "you", making of Martha an unclothed and unfallen Eve, in contrast to her fashionable but worldly sister. If this suggestion is really operative, it is worth considering how sharp the contrast is between the mythical landscape of Eden, its inhabitants innocently nude because they are unconscious of having anything to hide, and the mythical landscape of Pope's fantasy of the Last Judgment, with the "arrant squabs" stripped of their hypocritical coverings. Years later, in a letter to John Knight, Pope explicitly compared Martha to Eve:

> Her love for the place she banished herself from in so few days, resembles Eve's passion for Paradise, in Milton, when she had got herself turned out of it. However, like Eve, who raves upon tying up the rose-trees, and cultivating the arbours in the midst of her grief, this Lady too talks much of seeing the lawn enlarged, and the flocks feeding in sight of the parterre, and of administering grass to the lambs, and crowning them with flowers, etc.
>
> (8 November 1729; III, 68)

101

These and other fantasies function as the "courtly" witticisms function in many of Pope's earlier letters: aside from making entertaining reading, they allow Pope to dramatize his feelings toward Lady Mary or Martha in a form far enough from being explicit that his own feelings are protected. Consequently, Pope's occasional admissions that the fantasies are "the meer disguise of a discontented heart" (I, 383), though even those admissions themselves are couched in suspiciously dramatic language, are admissions of an important truth: the maker of the *persona* recognizes both his tools and his reasons.

Pope used similar tools to create the *persona* of the writer of his poetic love-letter "Eloisa to Abelard". He drew not only on John Hughes' English version of "those celebrated letters", and on Ovid and the whole tradition of the heroic epistle, but on his own experiences as a letter-writer. Eloisa's lines on letters,

> Heav'n first taught letters for some wretch's aid,
> Some banish'd lover, or some captive maid;
> They live, they speak, they breathe what love inspires,
> Warm from the soul, and faithful to its fires,
> The virgin's wish without her fears impart,
> Excuse the blush, and pour out all the heart,
> Speed the soft intercourse from soul to soul,
> And waft a sigh from *Indus* to the *Pole*.
>
> (51–8)

are in fact a pastiche of phrases from Pope's earlier letters. To Caryll, for example, he had described his own letters as "so many things freely thrown out, such lengths of unreserved friendship, thoughts just warm from the brain without any polishing or dress, the very *deshabille* of the understanding" (5 December 1712; I, 160). The similarity of phrasing here suggests a broader relationship between Pope's love-letters and the *Eloisa*.

Eloisa begins her letter with eight dense lines, which immediately establish a physical landscape, a psychological tension, and a dramatic situation:

> In these deep solitudes and awful cells,
> Where heav'nly-pensive, contemplation dwells,
> And ever-musing melancholy reigns;
> What means this tumult in a Vestal's veins?
> Why rove my thoughts beyond this last retreat?
> Why feels my heart its long-forgotten heat?

Yet, Yet I love!—From *Abelard* it came.
And *Eloisa* yet must kiss the name.

The Miltonic atmosphere of the first three lines gains force from
the muted personifications of "contemplation" and "melancholy".
Later in the poem, "Black Melancholy" is re-introduced as a
full-fledged goddess. The lines center upon their nouns ("soli-
tudes—contemplation—melancholy"), and the sudden contrast of
"tumult", similarly centered in the fourth line, couples with the
surprisingly physical rhyming word "veins" to create a dramatic
impression of something out of place. As Eloisa's questions show,
she finds her sudden emotional "heat" very much out of place
in the cold setting of the convent. A considerably milder version
of such a contrast between environment and emotion occurs in a
letter Pope wrote to the Blount sisters, describing a visit to Oxford,
a temporary cloistering of himself

> among those old walls, venerable Galleries, Stone Portico's,
> studious walks & solitary Scenes of the University. I wanted
> nothing but a black Gown and a Salary, to be as meer a Book-
> worm as any there. I conform'd myself to the College hours,
> was rolled up in books & wrapt in meditations, lay in one of
> the most ancient, dusky parts of the University, and was as dead
> to the world as any Hermite of the desart . . .
> Methinks I do very ill, to return to the world again, to leave
> the only place where I make a good figure, and from seeing my-
> self seated with dignity on the most conspicuous Shelves of a
> Library, go to contemplate this wretched person in the abject
> condition of lying at a Lady's feet in Bolton street.
>
> ([September 1717]; I, 430)

Bolton Street was, at this point, the London address of the sisters.
Neither Pope's account of the attractions of the retired life of the
University nor his sense of the ludicrousness of "lying at a Lady's
feet" ought to be dismissed as mere wit. They show, on the contrary, Pope's real comprehension of the impropriety of passion
for some people under some circumstances.

But people *do* have improper feelings. Pope's letter continues
with a powerfully emotional passage (of which more later), and
Eloisa, while recognizing that her "tumult" is far from proper,
holds in her hand a letter from Abelard; the "long-forgotten
heat" she feels has been kindled by that bit of paper. Pope claimed
similar tumult on receiving one of Lady Mary's letters:

103

Madam,—I wish I could write any thing to divert you, but it is impossible in the unquiet state I am put into by your letter. It has grievously afflicted me, without affectation.

(3 February [1716/1717]; I, 388–89)

His letter goes on to attempt a graphic equivalent of the tumult it claims:

I am now—I can't tell what—I won't tell what, for it would grieve you—This letter is a piece of madness, that throws me after you in a distracted manner. I don't know which way to write, which way to send it, or if ever it will reach your hands. If it does, what can you inferr from it, but what I am half afraid, & half willing, you should know; how very much I was yours, how unfortunately well I knew you, and with what a miserable constancy I shall ever remember you? . . . But it is foolish to tell you this—did I say, foolish? it is a thousand times worse, it is in vain!—

It is difficult to read these phrases without suspecting Pope of dramatic extravagance, of exaggerating, even by punctuation, his supposedly distraught state of mind. Quite simply, the letter is too well-written to make good its claim that its writer is out of control. Consider, for example, the careful gradation, in speed and length, of these clauses:

how very much I was yours,
how unfortunately well I knew you,
and with what a miserable constancy I shall ever remember you.

This is not the prose of a distraught man, but it may be the prose of a man trying eloquently to express the *idea* of being distraught.[19]

Surely this is the way we must read the poem, although I do not mean to suggest anything like a mindless equation of Eloisa and Mr. Pope. Pope learned, partly from writing his own letters, to find verbal and formal equivalents for emotions he sometimes felt, and to exaggerate those emotions for two reasons: first, to give them an immediacy, as writing, that he might have achieved in conversation by gesture; second (particularly in the letters to women), to protect his feelings by couching them in somewhat ambiguous or contradictory terms. So when the ladies to whom his pseudo-passionate ravings were addressed ignored them, Pope

could make believe that they had read his letters as merely conventional effusions, *and* that he had written them thus. Much of
this process was probably unconscious.

Eloisa, although she is sometimes treated with a kind of irony,
always means what she says. Her ravings, whether they spill across
the couplets or fall neatly within them, are meant to be read as a
dramatic expressive *representation* of Passion, not as a realistic
version of disorderly passion itself. D. W. Roberston has put this
distinction particularly well:

> The reader is not invited to enter the scene at all. Abstractions
> find a natural place in it, and there is a sense in which Eloisa
> herself is an abstraction—a representation of the "idea" of a
> woman torn between passionate memories of love and equally
> passionate but futile and unreasoned impulses toward devotion.
> If we try to consider her as a "personality", or a "psychological
> reality", we inject a discordant note into the scenery and destroy
> the fabric of the poem.[20]

But the fact that the picture of Passion in the *Eloisa* is painted in
a highly ornamented, rococo style did not mean, for Pope and his
readers, that it was not supposed to be moving. While working
on the poem, Pope wrote to Martha Blount:

> Madam,—I am here studying ten hours a day, but thinking of you
> in spight of all the learned. The Epistle of Eloise grows warm,
> and begins to have some Breathings of the Heart in it, which
> may make posterity think I was in love. I can scarce find in my
> heart to leave out the conclusion I once intended for it—
>
> ([March 1716?]; I, 338)

Posterity, especially nineteenth-century posterity, did think of the
poem and its author in this way. In writing the letter, Pope was
encouraging Martha to think of the poem she would soon read as
an outgrowth of their relationship, but it is hard to believe that
it was exclusively such an outgrowth, particularly in the face of
his similar claims in a later letter to Lady Mary:

> Among the rest, you have all I am worth, that is, my Workes:
> There are few things in them but what you have already seen,
> except the Epistle of Eloisa to Abelard; in which you will find
> one passage, that I can't tell whether to wish you should under-
> stand, or not?
>
> ([June 1717]; I, 407)[21]

105

By telling both women explicitly to look for "Breathings of the Heart" in the *Eloisa*, Pope was encouraging them to look beyond the careful formal patterns of the poem's surface to its generating emotions. He was insisting on the existence of those emotions, in himself and in Eloisa, but perhaps insisting a bit too much. As I have been arguing, Pope's portrayals of himself as the languishing lover are, in most cases, careful, formal, even conventional. This need not imply that there was no feeling at all behind the expressions, but it does suggest that the feeling was almost always controlled, as it found expression, by Pope's concurrent sense of the ludicrous physical figure he made as a lover, and his consequent need to protect himself from ridicule.

For similar reasons, Pope does not try to make Eloisa's letter look like an actual letter. Later in the century, Richardson would use all the resources of typography to insist on the reality of his heroines' letters, and it is not insignificant that Pope praised *Pamela*.[22] But in the *Eloisa*, the epistolary form is bent to accommodate a great deal of obviously non-epistolary matter. To be sure, Eloisa begins the poem by describing her surroundings and acknowledging her receipt of Abelard's letter—just as Pope begins many of his own letters—but she also recapitulates the story ("Thou know'st how guiltless first I met thy flame"), and a reader insistent on realism might well ask why Eloisa is telling Abelard what he already knows. In fact, Pope's poem intensifies Eloisa's feelings by the very devices that distance the reader from the actual incoherent and unpoetic form her feelings might have taken: the Ovidian tradition provides a rich frame of reference, an implicit claim that Eloisa's plight has the status of myth; the rhetoric borrowed from the drama and cast into tight couplets gives a pointedness to her dilemma; even the presence of such abstractions as nature, grace, passion, reason, forgiveness, contemplation, and melancholy should not, for readers aware of Boethius and Augustine, suggest coldness. Pope used the full force of the various traditions at hand to create his Eloisa. If she is an abstraction, she is an abstraction meant to exemplify the powerful pull on all of us of feelings we know are unreasonable.

One of Pope's ways of dramatizing the power of such feelings, both in the poem and in his letters, is the use of sympathetic landscape. This practice has often been described as "pre-Romantic",[23] but it had the sanction of Ovid himself. Pope had translated one typical passage in his *Sapho to Phaon*:

> [I] frantick rise, and like some Fury rove
> Thro' lonely Plains, and thro' the silent Grove,
> As if the silent Grove, and lonely Plains
> That knew my Pleasures, could relieve my Pains.
> I view the *Grotto*, once the Scene of Love,
> The Rocks around, the hanging Roofs above,
> That charm'd me more, with Native Moss o'ergrown,
> Than *Phrygian* Marble or the *Parian* Stone.
>
> (159–66)

Pope's letter from Oxford to the Blounts begins with a description of his ride to Oxford from Stonor which echoes many details of this and other Ovidian landscapes:

> Nothing could have more of that Melancholy which once us'd to please me, than that days journey: For after having passed thro' my favorite Woods in the forest, with a thousand Reveries of past pleasures; I rid over hanging hills, whose tops were edged with Groves, & whose feet water'd with winding rivers, listening to the falls of Cataracts below, & the murmuring of the Winds above. The gloomy Verdure of Stonor succeeded to these, & then the Shades of the Evening overtook me, the Moon rose in the clearest sky I ever saw, by whose solemn light I pac'd on slowly, without company, or any interruption to the range of my thoughts.
>
> (I, 429–30)

The fact that this self-consciously beautiful prose is related to Ovid's poetry does not constitute a reason to suspect Pope's melancholy on his ride. He was using the best tools at hand to express his feelings, and the casting of those feelings in a mode made rich by tradition was, for him, a way of increasing, not reducing, their intensity. The similar passage in the *Eloisa* is justly famous:

> The darksome pines that o'er yon rocks reclin'd
> Wave high, and murmur to the hollow wind,
> The wandring streams that shine between the hills,
> The grots that eccho to the tinkling rills,
> The dying gales that pant upon the trees,
> The lakes that quiver to the curling breeze;
> No more these scenes my meditation aid,
> Or lull to rest the visionary maid:

107

> But o'er the twilight groves, and dusky caves,
> Long-sounding isles, and intermingled graves,
> Black Melancholy sits, and round her throws
> A death-like silence, and a dread repose:
> Her gloomy presence saddens all the scene,
> Shades ev'ry flow'r, and darkens ev'ry green,
> Deepens the murmur of the falling floods,
> And breathes a browner horror on the woods.
>
> (155–70)

These lines have more intensity than the translation because Pope had become a better poet in the intervening years; they have more intensity than the letter because the context of the *Eloisa* allows him to call the winds not merely "murmuring" but (ominously) "dying". The introduction of the powerful personification "Black Melancholy", which would hardly have been possible in a letter, gives a focus and climax to the description; she sits over the entire scene as a brooding, all-controlling presence, making possible such sinister details as the "intermingled graves" and the "browner horror". Still, different as this Melancholy is from "that Melancholy which once us'd to please me", to which Pope alludes in the letter, both are abstractions whose purpose is to give palpable life to a mental state. Eloisa's state is more wrought up than Pope's; consequently her Melancholy is a more powerful figure.

Individual metaphors which Pope had used in his letters in a qualified or detached way gain a more naked intensity in the *Eloisa*. One example is Eloisa's almost metaphysical assertion that Abelard's "Idea" lies in her heart:

> Dear fatal name! rest ever unreveal'd,
> Nor pass these lips in holy silence seal'd.
> Hide it, my heart, within that close disguise,
> Where, mix'd with God's, his lov'd Idea lies.
>
> (9–12)

In a letter to Lady Mary, probably written about the time of the composition of the *Eloisa*, the very word "Idea" occurs in a context close to that of the poem:

> If you could see the heart I talk of, you would really think it a foolish, good kind of thing, with some qualities as well deserving to be half-laughed at and half-esteemed, as any in the

108

world. Its grand Foible in regard to you, is the most like Reason
of any Foible in nature. Upon my faith, this heart is not like a
great Ware-house stored only with my own Goods, with vast
empty spaces to be supplyd as fast as Interest or Ambition can
fill them up; but it is every inch of it let out into Lodgings for
its friends, and shall never want a Corner at your service: where
I dare affirm Madam, your Idea lyes as warm, and as close, as any
Idea in Christendom.

([1716–17]; I, 383)

To be sure, there is a great difference in tone. Eloisa would never
tell Abelard that her heart deserved "to be half-laughed at and
half-esteemed", nor does she think that her passion for him is
even "like Reason". She knows that her passion is unreasonable,
and makes no attempt to excuse it.   She uses the metaphor of
the idea in the heart, like others, to express the power of a passion
she would like to conquer, recognizing its hopelessness. Pope's
feelings about Lady Mary were not dissimilar, but because he was
aware of the ludicrousness of professing passionate love for a
woman who was married, taller, and several thousand miles away,
he undercut the force of the metaphor by slipping it into a paragraph which offhandedly calls his feelings for her a "Foible".
But he could not always maintain the self-mocking, self-protective tone. As Lady Mary's return approached, he began to
betray his excitement at the prospect of seeing her again:

> I can keep no measures in speaking of this subject. I see you
> already coming, I feel you as you draw nearer, My heart leaps
> at your arrival: Let us have You from the East, and the Sun is
> at her service.
>
> I write as if I were drunk, the pleasure I take in thinking of
> your return transports me beyond the bounds of common Sence
> and decency.

([Autumn 1717]; I, 440)

The quick qualification ("I write as if I were drunk") is Pope's way
of acknowledging what seems a momentary loss of control. Take
away the self-mocking humor, and you have a rhetoric of contrast
not unlike Eloisa's. Her appeals,

> Come, if thou dar'st, all charming as thou art!
> Oppose thyself to heav'n; dispute my heart!
> (281–82)

are as quickly denied:

> No, fly me, fly me! far as Pole from Pole;
> Rise *Alps* between us! and whole oceans roll!
> (289–90)

Eloisa reverses her appeals for Abelard's presence because she has equally powerful yearnings for God and the lot of the ":blameless Vestal" whose situation she describes (lines 207–22). One source of the poem's remarkable energy is the intensity with which Pope manages to portray both Eloisa's physical passion for her emasculated lover and her genuine desire for heavenly grace and acceptance. This particular opposition was not one he had himself literally experienced; what qualified his occasional outbursts to the Blounts and Lady Mary, in the passages just examined, was embarrassment or the fear of appearing ridiculous, not a powerful attraction to a higher devotion. But he had experienced, in other areas, the dilemma of conflicting impulses: his desire to "publish [his] own heart", which led to the publication of the letters, often conflicted with his need for concealment and even stratagem; his sincere attraction to the retired life conflicted with his interest in the hurry of the city; his good intentions about remaining insensitive to attack and aloof from his attackers conflicted with his natural resentment. And these are only the most obvious examples. Aware of the force of such conflicts, Pope was able to give Eloisa's conflicts poetic life, showing her fluctuating rapidly from one desire to another.

Eloisa's dialectic, despite the expectations of readers who define that word according to Marx, cannot resolve itself by synthesis.[24] Her love for Abelard and her love for God can never merge. One is an intense physical passion, rendered impossible of satisfaction by Abelard's emasculation; the other is a similarly intense desire for submission and acceptance, rendered impossible by her inability to forget her bodily longings. No earthly solution is possible; the picture the poem makes is the picture of a struggle without a solution. Like her Ovidian precursors, Eloisa imagines death as a final release from her quandary, but there is a crucial difference: her death will not be a suicide like Sappho's or Dido's, but a release granted by God:

> But all is calm in this eternal sleep;
> Here grief forgets to groan, and love to weep,

Ev'n superstition loses ev'ry fear:
For God, not man, absolves our frailties here.

(313–16)

The frailty of Pope's earthly body made him peculiarly conscious of death. In a letter he wrote Martha Blount in [1715], he
speculated about its consequences:

> I am growing fit, I hope, for a better world, of which the light
> of the sun is but a shadow: for I doubt not but God's works
> here, are what come nearest to his works there; and that a true
> relish of the beauties of nature is the most easy preparation and
> gentlest transition to an enjoyment of those of heaven; as on
> the contrary a true town life of hurry, confusion, noise, slander,
> and dissension, is a sort of apprenticeship to hell and its furies.
> I'm endeavoring to put my mind into as quiet a situation as I
> can, to be ready to receive that stroke which I believe is coming
> upon me, and have fully resign'd my self to yield to it. The separ-
> ation of my soul and body is what I could think of with less
> pain; for I am very sure he that made it will take care of it, and
> in whatever state he pleases it shall be, that state must be right:
> But I cannot think without tears of being separated from my
> friends, when their condition is so doubtful, that they may want
> even such assistance as mine. Sure it is more merciful to take
> from us after death all memory of what we lov'd or pursu'd here:
> for else what a torment would it be to a spirit, still to love
> those creatures it is quite divided from? Unless we suppose, that
> in a more exalted life, all that we esteemed in this imperfect
> state will affect us no more, than what we lov'd in our infancy
> concerns us now.
>
> (I, 319)

Eloisa also thinks of heaven as a place with beauties beyond those
of nature:

> I come, I come! prepare your roseate bow'rs,
> Celestial palms, and ever-blooming flow'rs.
>
> (317–18)[25]

She too recognizes that it would be "torment . . . to a spirit, still
to love those creatures it is quite divided from". As she imagines
her eventual death, she thinks of Abelard looking on

> Till ev'ry motion, pulse, and breath, be o'er;
> And ev'n my *Abelard* be lov'd no more.
>
> (333–34)

111

She too has had an "apprenticeship to hell and its furies", but her apprenticeship is not "town life" but her dreams of sexual gratification with Abelard, dreams in which "glowing guilt" and "Provoking Daemons" take part. That the dreams are hellish and sinful is beyond question. That they are attractive is also true. And much the same thing could be said about Pope's considerably more flippant remarks about the city. Much as he was attracted to the more heavenly life of the country, no reader of the *Dunciad* could deny that he was fascinated by the "hurry, confusion, noise, slander, and dissension" of the city.

Death, Eloisa realizes, will separate her at last from her hopeless passion for Abelard. In her imagined death scene, he is present in his function as a priest, but her imagination gives his presence other overtones:

> Thou, *Abelard*! the last sad office pay,
> And smooth my passage to the realms of day:
> See my lips tremble, and my eye-balls roll,
> Suck my last breath, and catch my flying soul!
> Ah no—in sacred vestments may'st thou stand,
> The hallowed taper trembling in thy hand,
> Present the Cross before my lifted eye,
> Teach me at once, and learn of me to die.
>
> (321–28)

Even when inviting Abelard to perform her last rites, she continues to think of him in sensual terms. He becomes, in the second of these couplets, the same demon lover she has imagined him earlier:

> Still on that breast enamour'd let me lie,
> Still drink delicious poison from thy eye,
> Pant on thy lip, and to thy heart be prest;
> Give all thou canst—and let me dream the rest.
>
> (121–24)

The imagery of both these passages suggests Faustus's damning encounter with Helen; reversing the sexual roles, Pope was able to use the same imagery at the emotional center of his letter to the Blounts from Oxford:

> I will not deny, but that like Alexander, in the midst of my Glory,
> I am wounded, & find myself a meer man. To tell you from

112

whence the Dart comes, is to no purpose, since neither of you
will take the tender care to draw it out of my heart, & suck
the poison with your lips; or are in any disposition to take in a
part of the venome yourselves, to ease me.

(I, 430)

The "taper" Abelard is to hold in his hand, a kind of graphic representation of Eloisa, trembling on the brink of extinction, was
an image Pope often used for his dying mother. For example, he
wrote Lady Mary:

I have yet a Mother of great age & infirmitys, whose last precarious days of life I am now attending, with such a solemn pious
kind of officiousness, as a melancholy Recluse watches the last
risings & fallings of a dying Taper.

([1718]; I, 469)

In this passage, Pope imagined himself as a "melancholy Recluse",
but in his stricken letter to the Blounts at the time of the severe
misunderstanding that led to his break with Teresa, he actually
imagined himself as a priest:

A Man that you love is a joy to your eyes at all times; a Man
that you Esteem is a solemn kind of thing, like a Priest, only
wanted at a certain hour to do his Office.

([Late 1717]; I, 455–56)

If Sherburn's date for this last letter is correct, it was written
five or six months after the publication of the *Eloisa*. Did the rejection Pope had experienced make him feel emasculated, and was
his echo of the poem (explicit in the word "Office") his way of
signalling his pain to the Blounts? The uncertainty of the date
renders this a mere speculation, but if, as I have been suggesting,
Pope paralleled certain formalized and unprotected versions of
phrasing and imagery from his letters in creating his Eloisa, it
would be a fascinating reversal of that process for him to draw on
his poem for an image to express his pain in a letter.

He used the ending of the poem as a signal to Lady Mary. After
describing the grave in which she hopes to be interred with Abelard, Eloisa continues:

And sure if fate some future Bard shall join
In sad similitude of griefs to mine,

113

Condemn'd whole years in absence to deplore,
And image charms he must behold no more,
Such if there be, who loves so long, so well;
Let him our sad, our tender story tell;
The well-sung woes will sooth my pensive ghost;
He best can paint 'em, who shall feel 'em most.

(359–66)

These must be the lines referred to in Pope's letter to Lady Mary as "one passage, that I can't tell whether to wish you should understand, or not?" (I, 407). She certainly *should* have understood them, for they serve precisely the function that the witty flashes in his otherwise passionate letters to her serve: they suggest that what has come before need not be taken too seriously. Again, Professor Robertson comments acutely:

> In a Providential world, as in the world of Ovid's *Heroides*, frustrated passion uncontrolled by reason is more than a little ridiculous, and Pope was the "bard" to whom his Eloisa clearly refers. In the last line of his poem, therefore, Eloisa is asking us, quite inadvertently, to smile a little at Alexander Pope. If Eloisa was unaware of this implication, Pope was certainly not; we may assume that he led the chorus of smiles.[26]

We may indeed so assume, for Pope was usually capable of laughing at himself. But we should perhaps look at this laughter in the context of the story of his claim to be amused by Cibber's attacks, with his features actually "writhen with anguish". Laughter can be, and frequently is for handicapped persons, a way of hiding and coping with pain. Pope's feelings for Lady Mary and the Blounts, irrational as they may have been, undeniably caused him pain. Without his experience of that pain, the *Eloisa* would be a less powerful poem.

Yet with the exception of the flippant final couplet, Pope had the good sense to keep himself out of the poem. He drew on his own experiences and his own language, but not in ways that would have been obvious to any reader but the Blounts and Lady Mary. The imagination that helped Pope dramatize himself in his letters serves in the poem to dramatize Eloisa, to give her quandary the poignance that made her appealing to both Johnson and Byron.

Thwarted in his early attempts to find a wife, aware that "no Child of mine (but a Poem or two) is to live after me" (27 March

114

[1739]; IV, 169), and constrained throughout his life to relations with women in which ridicule was a constant possibility, Pope emerged with the ability to look with a somewhat jaundiced eye on the sexual foibles of others. That attitude emerges with some bitterness in *Sober Advice from Horace* and with temperate sense in the *Epistle on the Characters of Women*, dedicated, although with typical modesty she would not allow the use of her name, to Martha Blount. Pope ultimately broke with Lady Mary,[27] as he had earlier broken with Teresa, but Martha remained his 'virtuous friend", and his mature relationship with her was a special and intimate one. The slanders, by no means now dead, which sought to describe her as his secret wife or mistress, pained Pope, and in the absence of evidence, I tend to believe his denials on this point.[28] His later letters record tender, protective, critical, and appreciative feelings about her; their most moving moments show Pope's sense of what might have been. He concludes one long letter with the hope that she might come to a country house near Stowe, where he was making a visit, but realizes that she will not and laments: "But this, I know, is a Dream; and almost Every thing I wish, in relation to You, is so always!" ([7 July 1739]; IV, 188). But dreams are the stuff of poetry, and surely Pope's poems, despite their relative lack of surface emotion and sexuality, gained much from his dreams—even those dreams which his physical shape rendered impossible of fulfillment.

NOTES

1 *The Letters of Mounsieur de Balzac Translated into English, according to the last Edition, by W*[illiam] *T*[irwhyt] *Esq.* (London, 1634), p. 94.

2 This and all subsequent citations of Pope's letters follow the text of *The Correspondence of Alexander Pope,* ed. George Sherburn, 5 vols. (Oxford, 1956).

3 Pope's letter "to a Lady, with a *Book of Drawings*" (I, 4) is based upon a letter from Voiture to Madame de Rambouillet, as even Curll realized (see III, 495). For other borrowings, see the correspondence between Pope and Cromwell in 1710, especially I, 89, 95, 98. For a full discussion, see Emile Audra, *L'influence Francaise dans L'oeuvre de Pope,* pp. 315–46.

4 Richelet's "Account of Voiture", which appears in the front-matter of *The Works of Vincent Voiture, Done from the Paris edition, by Mr.*

Ozell (London, 1715), p. xx. Ozell's translation, despite its title-page, in fact reprints earlier translations by Dryden, Dennis, Thomas Cheek, Henry Cromwell, and others.

5   In Ozell, I, lxxvii.

6   In Ozell, I, xxxvi.

7   In Ozell, I, lxxix.

8   Michael J. Pretina, Jr., *Vincent Voiture, Creation and Reality: A Study of his Prose* (unpublished Ph.D. dissertation, Yale, 1967), p. 105.

9   In Tom Brown's *Familiar Letters: Written by the Right Honourable John late Earl of Rochester, And several other Persons* . . . (London, 1697), I, 73–4.

10 See *The Early Career of Alexander Pope* (Oxford, 1934), p. 157. For an example of Pope's boasting, see p. 47.

11 Marjorie Nicolson and George S. Rousseau, *"This Long Disease, My Life"* (Princeton, 1968), p. 66.

12 Joseph Spence, *Observations, Anecdotes and Characters of Books and Men*, ed. James M. Osborn (Oxford, 1966), p. 111. The "slander" of which Cheselden spoke was Cibber's tale that he had rescued Pope from what might have been the dangerous embraces of a prostitute (in his *Letter from Mr. Cibber, to Mr. Pope* . . . , published in 1742). Cibber's letter occasioned a number of satirical prints; for one example, see J. V. Guerinot, *Pamphlet Attacks on Alexander Pope* (London, 1969), opposite p. 288. The account of the Pope-Cibber quarrel in Norman Ault's *New Light on Pope* (London, 1969), pp. 301–7, is thorough and judicious.

13 Martha Blount told Spence that she was "a very little girl" when she met Pope, but also said that the meeting occurred after the publication of the *Essay on Criticism*, i.e. 1711. Osborn, reckoning backwards from Pope's jocular phrase about "the three hundred eighty-ninth week of the reign of your most serene majesty" (I, 258), dates the meeting in May of June 1707. Pope's sense of time was never very precise, but in this case his numbers lead to a plausible date.

14 *Early Career*, p. 48.

15 William K. Wimsatt, Jr., in his introduction to *Alexander Pope; Selected Poetry and Prose* (New York, 1951), p. xii.

16 Pope was a contributor to this volume, so there can be little doubt that he knew the poem, which includes these lines:

> *Cynthio* was puzzel'd, and one may
> Give any one at least a Day
> To guess the Nymph that humbly su'd,
> And Swain so stubborn to be wo'd.
> Now who shou'd this *Adonis* be,
> But the King's ugly Dwarf! and she,
> In whose Embraces he was seen,
> The bright Astolpho's haughty Queen!
>   (pp. 342–43)

17 *New Light on Pope*, p. 359.

18 Quoted in *Early Career*, p. 92.

19 Cf. Murray Kreiger's somewhat similar point about the poem in " 'Eloisa to Abelard', The Escape from Body or the Embrace of Body", *Eighteenth-Century Studies* III (1969), p. 34.

20 *Abelard and Heloise* (New York, 1972), p. 188.

21 Geoffrey Tillotson, in his introduction to the *Eloisa*, argues plausibly that the letter to Martha, placed in Holy Week of 1716 by Elwin (and by Sherburn), actually belongs in Holy Week of 1717, suggesting that the poem was nearly finished and that "Pope *did* 'find in [his] heart to leave out the conclusion [he] once intended for it' " (TE II, 312). Pretty clearly, the lines in the conclusion about absence (361–62) fit Lady Mary far better than Martha, but Tillotson's postulation of an earlier, cancelled conclusion written specifically for Martha may be considered an attractive conjecture.

22 See IV, 335n. For a useful account of Richardson's typographical techniques, see the first of the two chapters on *Clarissa* in John Preston's *The Created Self* (London, 1970).

23 The introduction to the edition of James E. Wellington (Miami, 1965) is a particularly excessive example: "The inclusion of details of landscape absent from the Hughes letters and unknown at the site of the real Paraclete indicates Pope's determination to enlist all the 'Gothick' details of pre-Romantic poetry in dramatizing her plight" (p. 46). In fact, such details of landscape occur, for example, in *Heroides* II, 131–34; VII, 37–40; and X, 25–30.

24 The search for a synthesis for Eloisa has been carried out by Brendan P. O Hehir in "Virtue and Passion: Dialectic of *Eloisa to Abelard*", *Texas Studies in Literature and Language* II (1960), 219–32, and (refining on O Hehir) by Krieger in the article cited above (n. 19) and by Barret John Mandel in "Pope's 'Eloisa to Abelard' ", *Texas Studies* IX (1967), 57–68.

25 These lines represent a distillation of the imagery used earlier for the "blameless Vestal" (207–22), where the landscape is heavenly in the manner of a baroque painting. Still, the next couplet, with its talk of "flames refin'd" perhaps suggests the possibility of Purgatory, a possibility more dramatically implicit in the earlier line, "In seas of flame my plunging soul is drown'd" (275).

26 Robertson, p. 202.

27 Their separation may have been more gradual than violent, and cannot be dated with certainty. See Robert Halsband, *The Life of Lady Mary Wortley Montagu* (Oxford, 1956), pp. 129–32.

28 In the chronology at the beginning of *Alexander Pope: A Critical Anthology* (Harmondsworth, 1971), p. 24, Bateson and Joukovsky, without comment or proof, make the entry: "1727 . . . Martha Blount becomes Pope's mistress about this period." This bald statement represents the hardening into dogma of a position Professor Bateson once expressed more tentatively. In his notes for *Epistles to Several Persons*, which he edited for the Twickenham Edition in 1951, he provided a summary of the gossip (by Horace Walpole and others) upon which such an

assertion might be based, and concluded, "It is not improbable that she was Pope's mistress". However, Pope's letter to Caryll, denying such a rumor (II, 353–54), and a letter from Caryll's wife to Martha (see *Early Career*, p. 294) constitute strong evidence that the relationship was not a sexual one.

5

Pope on the Subject of Old Age: The *Iliad* Translation, Books XXII-XXIV

by FELICITY ROSSLYN

In Book XXI of the *Iliad*, Achilles slaughters an unarmed suppliant and runs amok among the Trojans. In Book XXIV, he honourably ransoms Hector's body and sheds tears with his enemy for their losses in the war—a change that might come as a jolt, if Homer had not shown how far Achilles was from the brute in Patroclus' funeral games, Book XXIII, where he presides with quick tact, generosity, and a sense of what is due to the competitors' honour. He offers Agamemnon a prize without his taking part; and gives one to Nestor because the old warrior cannot fight for it, a gesture which draws an interesting translation from Pope:

> Take thou this Token of a grateful Heart,
> Tho' 'tis not thine to hurl the distant Dart,
> The Quoit to toss, the pond'rous Mace to wield,
> Or urge the Race, or wrestle on the Field.
> Thy present Vigour Age has overthrown,
> But left the Glory of the Past thy own.
>   He said, and plac'd the Goblet at his side;
> With Joy, the venerable King replied.[1]

The translation suggests how warmly Pope recognized the delicacy of this behaviour towards an old man, and how concerned he was to make it appear. There is no "Token of a grateful Heart" in the Greek, to make Nestor feel his obligation less, and the graceful turn at the end, "But left the Glory of the Past thy own", is the reassurance Homer withholds. Pope's first draft was not so tactful,

Thy present vigor, Age has overthrown
& left ye Glory of ye past alone,[2]

but even this was a softened account of what he found in the Greek: "I give you this prize un-fought for, because you cannot show your prowess in the games: *khalepon gēras* is weighing you down"—old age, in its harsh intransigence. Homer's meaning is that Nestor cannot defend, or even lay claim to his honour; the penalty of old age is that it can only be given to him, and it is one part of what makes Achilles a hero, that he rescues Nestor's pride. Pope's adjustments disguise the starkness of the facts, but suggest how keenly he felt them, just as the approving couplet he inserts after Nestor's eloquent reply suggests how much there was to lose, had either of them behaved less well:

> Proud of the Gift, thus spoke the Full of Days:
> *Achilles* heard him, prouder of the Praise.[3]

Wherever the old men of the *Iliad* appear Pope shows the same sensitivity, with a corresponding reluctance to be as frank as Homer. His reluctance grows towards the end of the poem, where the loss of Hector turns Priam into the prototype of suffering old age in literature. He begins to inspire awe, like Lear or Oedipus, simply by his willingness to carry on living, and by the quantity of pain he is able to support without narrowing, in self-defence, his ability to feel. The story does not go as far as his death, but Homer foreshadows it in Priam's prophetic speech to Hector on the point of his last battle with Achilles, and it is perhaps this passage that finds Pope at his most sensitive:

> "So come inside the wall, my child, and guard the men and women of Troy from here; do not throw away your own life only to give glory to the son of Peleus. Have pity on me: I know that I am wretched and doomed; that father Zeus has a black end prepared for me, on the threshold of my old age. I shall see horrors before I die: my sons slaughtered and my daughters hauled away, my chambers ransacked, and my little ones dashed to the ground in the fury of battle, while my sons' wives are dragged off in the hands of the cruel Achaians. And I, last of all, will be stabbed or beaten to death by a sharp bronze weapon, and torn apart by flesh-eating dogs at my own palace doors; by the same dogs that I reared in my hall, and fed at table, as watch-dogs. They will lap my blood and lie in the gateway, with madness in their

120

hearts. It is fitting for a young man to lie slain in battle, showing the gashes made by sharp bronze; though he is dead, the sight is a fine one, no matter what can be seen; but when it is an old man who is down, and dogs are scavenging on his grey head, grey beard and private parts, it is the most pitiful sight of all for sad humanity."[4]

This speech is Homer's way of bringing the end of the war inside his narrative, but it is also, from Priam's point of view, conscious oratory: he is putting forward all the arguments that should move Hector as a son, and the order he presents them in suggests his own estimate of their respective pull. Terrible as the massacre of his other sons and the slavery of his daughters would be, his own death, unprotected, would be worse, and his horror is the greater for the kind of death he must expect. He is specific: a young man's death in battle is fitting, and whatever he looks like the sight is not abhorrent to the eye but *kalos*, fine, at once pleasant to the eye and welcome to the sense of right. But he, an old man, will be ravaged by dogs and made *aiskhros*, the very opposite —ugly to the sight and outrageous to the feelings. The dogs will maul the grey head and beard which, because of their greyness, should be revered, and last of all they will destroy his *aidō*, private parts, which are the object in himself of the same protective *aidōs*, reverence, on which the heroic code is founded. This is *oiktistos*, the most pitiful sight of all; one that undermines such grounds of understanding and acceptance as Priam's world has been able to wrest from tragedy. The heroic code, which justifies the death of the young warrior, bestows no meaning on a death like this. Priam will die meaninglessly, as animals die.

Pope's translation contains so many other considerations than these, however, that it may help to set it in the context of the translations that preceded it, and affected his reading. He was not the first to feel that Homer lays bare an almost intolerable truth here, and *ménagement* in handling it is at least as old as Virgil, who worked one version of Priam's death into the *Aeneid*, and attempted to arouse an equivalent horror without recourse to Homer's physical details. His Priam is much older than Homer's figure, and has a tremulous frailty that heightens our sense of the consideration due to him. But his opponent is Pyrrhus, who willingly agrees—when Priam denounces him—that he has none of the scruples of Achilles, and drags Priam through the blood of one of his sons to slaughter him, like an animal, on his own sacrificial altar:

> hoc dicens altaria ad ipsa trementem
> traxit et in multo lapsantem sanguine nati,
> implicuitque coman laeva, dextraque coruscum
> extulit ac lateri capulo tenus abdidit ensem.[5]

The outrage to all the Roman sanctities is so strongly drawn, that it may seem paradoxical to suggest that these atrocious details remove Priam's suffering to safer ground—that of wanton evil—and that Virgil's pathos is simpler than Homer's. But if Pyrrhus is the villain, he draws on himself the resentment that in the Greek remains without an object. Homer's Priam spoke of being mauled by dogs, who are not responsible for what they do, and of becoming an offence, not only to decency, but the eye; a kind of knowledge that is more evident in Chapman's plain-spoken version:

> A faire yong man, at all parts it beseemes,
> (Being brauely slaine) to lie all gasht; and weare the worst
> extremes
> Of warres most crueltie; no wound, of whatsoeuer ruth,
> But is his ornament: but I, a man so farre from youth;
> White head, white bearded, wrinkl'd, pin'd; all shames must
> shew the eye:
> Liue; preuent this then; this most shame, of all mans miserie.[6]

Chapman's additions, "wrinkl'd", "pin'd", show us the visual as well as the moral outrage, and his use of "shame" conveys something like Homer's mixture of the humiliating and the shocking. From this version we might divine an even harder meaning in the Greek: that Homer meant that to die in one's old age was a qualitatively different thing from dying in one's prime, and that it borrowed a dignity from externals that it could not supply from itself. Just as the intransigent burden of old age on Nestor could only be mitigated by Achilles' tact, so Priam's death in old age, however it came, could only be ameliorated by reverential care and funeral rites; and stripped of these, it is indeed the "most shame, of all mans miserie", a death for which there is no formal response.

Pope's difficulty in exposing Priam's fears as honestly as Chapman did stemmed partly from his allegiance to the tradition of linguistic delicacy in referring to the body, and partly from the wider demands of neo-classical "Politeness", which owed much to Virgil. "Politeness" shrank from eliciting strong responses in a context that might not contain them, and at worst, it shrank from eliciting strong responses at all. La Valterie, Homer's translator in the age of Racine, expunged all the details of the original save the drinking of Priam's blood by his dogs, and expected the general grounds of horror he supplied to be quite adequate to a reader of sensibility. Amid a series of rhetorical questions, his Priam asks, "Pouvoient-ils [les destins] me donner une fin plus miserable, que d'estre exposé à mon âge à la fureur de mes ennemis?"[7] Pope knew this version, which reflected his own scruples, and that of Madame Dacier, its successor; which with much more loyalty to what Homer actually said, still obscured the physical details, and wrote the translator's sympathy into the text:

> Un jeune homme mort en combattant peut estre vû sans horreur estendu à terre tout nud percé de coups & tout défiguré par le sang & par la poussiere; mais un vieillard, à qui les années ont blanchi les cheveux, & qu'elles ont depuis longtemps essoigné des combats, de le voir gisant sur la terre tout découvert à la face du ciel, & le jouet des bestes, c'est le plus horrible & le plus pitoyable de tous les spectacles qui peuvent estre exposez aux yeux des miserables mortels.[8]

She describes the old man as a compassionate bystander might, not Priam,

> à qui les années ont blanchi les cheveux, & qu'elles ont depuis longtemps essoigné des combats,

and "horreur", "horrible", are her nearest approach to the awkward feelings of the original, but she adds a note underlining her conviction that Homer is saying something important, beside which La Valterie's revisions are trifling:

> Il n'y a rien de plus touchant que l'image qu'Homere fait icy en comparant les differents effets que produit la veuë d'un jeune homme & celle d'un vieillard, tous deux percez de coups & estendus sur la poussiere. Il est certain que le vieillard touche d'advantage, & il me semble qu'on en peut donner plusieurs raisons. La principale est qu'un jeune homme s'est defendu, & que sa mort est glorieuse: aulieu qu'un vieillard n'a eu pour défense que sa foiblesse, ses prieres, ses larmes. Il faut estre insensible à ce qu'ily a de plus affreux & n'avoir aucun goust de la poësie pour

avoir retranché cet endroit dans une traduction, & pour avoir substitué à la place des choses tres triviales & tres froides.[9]

But the censorship "Politeness" operates over what she sees, as well as what she says, prevents her from deducing that the horror of the old man's death stems not only from his defencelessness, but from the fact that it is *not* "glorieuse"; like Virgil, she locates the pathos where she is able to control her feelings, and stresses the protection due to weakness, and the outrage wrought on the sanctity of old age.

Pope borrowed this note for his commentary, and set the passage in a similar light:

> Perhaps ev'n I, reserv'd by angry Fate
> The last sad Relick of my ruin'd State,
> (Dire Pomp of sov'reign Wretchedness!) mut fall,
> And stain the Pavement of my regal Hall;
> Where famish'd Dogs, late Guardians of my Door,
> Shall lick their mangled Master's spatter'd Gore.
> Yet for my Sons I thank ye Gods! 'twas well:
> Well have they perish'd, for in Fight they fell.
> Who dies in Youth and Vigor, dies the best,
> Struck thro' with Wounds, all honest on the Breast.
> But when the Fates, in Fulness of their Rage,
> Spurn the hoar Head of unresisting Age,
> In Dust the rev'rend Lineaments deform,
> And pour to Dogs the Life-blood scarcely warm;
> This, this is Misery! the last, the worst,
> That Man can feel; Man, fated to be curst![10]

The "hoar Head of unresisting Age", "spurned" and "deformed in Dust", expresses Pope's sense of the old man's vulnerability, and the outrage that his fate represents to civilized feelings. But his picture has more variety than Madame Dacier's: he increases the pathos by underlining what Priam was—not an old man merely, but King of Asia:

> Perhaps ev'n I, reserv'd by angry Fate
> The last sad Relick of my ruin'd State,
> (Dire Pomp of sov'reign Wretchedness!) must fall . . .

To stress the reversal of his destiny is a Roman thought. In the same way, Virgil dwells on what Priam was:

haec finis Priami fatorum; hic exitus illum
sorte tulit, Troiam incensam et prolapsa videntem
Pergama, tot quondam populis terrisque superbum
regnatorum Asiae. iacet ingens litore truncus,
avolsumque umeris caput et sine nomine corpus.[11]

More Roman still is Pope's reinterpretation of Homer's general
remark on the death of a young warrior:

Yet for my Sons I thank ye Gods! 'twas well:
Well have they perish'd, for in Fight they fell.
Who dies in Youth and Vigor, dies the best,
Struck thro' with Wounds, all honest on the Breast.

Priam is being assimilated to the idea of Roman fatherhood; in
the same way, Addison's Cato hears of the heroic death of one of
his sons with the simple observation, "I'm satisfy'd".[12] If Priam
is to stimulate pathos here, it is by his nobility rather than his
common humanity—a choice that makes it additionally hard for
Pope to descend to the physical details which arouse pathos so
naturally in the Greek. "Rev'rend Lineaments" and "Life-blood
scarcely warm" are metaphors for the sanctity of old age rather
than description; like the French translators, Pope balks at the
simplicity of an appeal to the defencelessness of a grey head, grey
beard, and private parts. Priam is talking about the penalty of
living in the flesh, that one must also die in it, whether or not
one is King of Asia, but it is only Chapman who allows him to
have a body: "White head, white bearded, wrinkl'd, pin'd; all
shames must shew the eye." The price Pope pays for his reluctance
to be concrete is to claim more of the reader's horror than he has
earned in the final lines; like La Valterie's prose, they do not so
much shock, as gesture in the direction where shock might be felt:

This, this is Misery! the last, the worst,
That Man can feel; Man, fated to be curst!

This reluctance, combined with Pope's decision to efface the
harsher meaning of Achilles' speech to Nestor, might only seem
to prove that Pope's very sensitivity to the pathos of old age made
him a repressive translator. But that this wasn't always the case is
clear from his treatment of Priam in Book XXIV, in a passage that
offered him its challenge less directly. It comes after Iris has
advised Priam to ransom Hector's body, and he has made prepar-

ations to visit the Greek camp. In Priam's mood of grief, fear and impatience, the presence of a crowd of townspeople is more than his temper can bear:

Then he drove all the Trojans off his portico, and attacked them bitterly: "Get away, you good-for-nothing gossips: haven't you enough grief to keep you at home? Have you come to add to my trials? Is it nothing to you that Zeus, son of Cronos, has inflicted the loss of the best of my sons on me? But you will learn what it means yourselves: you will be far easier for the Achaians to kill, now he is dead. As for me, may I go down to Hades' halls before these eyes see the city plundered and laid waste," he said, and drove them away with his staff. They fled from the fierce old man. Then he shouted for his sons, and picked a quarrel with them: Helenus and Paris and noble Agathon, Pammon, Antiphonus and Polites, famous for the war-cry, Deiphobus, Hippothous and proud Dius; he shouted out and gave them orders. "Stir yourselves, you poor apology for offspring, sons I'm ashamed to own; why didn't you all give your lives for Hector, fighting by the ships? Oh Gods! how low I have been brought, who had the finest sons in all Troy—not one of whom (I say) is left, not godlike Mestor, nor Troilus the chariot-fighter, nor Hector, who was a god among men, and not like the son of a mortal at all. Ares has destroyed these, and only the dregs remain, liars and dancers, heroes of the dance-floor only, men who pilfer lambs and kids from their own people. Prepare me a cart quickly and put all these things in it—we have a journey to make," he said; and cowed by their father's rough tongue, they brought out a new, lightly-running mule-cart.[13]

This outburst on the part of a father (not to mention a king) offended those who, like Rapin, believed in a "Decorum" that made it impossible for a father to be "dur et cruel",[14] and it may still be one of the more disconcerting strokes of the *Iliad*, unless we remember other models of pathos who spring the same surprise: King Lear and his satisfied, "I killed the slave that was a-hanging thee", or Oedipus' vigorous execration of Polyneices. Old men evidently do not become more sweet-natured for their suffering, but less apologetic; what they have been reduced to they are content to be, with a nakedness disturbing to those whom tragedy has not touched. Unlike Madame Dacier, Pope felt no need to defend Priam's character against Rapin's well-known censure, and these two speeches are perhaps the most immediate presentation of it that he gives. Speech that supplies its own commentary (like Priam's line, "Dire Pomp of sov'reign Wretchedness!") has given way to speech that acts out its passion:

> Lo! the sad Father, frantick with his Pain,
> Around him furious drives his menial Train:
> In vain each Slave with duteous Care attends,
> Each Office hurts him, and each Face offends.
> What make ye here? Officious Crowds? (he cries)
> Hence! Nor obtrude your Anguish on my Eyes.
> Have ye no Griefs at Home, to fix ye there?
> Am I the only Object of Despair?
> Am I become my People's common Show,
> Set up by *Jove* your Spectacle of Woe?
> No, you must feel him too; your selves must fall;
> The same stern God to Ruin gives you all.
> Nor is great *Hector* lost by me alone;
> Your sole Defence, your Guardian Pow'r is gone!
> I see your Blood the Fields of *Phrygia* drown,
> I see the Ruin of your smoking Town!
> Oh send me, Gods! e'er that sad Day shall come,
> A willing Ghost to *Pluto*'s dreary Dome!
>   He said, and feebly drives his Friends away;
> The sorrowing Friends his frantick Rage obey.
> Next on his Sons his erring Fury falls,
> *Polites, Paris, Agathon*, he calls,
> His Threats *Deïphobus* and *Dius* hear,
> *Hippothous, Pammon, Helenus* the Seer,
> And gen'rous *Antiphon*: For yet these nine
> Surviv'd, sad Relicks of his num'rous Line.
>   Inglorious Sons of an unhappy Sire!
> Why did not all in *Hector*'s Cause expire?
> Wretch that I am! my bravest Offspring slain,
> You, the Disgrace of *Priam*'s House, remain!
> *Mestor* the brave, renown'd in Ranks of War,
> With *Troilus*, dreadful on his rushing Car,
> And last great *Hector*, more than Man divine,
> For sure he seem'd not of terrestrial Line!
> All those relentless *Mars* untimely slew,
> And left me these, a soft and servile Crew,
> Whose Days the Feast and wanton Dance employ,
> Gluttons and Flatt'rers, the Contempt of *Troy*!

> Why teach ye not my rapid Wheels to run,
> And speed my Journey to redeem my Son?
>   The Sons their Father's wretched Age revere,
> Forgive his Anger, and produce the Car.[15]

The speech is re-imagined by Pope from the first: the Trojans, whose purpose in coming is not specified in the Greek, he represents as anxious servants, whose conscientious efforts only serve to irritate Priam's grief:

> Around him furious drives his menial Train:
> In vain each Slave with duteous Care attends,
> Each Office hurts him, and each Face offends.

Their good intentions help throw Priam's wildness into relief, and his rough sarcasm is elaborated by Pope into a display of self-pity, in which his emphasis on rank is only an addition to the pathos:

> Have ye no Griefs at Home, to fix ye there?
> Am I the only Object of Despair?
> Am I become my People's common Show,
> Set up by *Jove* your Spectacle of Woe?

The Cassandra-like vision of the end of Troy Pope lends him is coloured by the general denunciation—Troy is "your" town:

> I see your Blood the Fields of *Phrygia* drown,
> I see the Ruins of your smoking Town!

and through Priam's reference to himself as a "willing Ghost" for "*Pluto*'s dreary Dome" we glimpse the aggression that lurks in his self-pity. To Pope the pathos of the scene is so evident that he cannot imagine the Trojans will not have felt it too. The men whom Priam drives away, frightened, with his staff, in his version are "sorrowing", and Priam's fierce gestures are clearly ineffectual:

> He said, and feebly drives his Friends away;
> The sorrowing Friends his frantick Rage obey.

Priam's denunciation of his sons is introduced by a reminder not in the original, by which Pope forces the reader (as he says in his note) to "consider his Circumstances",

> for yet these nine
> Surviv'd, sad Relicks of his num'rous Line,

128

and the terms of Priam's insults are as vigorous as "Decorum" will allow. Pope suppresses the accusation of stealing sheep and kids as too antique and demeaning, but "soft and servile", "wanton" and "the Contempt of *Troy*" are his own additions to Homer, as is the honourable response of the sons, who like the Trojans are merely frightened in the original:

> The Sons their Father's wretched Age revere,
> Forgive his Anger, and produce the Car.

This quantity of rewriting, and the confidence of the poetry itself, suggest how certain he was of what Homer was doing here, and the impression is confirmed by his note:

This Behaviour of *Priam* is very natural to a Person in his Circumstances: The Loss of his favourite Son makes so deep an Impression upon his Spirits, that he is incapable of Consolation; he is displeased with every body; he is angry he knows not why; the Disorder and Hurry of his Spirits make him break out into passionate Expressions, and those Expressions are contain'd in short Periods, very natural to Men in Anger, who give not themselves Leisure to express their Sentiments at full length: It is from the same Passion that *Priam*, in the second Speech, treats all his Sons with the utmost Indignity, calls them Gluttons, Dancers and Flatterers. *Eustathius* very justly remarks, that he had *Paris* particularly in his Eye; but his Anger makes him transfer that Character to the rest of his Children, not being calm enough to make a Distinction between the Innocent and the Guilty.

That passage where he runs out into the Praises of *Hector*, is particularly natural: His Concern and Fondness make him as extravagant in the Commendation of him, as in the Disparagement of his other Sons: They are less than Mortals, he more than Man. Rapin has censur'd this Anger of Priam as a Breach of the *Manners*, and says he might have shewn himself a Father, otherwise than by this Usage of his Children. But whoever considers his Circumstances will judge after another manner. *Priam*, after having been the most wealthy, most powerful and formidable Monarch of *Asia*, becomes all at once the most miserable of Men; He loses in less than eight Days the best of his Army, and a great Number of virtuous Sons; he loses the bravest of them all, his Glory and his Defence, the gallant *Hector*. This last Blow sinks him quite, and changes him so much, that he is no longer the same: He becomes impatient, frantick, unreasonable! The terrible Effect of ill Fortune! Whoever has the least

Insight into Nature, must admire so fine a Picture of the Force
of Adversity on an unhappy old Man.[16]

The terms of Pope's enthusiasm show that, if the picture of Priam
physically desecrated by dogs was too powerful to be handled, the
picture of Priam warped away from his true nature by grief
touched the same depth of feeling in him, and in a way that could
be handled in poetry. He is a king and father wholly reduced:
"This last Blow sinks him quite", and under sufferings repeated
more often than a man can bear, "he is no longer the same: He
becomes impatient, frantick, unreasonable!" The opposition so
strongly drawn throughout the *Iliad* between unappeasable force,
and soft living matter, affects Pope most painfully here:

> The terrible Effect of ill Fortune! Whoever has the least Insight
> into Nature, must admire so fine a Picture of the Force of
> Adversity on an unhappy old Man.

We might guess that this passage always brought with it a
victory for disordered over ordered feelings in Pope, and that his
wish to "Rock the Cradle of reposing Age"[17] for his own mother
grew from a susceptibility almost beyond control, from a piece of
conversation preserved by Spence toward the end of his life:

> I always was particularly struck with that passage in Homer
> where he makes Priam's grief for the loss of Hector break out
> into anger against his attendants and sons, and could never read
> it without weeping for the distress of that unfortunate old prince.
> He read it then, [adds Spence] and was interrupted by his tears.[18]

NOTES

1   *The Iliad of Homer,* trans. A. Pope (1715–20), XXIII, 711–18.
2   B.L. MS Add. 4808, fol. 166 (verso).
3   *Iliad,* XXIII, 751–52.
4   *Ilias,* XXII, 56–76 (author's rendering).
5   *Aeneis,* II, 550–53.
6   *The Iliads of Homer,* trans. G. Chapman (1611), p. 300.
7   *L'Iliade d'Homere,* trans. De La Valterie (1681), vol. II, p. 404.
8   *L'Iliade d'Homere,* trans. A. Dacier (1711), vol. III, p. 255.
9   *Ibid.,* pp. 546–47.
10 *Iliad,* XXII, 92–107.
11 *Aeneis,* II, 554–58. Dryden's translation may have contributed some-
    thing to Pope's:

Thus *Priam* fell: and shar'd one common Fate
With *Troy* in Ashes, and his ruin'd State:
He, who the Scepter of all *Asia* sway'd,
Whom Monarchs like domestic Slaves obey'd,
On the bleak Shoar now lies th'abandon'd King,
A headless Carcass, and a nameless thing.

(*Aeneis*, II, 758–63)

Cf. "The last sad Relick of my ruin'd State".

12 *Cato, a Tragedy* (1713), p. 52. The Roman atmosphere and the word "honest" may also be owed to the *versio* in Barnes's edition (1711).
13 *Ilias*, XXIV, 237–67 (author's rendering).
14 *La Comparaison d'Homere, et de Virgile* (1684), p. 32.
15 *Iliad*, XXIV, 291–332.
16 Note to XXIV, 291.
17 *An Epistle from Mr. Pope, to Dr. Arbuthnot* (1735), 1. 409.
18 *Anecdotes*, ed. J. M. Osborn, vol. I, p. 223, no. 529.

6

Rhetoric and *An Essay on Man*

by SIMON VAREY

Readers of Pope's *Essay on Man* do not normally consider the poem to be satirical.[1] Yet the poem takes its place, chronologically, among Pope's most considerable satires, and it is well known that he originally envisioned a larger work to which the *Essay* and the *Epistles to Several Persons* were intended to belong. Further, Pope was at work on the *Essay* and the *Epistle to Burlington* during 1730 and 1731.[2] These two poems appear to have belonged, at the time of their composition, to a single conception, and their author clearly expected them to be substantially related to one another.[3] However, Pope was particularly concerned to conceal his authorship of the *Essay* at the time of publication of at least the first three epistles. He was keen to discourage his readers, including his friend John Caryll, from assuming that any relation existed between the anonymous *Essay* and his satirical poems.[4] He succeeded, at first, in separating the author of *An Essay on Man* from the author of the *Dunciad*.

In outlining the relationship between the *Essay on Man* and Pope's social and satirical poems of the 1730s, my concern is not with the poet's projected *"Opus Magnum"*.[5] Unlike Pope's other poems after the *Dunciad*, *An Essay on Man* is "optimistic", "philosophical" and defensive. There are obvious and important ways in which the *Essay* differs from its neighbours, but a significant relationship exists between the *Essay* and Pope's Horatian poems, a relationship established by Pope's development of a rhetorical speaking voice. Who narrates the poem, and whom does he address? Mack answers Everyman to both questions, and he is surely right,[6] but Pope's many shifts of narrative tone may have been intended for narrower and more immediate purposes than Mack's rather generous identification requires.

The poet opens the *Essay* with an address to its dedicatee,

Bolingbroke. But not until the collected editions of 1734 did the title or the opening lines include Bolingbroke's name.[7] The first two editions of Epistle I, published in February and April 1733, addressed in the title "to a FRIEND", begin:

> Awake, my LÆLIUS! leave all meaner things
> To low ambition, and the pride of Kings.[8]

Mack illuminatingly quotes the Elwin-Courthope edition: Laelius was

> celebrated for his statesmanship, his philosophical pursuits, and his friendship, . . . described by Horace as delighting, on his retirement from public affairs, in the society of the poet Lucilius. Thus the name was fitted to the functions of Bolingbroke, and the relation in which he stood to Pope . . .[9]

It was a point which Pope's audience could be expected to appreciate, even if Laelius was not immediately recognizable as Bolingbroke. This anonymous poet, then, analogizes Lucilius, the "inventor" of satire.[10] Whatever else may be said of this relationship, Pope opens the poem, in its earliest printed form, thinking of himself as a satirist.[11] Further, he exhorts his addressee to join him in looking down "o'er all this scene of Man" (I, 5). It is the privilege of the philosopher, but no less that of the satirist, to consider himself as standing "above" the men about whom he offers his conclusions.[12] The poet here urges Bolingbroke to "leave all meaner things" to the less worthy "low ambition, and the pride of Kings". Bolingbroke is above all that, and so too is Pope. The concept of superiority, itself belonging to a concept of hierarchy, is of central importance not only to the poem's expression of Pope's idea of universal order but also to his conception of himself standing above other men.[13] The introductory lines of the poem establish the superiority of both the addressee and the poet. The reader of those lines is in the position of witnessing one side of a conversation: the poet allows the reader to overhear remarks which determine that superiority.

The *Essay on Man*, as every reader quickly recognizes, is filled with imperatives: the reader or listener or addressee is continually urged to "look", "see", "know", "mark" and "go". As soon as Bolingbroke fades into an obscure background after sixteen lines, to return only in the fourth epistle, the poet begins to change his addressee, also shifting his tone in a long sequence of subtle variations of astonishing range.[14] Apart from his numerous imperative verbs, Pope demands, persuades, insists, cajoles, exclaims, asserts, describes, all with the apparent purpose of demonstrating the limitations of human reason, that "to be wise" is "but to know how little can be known" (IV, 260–61), but the conclusion we reach from reading Pope's poem is perhaps less in agreement with this sense of inadequacy than with the idea that we have seen the wise poet charting for us "a *general Map* of MAN".[15] As Pope alters his tone, from the relatively conversational intimacy of

> Modes of Self-Love, the Passions we may call. (II, 93)
>
> We, wretched subjects tho' to lawful sway. (II, 149)
>
> Yes, Nature's road must ever be prefer'd. (II, 161)

to the slightly less informal, philosopher's opening gambit designed to buttonhole the listener, "Grant that the pow'rful still the weak controul" (III, 49), to the descriptive "history" of man (III, 169 *et seq.*) and of political societies (III, 199 *et seq.*), so he speaks to different members of an audience of humankind. Kallich and Brower both emphasize a dominant conversational note, but although Pope's tone is assuredly conversational, the poem is not a conversation.[16] Where his tone is intimate, he addresses an equal, almost in conversation, but not quite. The use of the first person plural suggests a dialogue in which the poet is implicated as much as the other "wretched subjects" of the human race, but we do not usually hear the other side of the dialogue. On the other hand, Pope is also able to speak to Man of Man, again using the first person plural:

> Remember, Man, "the Universal Cause
> "Acts not by partial, but by gen'ral laws;"
> And makes what Happiness we justly call
> Subsist not in the good of one, but all.
> There's not a blessing Individuals find,
> But some way leans and hearkens to the kind.
> (IV, 35–40)

This time the "we" slips by almost unnoticed. In the second epistle Pope moves easily into intimate tones, especially when he is concerned with explanation. For example:

> Modes of Self-Love the Passions we may call;
> 'Tis real good, or seeming, moves them all;
> But since not every good we can divide,
> And Reason bids us for our own provide;
> Passions, tho' selfish, if their means be fair,
> List under Reason, and deserve her care;
> Those, that imparted, court a nobler aim,
> Exalt their kind, and take some Virtue's name.
>
> (II, 93–100)

After this, Pope begins to criticize the inadequacy of Stoic philosophy. Scorn replaces intimacy:

> In lazy Apathy let Stoics boast
> Their Virtue fix'd: 'tis fix'd as in a frost,
> Contracted all, retiring to the breast;
> But strength of mind is Exercise, not Rest:
> The rising tempest puts in act the soul,
> Parts it may ravage, but preserves the whole.
>
> (II, 101–6)

Let the Stoics make their mistakes: Pope knows better. He then returns to his former tone:

> On life's vast ocean diversely we sail,
> Reason the card, but Passion is the gale;
> Nor God alone in the still calm we find,
> He mounts the storm, and walks upon the wind.
>
> (II, 107–10)

Situated between the two passages that imply a kind of intimacy is a rather indignant outburst. The addressee, here no doubt including the reader, is flattered enough by the form and the conversational rhythms of the two "outer" passages to accept the sentiment of the intervening six lines, and also to accept the ideas that follow in the straightforward argument of the next dozen lines, in which Pope becomes by turns dogmatic, questioning, imperative, and descriptive (II, 111–22). The imperative, assertive tone which dominates large portions of the poem leaves no room for argument:

> Respecting Man, whatever wrong we call,
> May, must be right, as relative to all.
>
> (I, 51–2)

135

The slight hesitation of "May" is quickly brushed aside by the certainly of "must".[17] No one is expected to argue with this, nor with the famous assertion at the opening of Epistle II, nor with the instructions meted out in the same epistle:

> The action of the stronger to suspend
> Reason still use, to Reason still attend: ...
> (II, 77–8)

Pope uses such flexibility of approach throughout the poem. Man is not merely addressed, but addressed with some scorn (I, 35; I, 258; II, 19, 29–30) and called a fool (III, 27; IV, 173): a fool, it seems, for not knowing what the poet knows. But Pope is frequently not as clear as this. For example, who is addressed in these lines?

> What would this Man? Now upward will he soar,
> And little less than Angel, would be more;
> (I, 173–74)

> How Instinct varies in the grov'ling swine,
> Compar'd, half-reas'ning elephant, with thine:
> (I, 221–22)

> Honour and shame from no Condition rise;
> Act well your part, there all the honour lies.
> (IV, 193–94)

It is hard to say. Everyman, perhaps, or some imaginary antagonist, an ignorant pupil, or any reader? In these and other places it seems rather as if Pope is talking to himself, asking himself speculative questions, almost thinking aloud while still acting the part of the instructor. The method is of a piece with the rhetorical function of his deliberative questions. Once the opening address to Bolingbroke is completed, the poet sets about his subject:

> Say first, of God above, or Man below,
> What can we reason, but from what we know?
> Of Man what see we, but his station here,
> From which to reason, or to which refer?
> . . . . .
> But of this frame the bearings, and the ties,
> The strong connections, nice dependencies,

Gradations just, has thy pervading soul
Look'd thro'? or can a part contain the whole?
(I, 17–20, 29–32)

The identity of the addressee is no longer Bolingbroke alone. In using the first person plural, Pope indicates the human race, but he also draws the reader into agreement with him: that agreement is virtually demanded in the second person address in the last two lines quoted. Only a fool, it is implied, would fail to recognize that such questions as these embody implicit statements of "truth". This is, of course, one of their obviously persuasive rhetorical functions. The whole of the first epistle, to a greater degree even than the remaining three, employs a traditional oratorical framework.[18] It is a requisite of classical rhetoric that the speaker should be seen to be a man of good moral character, and according to Aristotle the successful persuasion of an audience also depends on the attitude of the audience, and the speech itself.[19] Consequently the speaker should be capable of argument and he should understand enough of human emotion and character to appeal to his audience. Anonymity at least helped to discourage accusations that the author of the *Dunciad* did not have a good moral character to equip him for a poem on man and the universe. More significantly, the poet, without speaking of himself, implies his superiority throughout the *Essay*, so that even if his moral character is only negatively implied, his good sense is visible through his attitude to fools, or pride, and through his ability to argue reasonably to a conclusion that strikes his reader as largely indisputable. His professed understanding of Man is visible on almost every page: the poet is ready and able to speak of character, motive, action, emotion, reason. His opponents, where they appear, are seen by contrast to be foolish, misled, blind. The poet's audience needs to be flattered, and will be flattered by recognizing that only the foolish or ignorant will dispute the validity of Pope's propositions. Further, statements about the *Essay*'s philosophical ideas show the poet acting in a morally responsible and sensible manner, so that the very narration of the poem constitutes evidence of the poet's reliability. In these ways, the audience is persuaded to climb to Pope's "level" of vision.

The poet's character is in fact consistent where that of his audience is not, for he speaks to a wide range, from philosopher to fool, from proud to humble. In the *Epistle to Dr. Arbuthnot* Pope uses dialogue to put himself in a favourable light;[20] in the *Essay on Man* he uses a variety of forms, none more effectively than questions, for the same purpose.

In Epistle I Pope poses questions whose literal answers would be ridiculous:

> What if the foot, ordain'd the dust to tread,
> Or hand to toil, aspir'd to be the head?
> What if the head, the eye, or ear repin'd
> To serve mere engines to the ruling Mind?
>
> (I, 259–62)

and he pushes home his point, supplementing his rhetoric by asserting the foolishness of anyone who attempts to offer those answers:

> Just as absurd for any part to claim
> To be another, in this gen'ral frame:
> Just as absurd, to mourn the tasks or pains
> The great directing MIND of ALL ordains.
>
> (I, 263–66)

The function of the rhetoric is twofold. Upon recognizing the absurdity, the audience is on the poet's side, and the poet expects his comparison to be accepted. In effect he contrasts the obviously ridiculous with the equally but less obviously ridiculous, using the inverted images to illustrate the absurdity of questioning apparent inconsistencies of God's will. Not only, as here, does the speaker oblige his audience to agree with him, he also asks straightforward questions which enable him to supply the answers, as in the celebrated lines

> Why has not Man a microscopic eye?
> For this plain reason, Man is not a fly.
>
> (I, 193–94)

These lines show us primarily that we need not doubt that the poet actually possesses all the answers. The same is true even at Pope's moments of apparent reservation.[21] Even when the poet does not supply the answers to his questions, the reader is encouraged to recognize the familiar (and this we all do)[22] and supply his own answers, as here:

> Who finds not Providence all good and wise,
> Alike in what it gives, and what denies?
> (I, 205–6)

Where the poet permits an invisible speaker the rare luxury of an utterance, he does so only to afford himself an opportunity to correct, overturn, or otherwise improve the ideas of his companion. This is perhaps the poem's nearest approach to dialogue. For instance, in the passage concerning greatness (IV, 217–30), once the invisible speaker's remark has been shown to be inadequate Pope reveals the identities of the truly great, Aurelius and Socrates: the "truth" of this revelation must come from none of Pope's listeners, but from the poet himself.

This attitude contributes to Pope's most persuasive tones in the long accumulation of revelations which bring Epistle I to its close (267–94). The ignorant addressee, told what to do and told what is proper, is enlightened step by step as the privileged poet unfolds the truth about Nature. The closing lines of the passage are the climax of a momentous sequence of revelations that "All are but parts of one stupendous whole" (267):

> All Nature is but Art, unknown to thee;
> All Chance, Direction, which thou canst not see;
> All Discord, Harmony, not understood;
> All partial Evil, universal Good:
> And, spite of Pride, in erring Reason's spite,
> One truth is clear, "Whatever Is, Is RIGHT."
> (I, 289–94)

All is "unknown to thee", but it is known to the God who directs the universe, and it is known to the poet, whose faith enables him to articulate his vision. The simple rhetorical devices place the poet in the best possible light, for here as elsewhere in the poem he is the spokesman for truth: the poet is in a position to say that "One truth is clear" but his listener is not. Despite the poem's apparently tentative title, the tone is frequently assertive, as poetic eloquence affirms a series of philosophical propositions which, the reader often finds, have a ring of truth about them.[23] "We", the poet and the reader, also the poet and his various addressees, are to stand above the fools, let them cherish their illusions, let them fail to see the truth:

> Let subtle schoolmen teach these friends to fight,
> More studious to divide than to unite,
> And Grace and Virtue, Sense and Reason split,
> With all the rash dexterity of Wit:
> Wits, just like Fools, at war about a Name,
> Have full as oft no meaning, or the same.
>
> (II, 81–6)

And again:

> Fools! who from hence into the notion fall,
> That Vice or Virtue there is none at all.
>
> (II, 211–12)

Above "us" is Heaven, on whose behalf the poet acts as spokes-man (II, 237–38). The poet, then, can see others' weaknesses and their repercussions.

A familiar theme of Pope's satirical works, that men are getting above themselves and must be checked, appears in the *Essay* too:

> All quit their sphere, and rush into the skies.
> Pride still is aiming at the blest abodes,
> Men would be Angels, Angels would be Gods.
> Aspiring to be Gods, if Angels fell,
> Aspiring to be Angels, Men rebel;
> And who but wishes to invert the laws
> Of ORDER, sins against th'Eternal Cause.
>
> (I, 124–30)

The poet tries to ensure that a hierarchical order is maintained in which no one usurps his superior. The kind of hierarchy de-sired by Pope is like "Th' according music of a well-mix'd State", a system

> Where small and great, where weak and mighty, made
> To serve, not suffer, strengthen, not invade,
> More pow'rful each as needful to the rest,
> And, in proportion as it blesses, blest,
> Draw to one point, and to one centre bring
> Beast, Man, or Angel, Servant, Lord or King.
>
> (III, 296–302)

The small and great may co-exist in such a world, but for the sake of harmonious order they must not leave their appointed places. Looking over this human hierarchy is Pope himself.

The reception of Pope's anonymous poem embodied as nearly as possible an unprejudiced judgment, as he desired, and it furnished him not merely with the pleasure of scoring off a dunce (as in the case of Leonard Welsted) and winning the unbiased, if not exactly unqualified, praise of John Caryll,[24] but also with the satisfaction of having won a higher public reputation. The *Essay* proved to the public that Pope (when his anonymity was penetrated) was a considerable poet who could write without recourse to the personal satire of the *Dunciad*, that he was a "philosophic" poet with whose philosophy many readers could readily agree; and the *Essay*'s rhetoric contributes to this attempt to cast the poet in such a favourable light by underlining his intellectual superiority. Geoffrey Tillotson notes that Pope "trusted to the reasonableness of the moral scheme he propounded"[25] so, if the poet's subject was reasonable—and fashionable—it was likely to follow that the poet was reasonable too. If a philosopher-poet possessed the right, which no one challenged, to place himself above men, and he then turned out to be, so to speak, a satirist in disguise, he was in a particularly advantageous position to place himself above the men he satirized. I suggest that the narration of *An Essay on Man* employs a simple kind of traditional rhetoric in order to elevate Pope in the public esteem, in preparation for the acceptance of his later satires.[26] The *Essay on Man* seems to me a necessary link in this way between the satires that preceded and followed it. The view is supported by our knowledge that

> though the years immediately following the *Essay*'s appearance were one of the fertile periods of hostile Popiana, a time when attacks on the poet's person, manners, morals, and works sprang up like dragon's teeth, the *Essay on Man* was left significantly alone[27]

for Pope may have reasoned,[28] erroneously as it happened, that if the public approved his writing of Man, it could more easily accept his writing of men.

NOTES

1 Few, however, deny that the poem contains elements of satire. Cf. Martin Kallich, *Heav'n's First Law: Rhetoric and Order in Pope's Essay on Man* (De Kalb, Illinois, 1967), p. 23; Geoffrey Tillotson,

Pope and Human Nature (Oxford, 1958), p. 216; and Donald Fraser, "Pope and the Idea of Fame" in Writers and their Background: Alexander Pope, ed. Peter Dixon (London, 1972), p. 297. This volume is hereafter cited as Dixon.

2   Maynard Mack, ed., An Essay on Man (London, 1950; reprinted 1958) p. xiii. All quotations from the Essay are taken from this edition, cited as Mack. See also Marjorie Hope Nicolson and G. S. Rousseau, "This Long Disease, My Life": Alexander Pope and the Sciences (Princeton, 1968), pp. 40, 44–5. Three epistles of the Essay on Man had certainly been completed by August, 1731; To Burlington was published four months later. Cf. F. W. Bateson, ed., Epistles to Several Persons, 2nd ed. (London, 1961), p. xx.

3   Cf. Nicolson and Rousseau, p. 45.

4   Pope issued the Essay anonymously through none of his usual booksellers, who continued to publish other of his works bearing his name. For his letter to Caryll, see The Correspondence of Alexander Pope, ed. George Sherburn (Oxford, 1956), III, 247.

5   Pope to Swift, 6 January 1734, Correspondence, III, 401. For a discussion of Pope's project, see Miriam Leranbaum, Alexander Pope's 'Opus Magnum' 1729–1744 (Oxford, 1977).

6   Mack, p. lxxvii. See also Kallich, pp. 40, 43.

7   James Reeves suggests the possibility "that Bolingbroke's name added status to the Essay, particularly in Tory circles" in The Reputation and Writings of Alexander Pope (London, 1976) p. 215, but the absence of Bolingbroke's name in the early editions could imply that Pope's initial aim was not to achieve such "status" but to let his poem win praise—or status—on its own merit.

8   "LÆLIUS" later became "ST. JOHN", of course. See Mack, p. 11. St. John is addressed by name in IV, 18, but again only in the collected editions: the first edition of IV (January, 1734), once more addressed "Lelius". Leranbaum, pp. 44–5, observes that "Memmius" had preceded "Lælius" in an early MS version.

9   Mack, loc. cit. Although Bolingbroke was certainly out of office, he had not retired from public affairs in 1733, when he was still conducting a campaign of opposition to Walpole and still writing regularly against him in the Craftsman.

10 Horace, Satires, I, x, 48.

11 Cf. also lines 9–14 and Mack's note.

12 Cf. Patricia Meyer Spacks, An Argument of Images: The Poetry of Alexander Pope (Cambridge, Mass., 1971), p. 44.

13 See, e.g., I, 241–46.

14 Cf. Mack, p. lxxix.

15 "The Design" (which was not prefixed to the separate editions of each epistle), Mack, p. 8.

16 Kallich, pp. 41, 132; Reuben A. Brower, Alexander Pope: The Poetry of Allusion (Oxford, 1959), p. 214. See also Douglas H. White, Pope and the Context of Controversy: The Manipulation of Ideas in An Essay on Man (Chicago, 1970), p. 9, and Mack, p. lxxiii.

17 Cf. A. R. Humphreys, commenting on I. 43–4 and 51–2, "Pope, God, and Man" in Dixon, p. 79.

18 Cf. R. E. Hughes, "Pope's *Essay on Man*: The Rhetorical Structure of Epistle I", *MLN* 70 (1955), 177–81, reprinted in *Essential Articles for the Study of Alexander Pope*, ed. Maynard Mack, rev. ed. (Hamden, Conn., 1968), 370–74).

19 Aristotle, *The "Art" of Rhetoric*, trans. J. H. Freese (London and Cambridge, Mass., 1926, reprinted 1967), I, ii, 3–7.

20 For an account of the *Epistle to Dr. Arbuthnot* in rhetorical terms, see Elder Olson, "Rhetoric and the Appreciation of Pope", *MP* 37 (1939), 13–35.

21 See, e.g., II, 133–44.

22 Cf. A. R. Humphreys, in Dixon, p. 67.

23 See Mack, pp. xlii–xlv. This attribute has led to the charge that the poem is commonplace, unoriginal, and perhaps therefore dull. For debate on this theme, see F. S. Troy, "Pope's Images of Man", *Mass. Rev.* 1 (1960), 361–62; John Laird, "Pope's *Essay on Man*", *RES* 20 (1944), p. 295; A. R. Humphreys, in Dixon, p. 68; and John Sutherland, "Wit, Reason, Vision, and *An Essay on Man*", *MLQ* 30 (1969), p. 358.

24 See Mack, p. xv, and Pope to Caryll, 28 February 1734 (*Correspondence*, III. 403). See also Pope to William Duncombe, 20 October 1734 (*id.*, 438).

25 *Pope and Human Nature*, p. 42.

26 Cf. John Sutherland, *art. cit.*, p. 369, on the *Essay's* rhetoric.

27 Mack, p. xvii.

28 Cf. *Correspondence*, III, 352–56.

7

Heirs of Vitruvius:
Pope and the Idea of Architecture

by HOWARD ERSKINE-HILL

Dryden's praise of Congreve as "the best *Vitruvius*" and Pope's command that Burlington

> Jones and Palladio to themselves restore,
> And be whate'er Vitruvius was before:

warrant a consideration of the meaning of architecture in their age. In seeking to add one or two suggestions to Maynard Mack's admirable exposition of Pope's villa in *The Garden and the City*, and to Paul Fussell's survey of the architectural metaphor in Chapter VIII of *The Rhetorical World of Augustan Humanism*, I want to keep in mind the comprehensive ancient and Renaissance significance of architecture, the interaction between the metaphor of building and the activity of building, and the architectural analogue as formative of poetic structure.

When, in his *Four Books of Architecture* (1570), Palladio wrote that he had taken Vitruvius as his master,[1] he would have had in mind three fundamental points about the Roman writer and his teaching. First, that architecture was the original art and science in one, by the development of which the advance of man from savagery to civilization might be measured.[2] As Perrault was to put it in his abridgement, translated into English in 1692, ". . . it is pretended that Architecture was the Beginning and Original of all other Arts."[3] Secondly, Vitruvius laid great stress on how the architect needs skill in almost all arts and disciplines: letters, history, philosophy, music, mathematics, medicine, and so on.[4] Thirdly, and perhaps most important, the *De Architectura* had been dedicated to the *princeps* Augustus when, as master of the world, he had shown his concern with the public buildings of

Rome.[5] The original art had now become the supreme art, expressing for present and future the majesty of the empire and the grandeur of Roman history. Vitruvius did not insist that the architect should be skilled in polity, but his opening paragraphs show that for him architecture was expressive of a political order. As Perrault summarized his importance, "He had the Honour to serve *Julius Caesar* and *Augustus*, the two greatest and most magificent Princes of the World, in an Age when all things were come to the highest degree of Perfection."[6]

All this was in the mind of John Evelyn when, in 1664, he penned the two dedications of his translation of Roland Fréart's *Parallel of the Antient Architecture with the Modern*, the first to the king, the second to Sir John Denham, the Surveyor of the King's Works. Charles is first paid the Augustan compliment:

> Since the Great *Augustus* vouchsafed to patronize a Work of this nature which was Dedicated to him by *Vitruvius*; I had no reason to apprehend Your *Majesty* would reprove these Addresses of mine . . .[7]

Evelyn refers to the "*Royal* . . . *Builder*'s intention to repair St. Paul's", and then turns an allusion to the English civil wars in order to develop the deeply Vitruvian inspiration of his panegyric:

> If there were such glorious *Hero*'s of old, who first brought Men out of *Wildernesses* into Walled and well built *Cities*, that chased *Barbarity*, introduced *Civility*, gave *Laws* to *Republiques* . . . how much cause have We in these *Nations* to rejoice, that *Architecture* ows her renascency amongst Us to your *Majesties* encouragements . . .[8]

The concept of architecture as a symbol, not only of a "renascency" of the arts of peace, but specifically of a political order, is brought out in the second dedication: "It is from the *assymetrie* of our Buildings, . . . that the irregularitie of our *Humors* and affections may be shrewdly discern'd . . ." and Evelyn argues that the promotion of building is a mark "of a *prudent Government*, of a *flourishing* and *happy People*".[9]

These meanings of architecture are certainly involved in those two famous places, *Absalom and Achitophel* and *To Congreve*, where Dryden deploys the architectural metaphor. In the first, the passage beginning "If ancient Fabricks nod, and threat to fall" (l. 801), Dryden applies the metaphor to the institutions of the body politic. As Alan Roper has observed, in *Dryden's Poetic Kingdoms*, the allusion here is not just to any ancient building: it contains the "Ark" and is therefore Solomon's Temple with the Ark of the Covenant in its inmost sanctuary.[10] Dryden refers in cryptic fashion to those "Divine and Humane Laws" which, in his view, sanctioned monarchy. Comparison of the Restoration itself to Solomon's Temple had not been unknown twenty years earlier.[11] This reminds us, as it would I think have reminded Dryden's readers, of the great English temple, St. Paul's, whose dilapidations Evelyn had lamented, and Charles commenced to make good before the Great Fire. When, in Charles I's reign, Inigo Jones was commissioned to restore St. Paul's, his radical design still did not "touch the Ark". The fourteenth-century choir, with its Gothic mouldings and ornaments, was restored without modernization; the foundations remained the same and the frame was not cast anew. John Summerson comments that Jones had thought himself into the original fabric, "converting the fabric itself into a powerful new design".[12] This is the St. Paul's Dryden would think of in 1681, with Wren's cathedral still far from completion. Even after the Great Fire it was not until the ancient fabric had actually begun to fall that Wren was allowed to start building on a new foundation.[13]

In *To Congreve* (1693), Dryden's reference to the temples of the Jews is made explicit.

> Our Age was cultivated thus at length;
> But what we gain'd in skill we lost in strength.
> Our Builders were, with want of Genius, curst;
> The second Temple was not like the first:
> Till you, the best *Vitruvius*, come at length;
> Our Beauties equal; but excel our strength.
> Firm *Dorique* Pillars found your solid Base:
> The Fair *Corinthian* Crowns the higher Space;
> Thus all below is Strength, and all above is Grace.
>
> (ll. 11–19)

The allusion of the passage is to Solomon's temple and the post-exilic temple, and it may be right to recall that the two Old Testament texts that lie behind this line reflect unfavourably on the second temple only because it was incomplete.[14] It did not yet contain the Ark. St. Paul's, England's second temple, was in

1693 still unfinished.[15] In the metaphor of the architectural orders Dryden now proceeds to express the ideal balance of vigour and beauty. Vitruvius assigned temporal priority to the Doric Order, characterized as masculine and plain. Next came the Ionic, graceful and matronly, lastly the Corinthian, more slender and graceful still and rich in ornament: Vitruvius called it maidenly.[16] The three Greek orders thus exemplify that development from strength to beauty in art which in other terms the poem has already assumed. Dryden, however, speaks of the use of two orders in one building. Vitruvius, in fact, said nothing of such combinations; Dryden is here following the precept of Palladio, at once practical and aesthetic, that: "the most strong and solid may be always undermost, for then it will be the better able to sustain the whole Weight, and the Fabrick will stand on a firmer *Basis*; . . . the *Dorick* must always be set under the *Ionick*, the *Ionick* under the *Corinthian*." Palladio specifically allows the combination used by Dryden: ". . . if the Architect is desirous . . . to set the *Corinthian* immediately over the *Dorick*, this may be done . . ."[17]

At this point it may be relevant to note that the architectural orders probably did not constitute for Dryden a purely classical conception. The derivation of Greek architecture from the Hebrew of Solomon's temple had been widely accepted (for example by John Shute, in *The First and Chief Groundes of Architectvre*, 1563);[18] less than a century before Dryden's poem Joannes Baptista Villalpandus argued that Solomon's temple had employed the Corinthian order, an opinion duly noted in the pages of Fréart.[19] Dryden has continued the metaphor of temple-building in a precise sense. Moreover the political meaning latent in the architectural metaphor is brought out here in the orders. To the Vitruvian account of the Corinthian order, there was a strong counter-tradition. Though the Corinthian be a *"maidenly Order"*, writes Fréart,

> . . . it may also be proper on some profane occasions, as in *Triumphal Arches* and the like Structures. In a Word, since it gave *Ornament* to that famous *Temple* of *Jerusalem*, which never yet had equal, we may with reason call it the *flower* of *Architecture*, and the *Order of Orders*.[20]

He lays down that "It is not therefore to be employed but in great and publick Works, Houses of *Princes*, and such Palaces as are built for magnificence onely . . ."[21] The Corinthian was thus both the most beautiful order and the royal order, as Dryden's line recognizes—"The *Fair* Corinthian *Crowns* the higher Space."—and suggests the part of kingship in an harmonious polity, as in civilization at large.

In the *laudando praecipere* tradition, Dryden's purpose is to relate the art of Congreve through the architectural metaphor to the most comprehensive possible ideal of what mankind may achieve: what civilization brings to nature. A series of analogues opens up, as we consider the architectural lines in the context of the whole poem. If we wish to look for a building it will not be, as has been argued, Wren's St. Paul's (which employed the Corinthian order throughout)[22] but his Chelsea Hospital, which has the right combination of orders, was founded by Charles II and extended by James II, and which had been opened in 1692.[23] At the next stage, Congreve's art has, as it were, combined the orders, infusing an authentic vigour into the sophisticated literary form he found. He is thus lineal to Dryden's lost laureateship, if right is to prevail. But on the political level, where might has prevailed, the temple of the kingdom will be uncrowned as long as the true king is in exile. If we recall Vitruvius, however, we shall see that, beyond particular states, architecture expresses civilization itself—as Dryden would have us see it, a temple built to God.

A well-known allusion in *The Dunciad* (I.6 —1729) reminds us that the Epistle *To Congreve* was familiar to Pope. The architectural analogue to literature is of course to be found early in Pope's work. When, in *An Essay on Criticism* (1711) Pope wishes to affirm that the power of art arises not from correctness or beauty of parts but from ". . . the joint Force and full *Result* of *all*", he does so first through the image of the human face and secondly through the image of architecture:

> Thus when we view some well-proportioned Dome,
> (The *World*'s just Wonder, and ev'n *thine* O *Rome*!)
> No single parts unequally surprize;
> All comes *united* to th'admiring Eyes;
> No monstrous Height, or Breadth, or Length appear;
> The *Whole* at once is *Bold*, and *Regular*.
>
> (ll. 247–52)

Pope's very move from human to architectural pays homage to a tradition, descending from Vitruvius through Palladio and Sir

Henry Wotton, which taught that architectural form recalled human form, and if architecture added to nature, yet it also derived principles from nature. Aristotelian precept on the relation of parts to whole was echoed in architectural as in other treatises of the Renaissance, and Palladio had laid it down that:

> . . . Beauty will result from the Harmony and Correspondence between the Whole and its Parts, and the several Parts between themselves; for then the Edifice will appear one entire and perfect Body, in which one Member answers to another, and all of them together to the whole . . .[24]

I must here pass by the extremely interesting use of architectural form and musical harmony in *The Temple of Fame* (1715) to focus briefly upon the negative and positive use of the architectural metaphor in *Windsor Forest*. As in the opening prospect of the ruins of Rome in *To Addison* (1720), architectural ruin conveys the sense of relapsed civilization:

> The levell'd Towns with Weeds lie cover'd o'er,
> The hollow Winds thro naked Temples roar;
> Round broken Columns clasping Ivy twin'd;
> O'er Heaps of Ruin stalk'd the stately Hind;
> The Fox obscene to gaping Tombs retires,
> And savage Howlings fill the sacred Quires.
>
> (ll. 66–72)

Though Pope is using an analogy between hunters and tyrants, it is hard not to see scenes like this as the consequence of war. The architectural image bears a full weight of meaning. The shattered forms amount, perhaps, to one temple unroofed, with the Ark gone. The tombs are despoiled and given up to beasts. Reverence for the past and orientation for the future are both lost. And, if we cast our mind back to Dryden (and to Sir Henry Wotton who in his *Elements of Architecture*, 1624, likened the Doric Order to a rank in society),[25] the broken column is the most evocative image of all. But this picture is balanced and answered by another later in the poem, for now a retrospect upon barbarism is supplanted by a prospect of peace. Upon Anne's decree, Pope, like Amphion in *The Temple of Fame*, raises a new architecture with his art:

> Behold! Augusta's glitt'ring Spires increase,
> And Temples rise, the beauteous Works of Peace.

I see, I see where two fair Cities bend
Their ample Bow, a new *White-Hall* ascend!

(ll. 377–80)

The fifty new churches ordained by Anne's Tory government are here part of Pope's vision, while the culmination of the passage with a new Whitehall is precisely expressive, for the old Whitehall, begun by Jones for Charles I before the Civil War, continued by Wren for James II before the Revolution, was the royal work of the original Stuart monarchy, for Pope's purposes most appropriately burnt down in 1698 in the reign of William III. But all had not gone. As in the last years of Anne it seemed to some that the best of the Stuart monarchy lived on, so the work of the first great architect associated with the Stuarts, Inigo Jones's Banqueting House, had survived: a piece of architecture, a piece of civilization, in whose harmony of forms an idealized seventeenth century lived on and a new eighteenth-century age of building waited to be released.

The Earl of Burlington, at once a Maecenas and Vitruvius of that new age, is said, when he saw the completed St. Paul's of Wren, to have remarked that when the Jews saw the second temple they remembered the first temple and wept.[26] Certainly that series of famous houses taking its origin from Colen Campbell's Wanstead designs (disseminated in his *Vitruvius Britannicus* of 1715): Pope's villa, Stourhead (1721), Mereworth (1723), Marble Hill (1724), Burlington's own Chiswick (begun 1725), have more in common with Jones's Palladian than the Baroque. It cannot be too much stressed that Pope was not just an enthusiastic onlooker, but a real participant in this second phase of English Palladianism; and sometimes the language of architecture becomes the language of his imagination: he writes to Jervas thus of his past projects and present plans:

> The History of my Transplantation and Settlement which you desire, would require a Volume . . . Much more should I describe the many Draughts, Elevations, Profiles, Perspectives, &c. of every Palace and Garden propos'd, intended, and happily raised by the strength of that Faculty wherein all great Genius's excel, Imagination . . . For you my Structures rise; for you my Colonades extend their Wings; for you my Groves aspire, and roses bloom.[27]

About the same time he wrote to Robert Digby:

My Building rises high enough to attract the eye and curiosity of the Passenger from the River, where, upon beholding a Mixture of Beauty and Ruin, he enquires what House is falling, or what Church is rising? So little taste have our common Tritons of *Vitruvius*; whatever delight the true, unseen, poetical Gods of the River may take, in reflecting on their Streams my *Tuscan* porticos, or *Ionic* Pilasters.[28]

Much later, after Kent had designed him a new portico, and Burlington approved, Pope was to relish a compliment of John Caryll, who might then more truly style the villa "little Whitehall."[29] Two architectural points may be made. First, Pope in including the Tuscan order used something regarded as more rustic and simple even than the Doric, though Jones had shown its plain dignity in St. Paul's Covent Garden. Pope moved *down* the architectural scale: not Corinthian and Doric, but Ionic and Tuscan. Secondly, Pope knew he was at the head of fashion, for it was Campbell's achievement to have followed Palladio in incorporating the full portico, hitherto mainly used for temples and churches, into domestic design. Beyond this, we notice how for Pope architectural symmetry has movement and life—"for you my Colonades extend their wings"—and how "poetical Gods" may, he thinks, delight in architectural form. The play of fancy, I suggest, has a pattern of truth.

The creative interplay between architectural and poetic, lightly enough intimated here, shows itself, I suggest, when we consider what Pope made of the generally fluid and asymmetrical form of the epistle. I have written in my book on Pope's milieu of the architectural passage at the end of *To Burlington*, and of how the architectural subject seems there to take on the most comprehensive Vitruvian meaning—a meaning which, I suggest, it also had for Dryden. In the final pages of this paper I want to argue that Pope's cultural inheritance as an heir to Vitruvius finds its fulfilment in his temple-building in verse,[30] in particular in the structure of *To Bathurst*, and of the total group of four *Epistles to Several Persons* which in the "death-bed" edition he abstracted from a wider and more miscellaneous group of epistles and printed on its own.

To compare *To Burlington* with *To Bathurst* is to see that the later and longer poem is composed of symmetries in a way in which the former is not. Pope, who was actually redesigning the front of his villa at the same time as he worked on the epistle, stressed to Tonson the great importance of placing and contrast in this work.[31] There is no question of numerological exactitude, but we notice the corrupt metropolitan setting of the opening and closing sequences, by which the poem may be thought to move "Downwards to darkness, on extended wings". We notice the balancing pairs of contrasting portraits (Old Cotta, Young Cotta; Buckingham, Cutler) on either side of the centrally placed moral figures of Oxford, Bathurst and the Man of Ross. In nearly all Palladio's villas the well modulated symmetries turn upon an architecturally emphasized central point, frequently that of a pediment surmounting a portico. In his own house Pope marked the mid-point by setting a pediment over the central window of the chamber level of his front; Campbell at Mereworth and Burlington at Chiswick used both pediment and dome. In all these cases the centre is marked by forms which point upwards, sometimes actually by standing figures with one higher than the rest. (Walpole's Houghton, by Campbell, had the figure of Justice in this position!) In *To Bathurst* it is the Man of Ross and the "heav'n-directed spire" of Ross church that mark the centre: the mid-point which is, as Pope, no doubt remembering Aristotelian and Horatian ethics, told Spence, "the point for virtue".[32] In addition, it may be thought that Pope uses architecture in this poem to point further the moral and religious contrast between a life truly heaven-directed and its opposite, for the spire of Ross church seems placed in opposition to another monument, which overlooks the activities of the pitiable and doomed Sir Balaam:

> ... London's column, pointing at the skies
> Like a tall bully, lifts the head, and lyes.
>
> (ll. 39–40)

The structure of the poem, thus articulated, invites us to compare true with false elevation.

To Burlington and *To Bathurst* were soon followed by *To Cobham* and *To a Lady*. I have no wish to press the architectural analogue to an extreme, but merely to suggest that it helps us see something of a larger structure in these otherwise flexible and miscellaneous couplet epistles. *To Cobham* opens with brilliantly expressed bewilderment at the enigmas of human nature, reveals (what is offered to us as) the key to the problem, the Ruling

Passion, soon after the centre of the poem, and can proceed from that to the confident summary "characters" at the end. The central area of the poem is crucial in the evolution from bewilderment to certainty. In *To a Lady*, as found in its final version, it is the strong portrait of the imperious Atossa that dominates the centre, the point for triumph as for virtue in many Renaissance poetic structures.[33] This is an ironical placing; she is masterful indeed, but not of the means to happiness. Atossa contrasts in various ways with other portraits of the epistle, but most with Martha Blount as Pope depicts her at the end. Likened not to the "glaring Orb" of the sun, but the "mild" and "sober" light of the moon, Martha has learnt how to submit to life without loss of the poise of her personality, the freshness and variety of her qualities—

> Reserve with Frankness, Art with Truth ally'd,
> Courage with Softness, Modesty with Pride
> (ll. 277–78)

—and the comparison with Atossa, another juxaposition of centre with end, as in *To Bathurst*, is pointed as Pope writes that Phoebus "Kept Dross for Duchesses" but to Martha gave "Sense, Good-humour, and a Poet".

These two later epistles are, apart from their individual form, of interest as parts of the patterned group of four *Epistles to Several Persons* which Pope seems to have wished to form towards the end of his life.[34] Pope is evidently speaking of this as early as February 1733, in a letter to Swift:

> I have declined opening to you by letters the whole scheme of my present Work, expecting still to do it in a better manner in person: but you will see pretty soon, that the letter to Lord Bathurst is a part of it, and a plain connexion between them, if you read them in the order just contrary to that they were publish'd in. I imitate those cunning tradesmen, who show their best silks last: or, . . . my works will in one respect be like the works of Nature, much more to be liked and understood when consider'd in the relation they bear with each other, than when ignorantly look'd upon one by one . . .[35]

This cannot apply to *An Essay on Man*, but *Burlington, Bathurst* and *Cobham* were always after printed in the inverse order to that of their publication. Once *To a Lady* appeared, it was always placed between *Cobham* and *Bathurst*, the "plain connexion" requiring that the epistle on the characters of men and women should constitute the first part of the sequence. It is in the placing of *Burlington* after *Bathurst*, involving the rejection by Pope of a process of increasing embitterment, that the poet keeps his best silks to the last. It is not that he necessarily thought *Burlington* the better poem, but that he sought to end his sequence with a resolution and glow of idealism rather than the darkness of Balaam's death. May not Pope have wished to conclude the sequence on this note of hope, this vision of human creativeness and the imperial work of civilization? If we look on the four epistles "ignorantly . . . one by one" they may seem to convey rather suddenly changing moods on Pope's part. If we see them "in the relation they bear with each other" (and we recall the human and architectural metaphor in *An Essay on Criticism*) we may see a whole poem whose four parts are indeed strongly articulated, but which together take us through the darkness of men's hearts and deeds to bring us out into the redemptive light of "Another age . . .". *Cobham* is a relatively buoyant introductory approach; in the imagery of *To a Lady* darkness increasingly comes on as we near the end, relieved only by the mild moonlight of that lady's character, just as the creative life of the Man of Ross interrupts and challenges the pervasive corruption of *To Bathurst*. In *To Burlington* the corruption of human nature seems once again less menacing; we have come through the worst and can hope once more. Yet even in the midst of the greatest moral darkness the Christian example of the Man of Ross could survive. I have suggested that the "heav'n-directed spire" of Ross is deliberately recalled by London's column at the end of *To Bathurst*. It is possible that both recall the futile imperiousness of Atossa, in the central area of *To a Lady*, whose "Temple[s] rise—then fall again to dust", and that these balancing opposites anticipate and are recalled by the false eminence of Timon's Villa to which we come at the centre of *To Burlington*, and that all these anticipate and are recalled by the hope for "Temples, worthier of the God" in the concluding Augustan idealism of the concluding poem of the group. Pope's letter to Swift suggests that in writing these epistles the poet had some idea of what would be their final order. We may suppose that once they were published Pope, always drawn to building, architectural relationship and rhythm, conceived not exactly a poetic structure in which (as it were) "Grove nods at

154

grove, each Alley has a brother", but certainly one in which, as in good landscaping and good building, "Parts answ'ring parts" might "slide into a whole".

NOTES

This essay was given as a paper at the American Society for Eighteenth Century Studies at the University of Victoria, B.C., Canada, in May 1977.

1 Andrea Palladio's *Five Orders of Architecture Translated and Revised by Colen Campbell* (London, 1729), Preface, np.; *I Quatro libri Dell' Architettvra Di Andrea Palladio* (Venice, 1570), Preface, np.

2 Vitruvii Pollionis *De Architectvra*, Bk. II, Ch. I (Venice, 1576), p. 50.

3 *An Abridgement of the Architecture of Vitruvius . . . First done in French by Monsr Perrault . . . now Englished, with Additions* (London, 1692), p. 18.

4 *De Architectvra*, Bk. I, Ch. I; ed. cit, pp. 3, 6.

5 *Ibid.*, Bk. I, Ch. I, pp. 2–3.

6 Perrault, *op. cit.*, p. 2.

7 Roland Fréart, *A Parallel of the Antient Architecture with the Modern . . .* [Translated] By John Evelyn (London, 1664), np. I am indebted to Mr. R. G. Knowles for this reference.

8 *Ibid.*, np.

9 *Ibid.*, np.

10 Alan Roper, *Dryden's Poetic Kingdoms* (London, 1965), pp. 17–18.

11 As Mr. R. G. Knowles has pointed out to me, Thomas Fuller had written of the peaceful restoration:

> So *Solomon* most wisely did contrive,
> His *Temple* should be STIL-BORN though ALIVE.
> That stately Structure started from the *ground*
> Unto the Roof, not guilty of the sound
> Of *Iron Tool*, all noise therein debarr'd . . .

(*A Panegyric to His Majesty On His Happy Return* [London, 1660], p. 4).

12 John Summerson, *Inigo Jones* (Harmondsworth, 1966), p. 99, and pp. 97–106 generally.

13 John Summerson, *Architecture in Britain, 1530–1830* (Harmondsworth, 1953; 4th. edn. revised and enlarged, 1963), p. 129.

14 *Ezra*, III, 11–13; *Haggai*, III, 2, 9.

15 In 1698, five years after Dryden's poem was finished, the dome, west front and west towers were still to add; Summerson, *Architecture in Britain*, ed. cit., p. 134.

16 *De Architectvra*, Bk. IV, Ch. I; ed. cit., pp. 122–24.

17 Andrea Palladio's *Five Orders of Architecture*, ed. cit., p. 21; *I Quatro Libri*, Bk. I, Ch. XII.

155

18 John Shute, *op. cit.*, f. 2.

19 Joannes Baptista Villalpandus, *In Ezechielem Explanationes et Apparatus Vrbis, ac Templi Hierosolymitani* (Rome, 1596–1604); see Vol. II, Part II, pp. 200, 455, 550–51 for his discussion of this and related matters. Fréart, *ed. cit.*, pp. 72–3.

20 Fréart, *op. cit.*, pp. 72–3.

21 *Ibid.*, p. 70.

22 A. W. Hoffman, "Various John Dryden: 'All, all of a piece throughout' " in *Dryden: A Collection of Critical Essays*, ed. B. N. Schilling (Englewood Cliffs, 1963), p. 168.

23 Summerson, *Architecture in Britain*, ed. cit., pp. 138–39; Plate 97.

24 Andrea Palladio's *Five Orders of Architecture*, ed. cit., p. 2; *I Quatro Libri*, ed. cit., pp. 6–7.

25 Sir Henry Wotton, *Elements of Architecture* (London, 1624), pp. 35–6. Joseph Spence, *Observations, Anecdotes and Characters of Books and Men*, ed. J. M. Osborn (Oxford, 1966), Item 617, shows that Pope knew this treatise.

26 James Lees-Milne, *Earls of Creation: Five Great Patrons of Eighteenth-Century Art* (London, 1962), p. 139.

27 *The Correspondence of Alexander Pope*, ed. George Sherburn (Oxford, 1956), Vol. II, pp. 23–4 (Pope to Jervas, 12 Dec. 1720).

28 *Ibid.*, Vol. II, p. 44 (Pope to Robert Digby, 1 May 1720).

29 *Ibid.*, Vol. III, p. 406 (Pope to Caryll, 10 April 1734).

30 For a similar approach to such literature, see F. W. Hilles, "Art and Artifice in *Tom Jones*", in Ian Gregor and Maynard Mack, eds., *Imagined Worlds: Essays Presented to John Butt* (London, 1968), pp. 93–8; Bernhardt Fehr, "The Antagonism of Forms in the Eighteenth Century", II; *English Studies*, Vol. XVIII (1936), pp. 193–94, and see the attempted but to my mind unconvincing refutation by G. Giovannini "Method in the Study of Literature in its Relation to the Other Fine Arts", *Journal of Aesthetics and Art Criticism*, Vol. VIII (1950), p. 194.

31 *Corr.*, Vol. III, p. 290 (Pope to Tonson, Sr. 7 June 1732).

32 Spence, *ed. cit.*, Item 297; cf. Aristotle, *Nicomachean Ethics*, Bk. III, Ch. XI; Horace, Odes, *Bk. II*, x, 1–8.

33 Alastair Fowler, *Triumphal Forms: Structural Patterns in Elizabethan Poetry* (Cambridge, 1970), Chs. II and IV, especially pp. 85–7. Caution is required in considering *To A Lady* since, as Frank Brady shows in "The History and Structure of Pope's *To A Lady*", *Studies in English Literature, 1500–1900*, Vol. IX (1969), pp. 439–62, it may not have come down to us in the exact form Pope planned. However the dominant position of the Atossa portrait in the central area of the Epistle is not much in question.

34 *The Twickenham Edition of the Poems of Alexander Pope*, Vol. III-ii, ed. F. W. Bateson (London, 1951, rev. edn. 1961), p. xxi; Howard Erskine-Hill, review of Pope, *Poetical Works*, ed. Herbert Davis, in *Review of English Studies*, N.S. Vol. XIX (1968), pp. 205–8.

35 *Corr.*, Vol. III, p. 348 (Pope to Swift, 17 Feb. 1732/33).

8

The Satirist in His Own Person

by I. D. MacKILLOP

1

> After the 32nd chapter of *Treasure Island*, two of the puppets strolled out to have a pipe before business should begin again, and met in an open place not far from the story.

In the "Advertisement" to *Imitations of Horace* Pope reminds his contemporaries that to treat vice and folly with indignation and contempt does not make a man a libeller. Horace and Donne did it, both "Authors acceptable to the Princes and Ministers under whom they lived". A reconstruction of their satires should teach a lesson to those who were shocked by the Moral Essays. An answer from Horace, especially, says Pope, would be more full and more dignified than "any I cou'd have made in my own person".

The reader of a modern edition has merely to flick his eye down the page to see that this disclaimer is disingenuous: the first lines of the Satire to Fortescue (Horace, II, i) are Pope speaking in his own person as never before. And quite right too, if his lesson is to be truly taught. To prove that respectable poets never shrank from speaking out Pope has to remind his readers of what their "Freedom" was like, and show that he possesses it as well. Frank self-exposure proved his mentors to be not libellers, or hypocrites, but men "*truly* Virtuous". Pope, to hold his position, must likewise make a strategic foray and show what kind of a man he is, to establish his probity. So he replies to the "Clamour" raised by the Moral Essays with a self-portrait, or a portrait of a pseudo-self, or a portrait of Horace.

In this essay I shall not explore Pope's strategies of self-presentation. Instead, I wish briefly to describe the rehearsal of similar strategies in the literary world of mid-seventeenth-century Paris, showing how Boileau and Molière met like clamours by appearing in their own persons. I shall not suggest straightforward influence

157

on Pope: he did not need, anyway, to learn how to present himself in verse from a European fracas because he had English and classical models to hand. The interest of the French episode, to be found in four works generated by "polite" criticism (from powerful quarters) of *L'école des femmes*, lies in seeing how a creative problem close to Pope's was handled elsewhere, especially when handled in quite major works which do not seem, nevertheless, all that well-known to readers of Pope. Two plays by Molière and two satires by Boileau supply a helpful analogue, which may even give a basis for some fresh evaluation. But the evaluation will not be attempted here: I shall simply lay out the story of how Boileau and Molière defended themselves in a game of masks (of themselves) in the mid-seventeenth century.

2

In December 1662 Molière's *L'école des femmes* was produced, and, despite its popular success was soon attacked, principally on grounds of supposed indecency. In the following June Molière replied with *La critique de l'Ecole des femmes*, which in turn was attacked by one of the original assailants, and by Edme Boursault in a play called *Le portrait du peintre ou la contre-critique de l'Ecole des femmes*. Molière followed this up with the performance, still in 1663, of *L'impromptu de Versailles*.

In Scene v of *La critique de l'Ecole des femmes* there is an exchange between the Marquis and Dorante, representing Molière's polite critics and his defenders respectively. In Scene v Dorante makes fun of those who claim to have been shocked by *L'école des femmes* and the Marquis reproves him, much as Addison reproved Pope for the satirical touches in the *Essay on Criticism*: "Enfin, Chevalier, tu crois défendre ta comédie en faisant la satire de ceux qui la condamnent." ("*In short, Chevalier, you think to defend your Play, by satyrizing those that condemn it?*") He is right, but Dorante's satire on the unappreciative is more than exasperated indulgence, reducing the debate *ad hominem*. The legitimacy of his satire comes out if Dorante's (and Molière's) literary critical problem is considered.

Dorante's predicament was awkward. *L'école des femmes* was a popular hit, especially satisfactory to Dorante who believed that the greatest rule of art was to please, declaring in Scene vi, "Je voudrois bien savoir si la grande règle de toutes les règles n'est pas de plaire, et si une pièce de théâtre qui a attrapé son but n'a pas suivi un bon chemin." (*"I'd fain know if the grand Rule be not to please, and whether a Play is not right if it has gain'd that End."*)

It was open to Dorante to make a simple assertion. The age of Boileau saw the discovery of an exhilarating critical option, to make an impudent refusal of the authority of rules. When it was believed that the potency of verse depended on *un je ne sais quoi* such an assertion of independence could be clothed in a certain mystique. But this did not satisfy Boileau (though he was a *je ne sais quoi* man) or Molière who, under fire, was in no position to be critically impudent.

The other way open to Molière-Dorante to justify his taste and that of the public at large against the strictures of refined criticism was to *substantiate* his taste, showing more fully what it was like to be the person who was pleased and that his preferences were other than isolated quirks. The besieged critic needs to make it felt that it is not "just" he who is doing the judging, that the judgment is part of a system of preferences, that this system may be shared by a party worth joining, and that it is directly related to recognized needs of human nature. The critic needs to give his taste voice.

Dorante's satire in *La critique* accomplished some of this negatively: he shows what his taste is not like. He argues that the intelligentsia is so blinkered that it hardly sees the play before its eyes:

> . . . il y en a beaucoup que le trop d'esprit gâte, qui voient mal les choses à force de lumière, et même qui seroient bien fâchés d'être de l'avis des autres, pour avoir la gloire de décider. (Scene v)

> (. . . *there are a great many who are spoilt by too much Wit; who have but an ill Perception of things, because they have too much Light, and who, to have the Glory of deciding, hate to be of another's Opinion.*)

Such critics fail morally because they do not take sincere offence, but condemn to fulfil a series of private stratagems. The Marquise snuffs out indecency to show her refinement. The Marquis has a stake in not thinking about what kinds of things lovers really say:

> *Dorante:* . . . Et quant au transport amoureux du cinquième acte, qu'on accuse d'être trop outré et trop comique, je voudrois bien savoir si ce n'est pas faire la satire des amants, et si les honnêtes gens même et les plus sérieux, en de pareilles occasions, ne font pas de choses—
> *Le Marquis:* Ma foi, Chevalier, tu ferois mieux de te taire.
> *Dorante:* Fort bien. Mais enfin si nous nous regardions nous-mêmes, quand nous sommes bien amoureux—?
> *Le Marquis:* Je ne veux pas seulement t'écouter.
> *Dorante:* Ecoute-moi, si tu veux. Est-ce que dans la violence de la passion—?
> *Le Marquis:* (*il chante*): La, la, la, la, lare, la, la, la, la, la, la, (Scene vi)
> (*Dorante:* . . . *And as for the Amorous Transport of the Fifth Act, which is accused of being too Extravagant and Comical; I'd fain know if that is not Satyrizing Lovers, and if even Men of Sense and the most Serious, wou'd not on such an Occasion do things*—
> Marquis: *Faith Chevalier, you'd better hold your Peace.*
> Dorante: *Very well. But if we consider our selves, when we are deeply in Love*—
> Marquis: *I won't so much as hear you.*
> Dorante: *Hear me I say. In the Violence of a Passion*—
> Marquis: (Sings): *La, la, la, la, lare, la, la, la, la, la, la.*)

The Marquis, who found the "ordures" of *L'école des femmes* "épouvantables", and the Marquise are interested parties, their judgment propelled by what Pope later called the "Casting-weight" of pride. By demonstrating the openness of real taste Dorante becomes perforce a moralist, though an unheeded one.

It cannot be stated as a matter of fact that the satire of *La critique* is other than invective. Whether it is depends on whether the reader feels that Dorante-Molière is describing failings general to human nature. It seems to me that in the episode just quoted Molière is decisively, and sunnily, succeeding to do so. in the next stage of the fracas Molière abandons the mask of Dorante and in *L'impromptu de Versailles* presents himself in his own person, giving direct, so it seems, expression to his taste and sensibility.

In *L'impromptu de Versailles* we see Molière rehearsing his own actors in the nerve-racking circumstances of a command performance at Versailles. Much could be said about this moving and lextrous play; I wish simply to make one remark about Molière's dramatization of himself. As was mentioned above an attempt was made to cap *La critique* by a "contre-critique", *Le portrait du peintre* by Edme Boursault. There is evidence that Boursault did not have much enthusiasm for attacking Molière, but was angled into it by his patron Corneille. Probably he only tacked together and subscribed the gibes of a cabal; certainly he found himself underwriting a libellous song from the hand of another which was included in the performance but not in the published version of the play. In *L'impromptu* Molière has no doubts about Boursault's part in the effort. One of his actors, Du Croisy, playing the part of a poet (roughly the equivalent of Lysidas in *La critique*) says about him:

> . . . Comme tous les auteurs et tous les comédiens regardent Molière comme leur plus grand ennemi, nous nous sommes tous unis pour le desservir. Chacun de nous a donné un coup de pinceau à son portrait; mais nous nous sommes bien gardés d'y mettre nos noms: il lui auroit été trop glorieux de succomber, aux yeux du monde, sous les efforts de tout le Parnasse; et pour rendre sa défaite plus ignominieuse, nous avons voulu choisir tout exprès un auteur sans réputation. (Scene v)
>
> ("*As all the Authors, and all the Comedians regard* Molière *as their greatest Enemy; we are all united to run him down; every one of us has given a stroke to his Picture, but we took care not to put our Names to it, it wou'd ha' been too glorious for him to have sunk, in the Eyes of the World, under the Efforts of all* Parnassus; *and to make his Defeat the more ignominious, we resolved to chuse an Author without Reputation, on purpose.*")

Boursault is diagnosed as a marionette satirist; the harassed Molière on the stage appears by contrast an even more nobly independent and autonomous figure. By so presenting himself Molière makes a critical point about the enemy position whose central weakness is its *herd* instinct (a central theme, of course, in Pope's Horatian imitations, especially in the "Epistle" to Arbuthnot and "The Second Epistle of the Second Book"). The move to dramatize himself is a brilliant one for another reason. There is a sense in which the stage Molière of *L'impromptu* is even more of a mask than Dorante in *La critique*, but a mask also of even more effectiveness. Dorante is the spokesman for *L'école des femmes* and so in the circumstances can be interpreted (and if necessary dis-

credited) as the spokesman for a Molière lurking behind the
scenes. But in *L'impromptu* Molière is there—or is he?—before
the very eyes of the audience. The stage Molière is such a winning
figure that the audience has hardly a chance to remember that
there is a "real" Molière who wrote his part. By committing his
personality to the stage Molière becomes an impersonal figure.

3

Molière acted himself in a play; Boileau did so in Horatian
satire for which it is a pity he is not better known. Boileau seems
to be lodged as the respectable figure of *L'art poétique* (1674) and
after, rather than the satirist of the sixties whom Chapelain called
"un Calmoniateur audacieux". Two of Boileau's satires are especially relevant to the theme of the satirist speaking in his own
voice, and relevant to Molière's self-defence of his plays; they are
Satires VII and II. Both were written at some time between June
1663 and the end of the year. Satire VII is an explosive defence of
the genre:

> Muse, changeons de stile, et quittons la Satire:
> C'est un méchant métier qui celui de médire:
> A l'Auteur qui l'embrasse, il est toûjours fatal. (1–3)

> (*No more, my Muse, tho' Satire may prevail,*
> *Let's change our Style for once and cease to rail:*
> *'Tis an ill Trade, and we have often found,*
> *Instead of giving, we receive the Wound . . .*)

The poem expresses the frustration of a man who realizes that
there is no future in his vocation, or no future in his own kind of
candour about the difference between fake and genuine art. Boileau
at this date could hardly have been defending his own satirical
oeuvre as it hardly existed. More likely the poem is a statement
of intent and a defence of Molière the satirist, the author of what
is to our eyes the relatively gentle performance of *La critique*,
for Boileau takes as his targets just those writers who responded
viciously to Molière's riposte. So in this early work Boileau is taking Molière's part, writing a bold manifesto for a violent profes-
sion:

> Un discours trop sincere aisément nous outrage.
> Chacun dans ce miroir pense voir son visage,

Et Tel en vous lisant admire chaque trait,
Qui dans le fond de l'âme, et vous craint et vous hait.
(17–20)

(*A Poem soon offends, if too severe,*
For each will think he sees his Image there;
And he who reads it may applaud your Art,
Yet fear its Force, and hate you from his Heart.)

Satire II is a subtler poem in which Boileau uses the trick of presenting himself in his own person to define literary qualities that he admires. According to tradition La Fontaine, Molière and Boileau's friends had decided that it was impossible to find a rhyme for "Malherbe" Boileau's satire begins on just this subject, the difficulty of finding rhymes:

Enseigne-moi, Molière, òu tu trouves la rime. (6)

(*Teach me to Rhyme; to me your Art disclose,*
And how it from your Pen so freely flows.)

Molière sails over difficulties, but poor Boileau strains hopelessly (or so he pretends):

Mais moi qu'un vain caprice, une bizarre humeur,
Pour mes pechez, je croi, fit devenir Rimeur:
Dans ce rude métier, où mon esprit se tuë
En vain pour la trouver, je travaille, et je suë.
Souvent j'ai beau rêver du matin jusqu'au soir:
Quand je veux dire *blanc*, la quinteuse dit *noir*.
Si je veux d'un Galant dépeindre la figure,
Ma plume pour rimer trouve l'Abbé de Pure:
Si je pense exprimer un Auteur sans defaut,
La raison dit Virgile, et la rime Quinaut.
Enfin quoi que je fasse, ou que je veüille faire,
La bizarre toûjours vient m'offrir le contraire.
De rage quelquefois ne pouvant la trouver,
Triste, las, et confus, je cesse d'y rêver . . .
(11–24)

(*While I, who only by Caprice and Whim,*
I doubt, am for my Sins condemn'd to Rhyme
My Fancy rack on such rude Tasks as these,
And Sweat in vain, for what you find with ease.

When the Fit takes me thus, from Morn to Night
I labour hard, but oft put Black *for* White.
Am I to paint an humble, Priest *or* show
A just Example *of a well drest* Beau,
Purely for sake of Prosody *and* Tag,
I put Sacheverell *and* Captain Rag.
Quote I an Author of the first Degree?
Reason's for DRYDEN, *but the Rhyme for* LEE.
Thus spite of my Endeavors, or my Will,
The Humorous Gypsie is against me still.
I rage that Rhymes shou'd puzzle me, and grieve,
And balk'd, at last the tiresome study Leave,
I curse the Sprite, with which I am possesst,
And swear to drive the Daemon *from my Breast.)*

But come the fit, he will write again, with "verve indiscrete".
Clichés flood in:

Avec tous ces beaux mots souvent mis au hazard,
Je pourois aisément, sans génie, et sans art,
En transposant cent fois et le nom et le verbe,
Dans mes vers recousus mettre en pieces Malherbe.

(43–6)

The paragraph concludes:

Ainsi, recommençant un ouvrage vingt fois,
Si j'écris quatre mots, j'en effacerai trois.

(51–2)

(With all these shining Words, by Chance compos'd,
The Noun and Verb a hundred times transpos'd,
All WALLER *I might make my own with Ease,*
And without Genius steal him Piece by Piece:
But in my Choice of Words I can't dispence
With one improper, or which clogs the Sense.
I can't allow that an insipid Phrase
Shou'd justle in to fill a vacant place,
I write, and add, and rase, and when I've done,
'Tis rare that in four Words I suffer one.)

Note what Boileau is *not* saying—that the artist takes endless
pains to work up the illusion of naturalness. The fact that Boileau's own verse is natural, and that (as he says) he works hard at it,
should not make one think that he is optimistic about the value of

painstaking labour. As he says in the longest quotation above, he often comes up with the comically wrong word when he strains for rhyme. It is true that "esprit" is crucial: it shudders at the wrong word, decreeing the deletion of three-quarters of Boileau's choices. Its censorship saves him from being a mindlessly fluent poetaster, though this is not *said* and is incompatible with the mask of incompetent writer that Boileau is wearing. But "esprit" is seen only as a negative force, the literary conscience that reminds the writer to hold on until light penetrates the clouds of *le bizarre*. The implication is that you can only wait for naturalness. Apparently the great Molière never has to wait, being unconscious of "le travail et la peine". His art is continuously natural. This is the point of the seeming solecism in the first lines of this poem in which Molière verse is described as writing itself. Boileau is fortunate to possess a censor in "l'esprit". But how much greater is "l'esprit de Molière", "rare et fameux", "un esprit sublime" (significant praise from the translator of Longinus). His mind is at ease with the medium, for "la rime" embraces more than rhyming. Boileau, claims his poem, lacks this instinct, and possesses a nagging "esprit" that censors fatuity.

In Satire II Boileau proceeds in the manner of Dorante to show what the creative spirit is like. He is as subtle in his use of a mask as Molière in *L'impromptu de Versailles*. Ostensibly the poem is Boileau speaking—but the real Boileau can, of course, find rhymes even for "Malherbe", the prize problem. The *persona* of the poem is cleverly described as "pseudo-Boileau" by Jules Brody in his first-class study of it in *Boileau and Longinus* (Geneva, 1958). Because the poem before us is so successful we may forget that it is meant to be the testimony of a failure. Towards the end pseudo-Boileau wails that he cannot turn out daily sonnets like Pelletier or Scudéry. This is not commonplace writers' conceit ("I am too intelligent and conscientious to churn out books like that"). In fact, Boileau is ranging himself quite closely with the Pelletiers and Scudérys, assuming that they, too, know the sterilities of composition, but are fatally weak because they pull themselves together and let the clichés roll. The joke is that Boileau tells the truth about what goes on in the poet's workshop, and it goes against Pelletier and Scudéry that they never do. If they did they might be more critically self-conscious and be able to voice Boileau's final exhortation—

165

. . . Molière, enseigne-moi l'art de ne rimer plus. (100)

> (*But least I shou'd in vain your Care implore,*
> *Teach me then, dear* Molière, *to Rhyme no more.*)

Criticism of current poetic fluency is enforced by a dose of reality. The pseudo-Boileau of Satire II shows what the conditions of writing are really like; they are the ones that must be admitted even by his enemies: do they wish to claim that finding rhymes is easy? In so doing Boileau substantiates his position much as Molière does in *L'impromptu*, and, indeed, as Pope was to do when answering the clamours of his critics in his imitations of Horace.

It would be a pity to leave this subject without a reference to the famous occasion on which Boileau remarked critically on Molière's presentation of himself in public. In Chant iii of *L'art poétique* the literary genres are described, climactic treatment being given to comedy, and to Molière who becomes the hero of this part of the poem. Boileau has one criticism to make, of Molière's propensity for coarsening his art, shifting from comedy to farce, having on occasion—

. . . sans honte à Terence allié Tabarin. (iii, 398)

> (*And* Harlequin *with Noble* Terence *joyn'd.*)

—that is, dropping from the comedy of nature into the farce of quick returns. Boileau illustrates this point by giving the reader a picture of Molière the actor (on the stage in someone else's person) in conflict with Molière the dramatist. He refers to the funny but "low" moment in *Les fourberies de Scapin* in which Scapin hides an old gentleman in a sack and pretends that he is protecting him, Geronte, from robbers:

> Dans ce sac ridicule où Scapin's s'enveloppe,
> Je ne reconnois plus l'Auteur du Misanthrope.
> (iii, 399–400)

> (*When in the* Fox *I see the* Tortois *hist,*
> *I lose the Author of the* Alchymist.)

Given that Molière had himself played the part of the old man you would expect Boileau to have written "*Geronte* s'enveloppe", not Scapin, so making a fair point about the dramatist demeaning himself. But this is not so fine a point as the one actually made, which is that Boileau cannot see the great artist in the whole spectacle of the sack episode. The lines refer to Scapin enveloped, not Geronte: the sight of Scapin, carrying his copious sack on to the stage, the audience surmising promptly for whom it is destined, personifies Molière's weakness for farce. He is momentarily identified with Scapin, the inventive trickster.

4

Molière and Boileau, then, presented themselves in their own persons. They did so to communicate a source of authority to their enemies, attempting to be fully themselves in public, and also to win their audience into believing that it was more than they themselves who spoke, by means of the strategy by which it was not *really* themselves presented in drama or satire. They sought a means of being highly specific about their taste, about what pleased them ("la grande règle de toutes les règles n'est pas de plaire?"), and at the same time impersonal. Pope sought the same seventy years later in his imitations of Horace. But before that in the youthful *Essay on Criticism* he provided a formula by which the endeavours of Molière and Boileau may be described:

> But where's the Man, who Counsel *can* bestow,
> Still *pleas'd* to *teach,* and yet not *proud* to *know* . . .
> (631–32)

Pope then proceeded to describe this man in general terms. Molière and Boileau had earlier, in drama and satire, attempted to *be* the man.

NOTE

My epigraph is by Robert Louis Stevenson in "The Persons of the Tale", *The Strange Case of Dr. Jekyll and Mr. Hyde with Other Fables* (1896). Texts cited in this essay are as follows: for Pope, "Twickenham" text (1963) edited by John Butt; for Molière, *Théâtre complet* (1962), edited by Robert Jouanny, 2 volumes; for Boileau, *Oeuvres complètes* (1966), introduced by Antoine Adam, text edited by Françoise Escal. For the date of composition of Boileau's Satires II and VII I follow Adam in *Les premières satires de Boileau (I–IX): édition critique et commentaire* (Lille, 1941). English translations are by John Ozell, *The Works of Mr. de Molière* (1714) and Nicholas Rowe, *The Works of Monsieur Boileau Made English from the last Paris Edition, By several Hands* (1712).

9

Pope's *Epistle to Bolingbroke* and *Epistle I. i*

by FRANK STACK

Pope's *Imitations of Horace*, produced between 1733 and 1738, were written in a distinctive mode. By freely adapting famous Horatian satires and epistles Pope created new poems which were genuine expressions of his own thought and feeling. But there is no doubt that Pope expected his readers to recognize these poems as versions of the particular poems on which they were based. Indeed he actively encouraged his readers to compare each imitation with its source by printing Horace's original poems next to his own, with a system of symbols to connect precise points in the two texts, and with key Latin words and phrases in different type to facilitate detailed comparison. No critic of the *Imitations*, I feel, has yet taken this practice fully into account, although its importance has been constantly emphasised.[1] The aim of this essay is to consider one complete imitation—the important *Epistle to Bolingbroke*—specifically from this point of view.

This poem published in March 1738 and based on Horace's *Epistle I. i* was Pope's last imitation of Horace, and in it Pope exploited fully all the possibilities of imitation. Pope here both follows Horace closely and radically departs from him, and the poem which results is characterized by sharp changes of perspective. From one point of view this is a very public poem, a vigorous attack on the city and the court written at a time of mounting political tension and boldly addressed to the government's long-standing enemy Bolingbroke.[2] But from another point of view it is a very personal poem in which Pope speaks to his close friend about his own yearnings, weaknesses, and failures. Through a detailed analysis of Pope's parallel texts I hope to show how this intriguing poem grows out of its Horatian model, and how as a complete work it compares and contrasts with that epistle.

I must say clearly however that my approach to the *Imitations* in this respect is different from that of Thomas E. Maresca in his *Pope's Horatian Poems* (1966). Maresca argues specifically that Pope as an imitator was not interested in the surface of Horace's poetry—its play of tone and irony—but rather in its moral content; and he argues further that Pope's Horace was not the classical Horace but rather a "Christianised" Horace as interpreted by a long tradition of Christian commentators. Working from these premises he suggests that the *Epistle to Bolingbroke* is about the conflict of material and spiritual values ending with Pope's confident assertion of the triumph of the spirit.[3] While Maresca has demonstrated admirably that Pope's Horace was in part a Christianized Horace, I think he gives in general too narrow a view of both the Horace Pope knew and of Pope as an imitator. I want to show that Pope was much more sensitive to the subtle texture of Horace's poetry than Maresca allows, and to suggest that Pope's point of departure for this imitation was essentially Horace's Latin poem in its classical form and meaning.

In interpreting the Latin I have attempted to keep in mind how Pope would have read the poem. A very useful guide to this is, of course, the detailed commentary in André Dacier's complete edition of Horace, which Pope knew and respected.[4] It is significant, I think, that this important edition gives a very full and rich view of the classical Horace. Dacier emphasises the moral seriousness of Horace, commenting in particular on the praise of virtue in the *Epistle*, and to point this up he draws parallels between Horatian passages and Biblical texts; but he also comments frequently and perceptively on Horace's tone and irony, attempting to show the distinctive nature of Horace's personality and moral vision. I think Pope found all these perspectives important. But I would like to emphasize also in this context the value of Pope's own Latin text, since the key words and phrases in different type are themselves a very subtle guide to Pope's own reading of Horace. As we read the *Imitations* what we are primarily aware of is the rich life of one language giving rise to the new life of another.

Horace's famous *Epistle* I. *i* addressed to his patron Maecenas is a mature Horatian epistle, probably written around 20 BC when Horace was forty-five. It is about Horace's desire to live the "moral life", for only this he claims can truly fulfil the needs of the self. This idea is of course central to Horace, and it is no accident that this poem serves as the introduction to his first book of epistles—it sets the tone for the poems that follow. Three features of this epistle are particularly important for Horace and also, I think, for Pope. First, Horace makes a central feature of his poem his own resolve to turn to philosophy and lead the good life. It is in this sense a very personal poem. Second, while Horace's moral earnestness is at the heart of the poem, it is tempered throughout by a wry scepticism about the actual possibilities of moral achievement. Horace is careful not to make too many claims for the lasting effect of the high ideals to which he is drawn. Third, like all Horace's hexameter poems, this epistle is characterized by the freedom and flexibility of its form, by the range and variety of its tones and its fine movement from one subject to another; but this is also the poem in which Horace makes his clearest assertion of his natural eclecticism so clearly embodied in that form. "Nullius addictus jurare in verba Magistri" ("I am not bound over to swear as any master dictates"). He asserts in this poem that his approach to life is essentially his own. As we shall see, Dacier particularly emphasises the importance of this.

These features of the poem are of course inter-related, and they spring from something deep in Horace—his capacity to see himself imaginatively in relation to other people. This indeed gives rise to the whole shape of this poem. At the beginning of the epistle he shares with us his desire to know what is right and fitting ("Quid verum atque decens"), making us feel that such thoughts eventually come to every person. But then he goes on to show that his attempt to know himself and his real needs in fact sets him apart from most of his contemporaries. Their whole attitude to life is different. They rush frantically to India to flee poverty, build larger and larger fortunes, are carried by mere whim from one fashionable resort to another, while he stands back, asking sceptically if these desperate attempts to achieve fulfilment will really satisfy their needs. Yet after ridiculing others for failing to be contented with anything they actually possess, Horace then identifies himself with everyone else, and with wry humour admits his own inconsistencies and his own inner discontent. At the end of the epistle we have an engaging picture of Horace as much in need of his own wisdom as everyone else; and he sardonically chastises Maecenas for not helping him to escape from the folly of his own inconsistencies. But in the very last line he cracks a witty joke and ends the poem on a note of buoyant confidence in himself.

Pope's imitation of this poem shows a fine understanding of the inner life of Horace's epistle. His own poem is partly about the need for inner contentment, and he too is at once confident and sceptical about the possibilities of success. His epistle has the overall shape of Horace's and the freedom and flexibility of its form. He too compares himself with his contemporaries, and he thinks of Bolingbroke as being his own Maecenas. But Pope cannot be Horace: the times are different and his temperament is different, and from that arise the tensions in this poetry of imitation.

We can see this if we compare the openings of the two poems. Horace begins by telling Maecenas he cannot write any more poems; the time has come for him to think about himself, and to discover the right way to live:

> *Prima* dicte mihi, summa dicende Camena!
> Spectatum satis, & donatum jam rude, quaeris
> (Maecenas) iterum antiquo me includere ludo?
> Non eadem est aetas, non mens. Vejanius Armis
> Herculis ad postem fixis, latet abditus agro,
> Ne populum extrema, toties, exoret arena.
>   Est mihi, purgatam crebro qui personet aurem;
> "Solve senescentem mature sanus equum, ne
> "Peccet ad extremum ridendus, & ilia ducat."
>   Nunc itaque, & Versus & *caetera ludicra* pono,
> Quid *verum* atque *decens*, curo & rogo, & *omnis* in hoc sum.
> Condo & compono quae *mox* depromere possim.[5]

(You, of whom my earliest Muse has told, of whom my last shall tell—you Maecenas, seek to shut me up again in my old school, though well tested in the fray, and already presented with the foil. My years, my mind, are not the same. Veianius hangs up his arms at Hercules' door, then lies hidden in the country, that he may not have to plead with the crowd again and again from the arena's edge. Some one there is who is always dinning in my well-rinsed ear: "Be wise in time, and turn loose the ageing horse, lest at the last he stumble amid jeers and burst his wind." So

now I lay aside my verses and all other toys. What is right and seemly is my study and pursuit, and to that am I wholly given. I am putting by and setting in order the stores on which I may some day draw.)

This is mature Horatian poetry, notable for its play of tone. The first line is impressively phrased ("Prima . . . summa", "dicte . . . dicende"); "Camena" for the Muses is a poetic touch; and the vocative "(Maecenas)" delayed until the third line is respectful. This prepares for a simple statement in which for a moment Horace's feelings deepen, "Non eadem est aetas, non mens". But there is wry irony in the sustained comparison with the gladiator Vejanius who has left the arena so as not to have to plead with the crowd again and again ("toties") and then the self-deprecation becomes more overt: the inner voice is amusingly powerful ("personet"), and Horace as the ageing horse clearly ridiculous. Drawing on all these feelings Horace then makes his central statement, with of course a touch of warm humour:

> Nunc itaque, & Versus & *caetera ludicra* pono,
> Quid *verum* atque *decens*, curo & rogo, & *omnis* in hoc sum.
> Condo & compono quae *mox* depromere possim.

The "*caetera ludicra*" is amusing, but "& *omnis* in hoc sum" suggests how absorbed Horace is in this pursuit; and by using pairs of verbs he takes us unobtrusively into that very activity of thought: "curo & rogo", "Condo & compono". The metaphors in the last line are of storing and arranging for future use.

Pope's imitation of this opening shows just what such poetry means to him. In March 1738 Bolingbroke was in retirement in France, but due back in England imminently, and Pope was almost fifty.

> St. John whose love indulg'd my labours past
> Matures my present, and shall bound my last!
> Why will you break the Sabbath of my days?
> Now sick alike of Envy and of Praise.
> Publick too long, ah let me hide my Age!
> See modest Cibber now has left the Stage:
> Our Gen'rals now, retir'd to their Estates,
> Hang their old Trophies o'er the Garden gates,
> In Life's cool evening satiate of applause,
> Nor fond of bleeding, ev'n in BRUNSWICK'S cause.

> A Voice there is, that whispers in my ear,
> ('Tis Reason's voice, which sometimes one can hear)
> "Friend Pope! be prudent, let your Muse take breath,
> "And never gallop Pegasus to death;
> "Lest stiff, and stately, void of fire, or force,
> "You limp, like Blackmore, on a Lord Mayor's horse."
> Farewell then Verse, and Love, and ev'ry Toy,
> The rhymes and rattles of the Man or Boy:
> What right, what true, what fit, we justly call,
> Let this be all my care—for this is All:
> To lay this harvest up, and hoard with haste
> What ev'ry day will want, and most, the last.

In so many ways this verse is Horatian. We recognize in the poetry the calm rhythms of Horace's verse, and hear again so many of Horace's tones. In the address to Bolingbroke the formality of Horace's first line is carefully echoed, though "St. John" comes impressively first. The meaning of Horace's "Non eadem est aetas, non mens" is caught in:

> Why will you break the Sabbath of my days?
> Now sick alike of Envy and of Praise.
> Publick too long, ah let me hide my Age!

And to balance this there is a fine touch of dry irony: "See modest Cibber now has left the stage." Cibber had officially retired from the theatre four years before but unlike Horace's gladiator kept returning periodically for the next eleven years. The humour is Horatian and the surface of the poetry is unruffled. Pope then brings out the idea of retirement. Developing imaginatively Horace's "latet abditus agro" he speaks of Peterborough's retirement at Southampton and here there are deeper feelings again: "In Life's cool evening satiate of applause". Even the final note is nicely subdued, "Nor fond of bleeding, ev'n in BRUNSWICK's cause". Originally it was "Br—s", which could have been simply "Britain's".[6]

What follows is almost more Horatian than Horace. Horace says something speaks to him clearly, "Est mihi, purgatam crebro qui personet aurem". In Pope there is a subtler self-deprecating irony:

> A Voice there is, that whispers in my ear,
> ('Tis Reason's voice, which sometimes one can hear) ...

For "personet" there is "whispers", and for "purgatam . . . aurem" the sceptical and delicate "which sometimes one can hear". After this there is more obvious amusement in the idea that he might sink into poetry as dull as Blackmore's and in Pegasus declining into a Lord Mayor's horse. But this leads directly to a fine version of Horace's claim that he has turned from poetry to philosophy, and here we see Pope blending Horatian tones with others. The tone of Horace's *"caetera ludicra"* is caught in Pope's sardonic "rhymes and rattles of the Man or Boy", but the farewell to "Love" is Pope's own touch. He dwells on the *"omnis"* in Horace's "& *omnis* in hoc sum" but also gives Horace's lines Christian overtones:

> What right, what true, what fit, we justly call,
> Let this be all my care—for this is All . . .

And he ends by nicely modifying Horace's idea of goods stored away to be used by and by (*"mox"*) to speak of spiritual goods needed at death, "What ev'ry day will want, and most, the last".[7]

From these opening lines we can begin to see the complexities of Pope's art of imitation. Pope's poetry is his own, but it is to a remarkable extent actually made out of Horace's verse and inspired by Horace's individual thoughts and feelings. Pope's attention to detail is very impressive, I think, and the key Latin words are always illuminating. Futhermore Pope's own feelings in those last lines only emerge in the comparison with Horace: to appreciate them fully we must know that Pope is emulating Horace's famous resolve and see the Horatian idea of self-discovery blending with the Christian idea of spiritual wisdom.

The whole first third of Pope's poem is in fact concerned with Pope's yearning to attend like Horace to his true needs, and it is very closely modelled on Horace's epistle. He makes imitating Horace here an opportunity to show how genuine that yearning could be, as we see in his treatment of the passages that follow. Having said that he has turned to philosophy, Horace makes his important point that he is not bound to any single type of ethics ("Nullius addictus jurare in verba Magistri"). After that he goes on to complain that he cannot yet find the time to attend wholly to the important task of setting himself aright:

> Ut nox longa quibus mentitur amica, diesque
> Longa videtur *opus debentibus*, ut piger annus

175

Pupillis, quos dura premit custodia matrum:
Sic mihi tarda fluunt *ingrataque* tempora, quae spem
Consiliumque *morantur* agendi gnaviter *id*, quod
Aeque *pauperibus* prodest, *locupletibus* aeque,
Aeque neglectum *pueris, senibusque* nocebit.

(*As the night seems long for one whose mistress proves false,
and the day long for those who work for hire; as the year lags
for wards held in check by their mother's strict guardianship:
so slow and thankless flow for me the hours which defer my
hope and purpose of setting myself vigorously to that task which
profits alike the poor, alike the rich, but, if neglected, will be
harmful alike to young and to old.*)

Pope's imitation of this passage is particularly revealing. Pope has
turned Horace's description of his eclecticism into a lively account
of his commitments to different causes ("Sometimes a Patriot . . ."
etc.); and after that the "return" to Horace seems particularly
significant:

> Long, as to him who works for debt, the Day;
> Long as the Night to her whose love's away;
> Long as the Year's dull circle seems to run,
> When the brisk Minor pants for twenty-one;
> So slow th'unprofitable Moments roll,
> That lock up all the Functions of my soul;
> That keep me from Myself; and still delay
> Life's instant business to a future day:
> That task, which as we follow, or despise,
> The eldest is a fool, the youngest wise;
> Which done, the poorest can no wants endure,
> And which not done, the richest must be poor.

Pope here recreates beautifully the long, slow rhythm of Horace's
lines, with their touches of wit and pathos. He echoes, but
slightly adjusts, Horace's movement from "nox" to "dies" to
"annus", and sympathetically gives prominence to those whose
work is an obligation ("*opus debentibus*"). But the key lies in his
rendering of "Sic mihi tarda fluunt *ingrataque* tempora . . .":

> So slow th'unprofitable Moments roll,
> That lock up all the Functions of my soul;
> That keep me from Myself . . .

That last touch gives real depth to the passage, and it is perfectly Horatian for Horace is *the poet* of that yearning to be oneself: "Vilice silvarum et mihi me reddentis agelli" (*"Bailiff of my woods and of the little farm which makes me myself again"*) (*Epistle I. xiv. i.*).[8] Pope's version of the last lines of the Horace are impressive too, but here there are some tensions. Pope's verse is thoughtful and pointed, echoing even in its rhythms Horace's careful turning on words ("Aeque *pauperibus* prodest, *locupletibus* aeque"); but Pope unlike Horace commits himself to superlatives ("eldest . . . youngest", "poorest . . . richest"). Both poets are momentarily touched by the universal benefits of wisdom, but Pope is much more idealistic than Horace.

Yet Pope is also aware of the limitations of wisdom, and as he goes on we soon see how much he has been influenced by Horace's wry scepticism. Horace points out that even if our physical potentialities are not very great we still care for ourselves, and asks sardonically if the same might not apply to our moral life. In a single line he states his own position, that he has time only for the basic principles; and then he slips into the satiric second person singular addressing the general reader:

> Restat, ut his ego me ipse regam, solerque, *Elementis.*
>   Non possis oculo quantum contendere Lynceus,
> Non tamen idcirco contemnas lippus inungi:
> Nec, quia desperes invicti membra Glyconis,
> Nodosa corpus nolis prohibere chiragra.
> Est quadam prodire tenus, si non datur ultra.
>   Fervet Avaritia, miseroque Cupidine pectus?
> Sunt *verba* & *voces,* quibus hunc lenire dolorem
> Possis, & magnam morbi deponere partem.
> Laudis amore tumes? sunt certa *piacula,* quae te
> *Ter* pure lecto poterunt recreare libello.
> Invidus, iracundus, iners, vinosus, *Amator,*
> Nemo adeo *ferus* est ut non mitescere possit,
> Si modo culturae patientem commodet aurem.

(*What remains is for me to guide and solace myself with these poor rudiments. You may not be able, with your eyes, to see as far as Lynceus, yet you would not on that account scorn to anoint them, if sore. Nor, because you may not hope for unconquered Glycon's strength of limb, would you decline to keep your body free from the gnarls of gout. It is worth while to*

*take some steps forward, though we may not go still further.
Is your bosom fevered with avarice and sordid covetousness?
There are spells and sayings whereby you may soothe the pain
and cast much of the malady aside. Are you swelling with ambition? There are fixed charms which can fashion you anew, if
with cleansing rites you read the booklet thrice. The slave to
envy, anger, sloth, wine, lewdness—no one is so savage that he
cannot be tamed, if only he lend to treatment a patient ear.)*

Horace's tone here is at once consoling and ironical. The references to Lynceus, the Argonaut famed for his keen eyesight, and
Glycon, a famous contemporary athlete, are clearly amusing; and
Horace's promises of moral cures are nicely qualified by words
like "lenire" ("*soothe*"), "magnam . . . partem" ("*a large part*"),
"*Ter*" (the magical three times), and the ironical "mitescere"
("*tame*").

Pope shows that he understands perfectly this blending of
assurance with dry irony, but he disarms us completely at first
by taking Horace's metaphor about physical weakness quite literally:

> Late as it is, I put my self to school,
> And feel some comfort, not to be a fool.
> Weak tho' I am of limb, and short of sight,
> Far from a Lynx, and not a Giant quite,
> I'll do what MEAD and CHESELDEN advise,
> To keep these limbs, and to preserve these eyes.
> Not to go back, is somewhat to advance,
> And men must walk at least before they dance.
>   Say, does thy blood rebel, thy bosom move
> With wretched Av'rice, or as wretched Love?
> Know, there are Words, and Spells, which can controll
> (Between the Fits) this Fever of the soul:
> Know, there are Rhymes, which (fresh and fresh apply'd)
> Will cure the arrant'st Puppy of his Pride.
> Be furious, envious, slothful, mad or drunk,
> Slave to a Wife or Vassal to a Punk,
> A Switz, a High-dutch, or a Low-dutch Bear—
> All that we ask is but a patient Ear.

That is pure Horace, touched at every point by Pope; and here the
tensions between Pope and Horace become remarkably subtle.
The first couplet is a very personal version of Horace's first line;

but when Horace turns to satirize others, Pope speaks only of himself. The pathos of the lines on his physical weakness is finely enhanced by the allusions to Lynceus and Glycon in the Horace, and Pope for a moment seems terribly vulnerable. There is an almost childlike play on words in his "Far from a Lynx"; and for Horace's dry "Est quadam prodire tenus, si non datur ultra" (*"It's worth going forward even if one can't go far"*) there is something personal and poignant:

> Not to go back, is somewhat to advance,
> And men must walk at least before they dance.

But at once Pope becomes Horatian again. He carefully mirrors the phrasing of Horace's assurances ("Sunt *verba* & *voces* . . . sunt certa *piacula*"; *"Know, there are Words, and Spells . . . Know, there are Rhymes"*). And he captures perfectly the note of Horatian scepticism in words and phrases like "controll", "(Between the fits)", and "(fresh and fresh apply'd)". But at the end he modifies Horace again. Horace's extraordinary line "Invidus, iracundus, iners, vinosus, *Amator*", resolves through irony to a positive conclusion:

> Nemo adeo *ferus* est ut non mitescere possit
> Si modo culturae patientem commodet aurem.

In Pope we hear the first notes of the attacking satirist. The *"Amator"* (*"paramour"*) and the *"ferus"* (*"wild"*) are spelt out, and Horace's calm "patientem . . . aurem" becomes a sarcastic pun:

> Be furious, envious, slothful, mad or drunk,
> Slave to a Wife or Vassal to a Punk,
> A Switz, a High-dutch, or a Low-dutch Bear—
> All that we ask is but a patient Ear.

If the *Imitations* offered only such deeply felt re-creations of Horace they would be impressive, but of course they offer this and more. In the first part of this imitation Pope writes about the yearnings of his Horatian self and explores his capacities for calm contemplation, sardonic amusement, and Horatian seriousness. As we read Pope's poetry next to Horace's we feel that Horace is very much Pope's guide. But in the middle part of the poem we find something almost totally different. When Pope follows Horace into a satiric attack on materialism the other side of Pope, felt only under the surface before, emerges; and as Pope begins an impassioned attack on the city and the court, Horace is not so much a guide to Pope as a strong moral ally. Though still made out of Horace, Pope's poetry is no longer Horatian; but it is still enough like Horace for Pope to draw on the power of Horace's moral authority. We see here the full flexibility of Pope's art of imitation, as we watch Pope turn Horace's satire on Roman materialism into a tremendous attack on contemporary corruption.[9]

Pope's poetry now moves with its own self-generating energy, and his satire is quite different in kind from Horace's. The satire of Horace's central section is finely attuned to his poem's general spirit of questioning. Indeed the subtlety of Horace's satire springs from this, for he makes his points by encouraging us to think and speculate, and by asking which of two alternatives is the better way of life. He dramatizes the voice of the city to show what pressures people are under to make money and seek position—" 'O cives, cives! quaerenda Pecunia primum est, / Virtus post nummos—' " (" 'O citizens, citizens, money you first must seek; virtue after pelf.' "); but he tries also to show the real strength of moral independence. To the man fleeing to India's riches he says:

> Ne cures ea que *stulte* miraris & optas
> Discere, & audire, & meliori credere non vis?

> (*That you may cease to care for the things which you foolishly admire and crave, will you not learn and listen and trust one wiser than yourself?*)

Verbs of caring ("miraris & optas") give way to verbs of listening and hearing ("Discere, & audire"). Who advises best, Horace asks, the man who urges obsessively " 'Rem facias, rem, / Si possis, recte, si non, quocunque modo rem' " (" '*make money, money by fair means if you can, if not, by any means money*' "), or he who encourages you to be your own master, ". . . qui Fortunae te responsare superbae / Liberum & erectum, *praesens* hortatur, & aptat?" (". . . *he who, an ever present help, urges and fits you to stand free and erect, and defy scornful Fortune?*").

Pope takes all this and casts it into a contemporary mould, and the key here is the fact that his poetry is now overtly political. Pope is no longer the man seeking retirement, but the Opposition poet attacking the city and the court in some of his most daring lines. Horace's idea of independence now means freedom from Walpole and his corrupt age. Horace's sarcastic lines on an anonymous Roman aspiring to be a Knight—

> Est animus tibi, sunt mores, est lingua, fidesque—
> Si quadringentis sex, septem millia desint,
> *Plebs* eris—

> (*You have sense, you have morals, eloquence and honour; if there are six or seven thousands short of the four hundred, you will be in the crowd.*)

are turned into a backhanded compliment to John Barnard, the independent M.P. for the City of London:

> BARNARD in spirit, sense, and truth abounds.
> "Pray then what wants he?" fourscore thousand pounds,
> A Pension, or such Harness for a slave
> As Bug now has, and Dorimant would have.
> BARNARD, thou art a *Cit*, with all thy worth;
> But wretched Bug, his *Honour*, and so forth.

Two lines in Horace on the power of conscience—

> Hic *murus aheneus* esto,
> Nil *conscire* sibi, nulla pallescere culpa!—

> (*Be this our wall of bronze, to have no guilt at heart no wrong-doing to turn us pale.*)

become a brilliant and bold jibe at Walpole's "screening": [10]

> True, conscious Honour is to feel no sin,
> He's arm'd without that's innocent within;
> Be this thy Screen, and this thy Wall of Brass;
> Compar'd to this, a Minister's an Ass.

And throughout the very word "Virtue", Horace's "virtus", is charged with the political connotations given it by the Opposition of the 1730s. [11]

The boldness of this political satire emerges clearly at one place in particular, and the contrast with Horace is very striking. It is at the point where Horace pauses to justify his own independent way of life:

> Quod si me Populus Romanus forte roget, cur
> Non, ut porticibus, sic judiciis fruar iisdem,
> Nec sequar aut fugiam, quos diligit ipse, vel odit?
> Olim quod Vulpes aegroto cauta Leoni
> Respondit, referam: "Quia me vestigia terrent
> "Omnia te adversum spectantia, nulla retrorsum".

(*But if the people of Rome should ask me, perchance, why I do not use the same judgements even as I walk in the same colonnades as they, why I do not follow or eschew what they love or hate, I should reply as once upon a time the prudent fox made answer to the sick lion: "Because those footprints frighten me; they all lead toward your den, and none lead back".*)

Pope takes these lines on the ordinary people, turns them upside down, and produces a daring attack on the Court and its "well-drest Rabble":

> If such a Doctrine, in St. James's air,
> Shou'd chance to make the well-drest Rabble stare;
> If honest S*z take scandal at a spark,
> That less admires the Palace than the Park;
> Faith I shall give the answer Reynard gave,
> "I cannot like, Dread Sir! your Royal Cave;
> "Because I see by all the Tracks about,
> "Full many a Beast goes in, but none comes out."
> Adieu to Virtue if you're once a Slave:
> Send her to Court, you send her to her Grave.

But when Pope does turn to "The People" he produces the climax of the central section of his poem. Horace says it is impossible to follow other people anyway, because their desires are all different; and he cryptically caricatures a few sordid ways of making money:

> *Bellua multorum* est *capitum*, nam quid sequar aut quem?
> Pars hominum gestit conducere *Publica*. Sunt qui
> Crustis & *Pomis*, Viduas venentur avaras,
> Excipiantque Senes quos in vivaria mittunt.
> *Multis* occulto crescit res faenore—

(*You are a many-headed monster-thing. For what am I to follow or whom? Some men rejoice to farm state-revenues; some with titbits and fruits hunt miserly widows, and net old men to stock their preserves; with many their money grows with interest unobserved.*)

In these few lines we see Horace's talent for grotesque comedy: "gestit" conveys how eagerly some long for public contracts, and strange metaphors characterize other weird activities—hunting ("venentur") miserly widows, and catching ("excipiant") old men to put in game preserves ("vivaria") like animals. In the last sinister line money grows for many through the secret power of interest ("faenore").

Taking the hint from Horace's *"Publica"* and *"Multis"*, Pope brilliantly turns all this into an intense vision of inner corruption on a national scale:

> Well, if a King's a Lion, at the least
> The People are a many-headed Beast:
> Can they direct what measures to pursue,
> Who know themselves so little what to do?
> Alike in nothing but one Lust of Gold,
> Just half the land would buy, and half be sold:
> Their Country's wealth our mightier Misers drain,
> Or cross, to plunder Provinces, the Main:
> The rest, some farm the Poor-box, some the Pews;
> Some keep Assemblies, and wou'd keep the Stews;
> Some with fat Bucks on childless Dotards fawn;
> Some win rich Widows by their Chine and Brawn;
> While with the silent growth of ten per Cent,
> In Dirt and darkness hundreds stink content.

There is nothing like this in Horace's poem, indeed nothing like it in the whole of Horace, except perhaps in the last Roman Ode (*Odes, III, vi*). The moral intensity and bitter cynicism here are all Pope's own. Horace is detached from the absurdities of avarice; but Pope is utterly gripped by the profound corruptions of the heart he discovers in a sinister association of avarice and sexual desire— "one Lust of Gold". Here human yearning has been perverted by the power of evil, the driving forces of human experience have been tainted, and the purpose of life has been lost.

After this it must have been hard to be Horatian again, and indeed these lines cast their shadow over the rest of Pope's poem, particularly, as we shall see, its conclusion. But in fact Pope does return to the Horatian style once more. When Horace turns his attention from avarice to inconsistency Pope follows suit, though Horace of course makes the transition with perfect ease—

> —Verum
> Esto, aliis alios rebus, studiisque teneri:
> Iidem eadem possunt horam durare probantes?—

> (But let it be that men are swayed by different aims and hobbies; can the same persons persist for one hour in liking the same things?)

while Pope can modulate to something lighter only by means of grim sarcasm:

> Of all these ways, if each pursues his own,
> Satire be kind, and let the wretch alone.
> But show me one, who has it in his pow'r
> To act consistent with himself an hour.

Pope produces an amusing sketch of a nouveau riche "Sir Job" closely modelled on Horace's "*Dives*"; and in his couplets he reproduces the quick turns of Horace's sharp satiric wit:

> —Lectus genialis in aula est?
> Nil ait esse prius, melius nil caelibe vita:
> Si non est, jurat bene solis esse maritis.

> (Is the bed of his Genius in his hall? "Nothing," he says, "is finer or better than a single life." If it is not, he swears that only the married are well off.)

> At am'rous Flavio is the Stocking thrown?
> That very night he longs to lye alone.
> The Fool whose Wife elopes some thrice a quarter,
> For matrimonial Solace dies a martyr.

Most important of all, Pope alludes persistently to the aimlessness of human lives. Speaking of the common people he had asked:

> Can they direct what measures to pursue,
> Who know themselves so little what to do?

Now in characterizing Sir Job, he mentions ". . . that Dev'l within / Which guides all those who know not what they mean", and he ridicules the poor who

> . . . change their weekly Barber, weekly News,
> Prefer a new Japanner to their shoes,

Discharge their Garrets, move their Beds, and run
(They know not whither) in a Chaise and one . . .

In contrast to the aggressive satire of the middle section this is
very Horatian. Both Pope and Horace here make us laugh at something which is actually quite serious and make us think of the
universal need for direction.

It is this that makes the endings of these two poems particularly
interesting. After encouraging us to laugh at the inconsistencies
of others—"Quid *pauper? ride . . ."*—Horace now admits his *own*
inner contradictions. At first we can hardly believe he is speaking
about himself: he uses a generalized "I" and an ambiguous "you".
We accept it only as we gradually realize that he is actually talking not to us but to Maecenas. The whole passage is masterful:

> Si curtatus *inaequali* tonsore capillos
> Occurro, rides; si forte subucula pexae
> Trita subest tunicae, vel si toga *dissidet impar,*
> Rides: quid? mea cum pugnat *Sententia* secum,
> Quod petiit, spernit; repetit quod nuper omisit;
> Aestuat, & Vitae disconvenit ordine toto;
> Diruit, aedificat, mutat quadrata rotundis?
> Insanire putas solennia me; neque rides,
> Nec *Medici* credis, nec *Curatoris* egere
> A *Praetore* dati? rerum Tutela mearum
> Cum sis, & prave sectum stomacheris ob unguem,
> De *te pendentis, te suspicientis,* Amici.

*(If, when some uneven barber has cropped my hair, I come your
way, you laugh; if haply I have a tattered shirt beneath a new
tunic, or if my gown sits badly and askew, you laugh. What,
when my judgement is at strife with itself, scorns what it craved,
asks again for what it lately cast aside; when it shifts like a tide,
and in the whole system of life is out of joint, pulling down,
building up, and changing square to round? You think my madness is the usual thing, and neither laugh at me nor deem that I
need a physician or a guardian assigned by the court, though
you are keeper of my fortunes, and flare up at an ill-pared nail of
the friend who hangs upon you and looks to you in all.)*

Horace's self-criticism here is ironical but pointed: the "rides . . .
rides . . . rides" is persistent; his mind fights itself ("pugnat");
conflicting verbs fall upon each other ('Quod petit, spernit; repetit

185

quod nuper omisit"); and "quadrata" and "rotundis" are pushed together. With nice irony he chastizes Maecenas for considering this madness to be quite normal ("solennia"). The final note is beautifully controlled: "stomacheris" (*"you flare up"*) is amusing, but literally hanging up the ill-pared nail is that appealing personal last line with its suspended genitives (*"pendentis"*, *"suspicientis"*) and perfectly placed, warm "Amici". He is first "everyone" and then "Horace".

But at once he breaks off. In one sentence he sums up rapidly, asserting that the Stoics are right, but then ends with his witty joke:

> Ad summam, *Sapiens* uno minor est *Jove!* Dives!
> Liber! honoratus! pulcher!—
> > —Rex denique regum!
> Praecipue sanus—
> > —Nisi cum pituita molesta est.

> (*To sum up: the wise man is less than Jove alone. He is rich, free, honoured, beautiful, nay a king of kings; above all, sound—save when troubled by the 'flu'!*)

The rapid list of Stoic terms ("*Sapiens*", "Dives", "Rex denique regum") leads straight to a neat pun on "sanus" ("sane", but also "healthy") and a quick thrust at the Stoic wise man. This joke is pure Horace: it is both a final reminder of the need to recognize human limitation, and a witty assertion of himself. As Dacier acutely remarked: "Et le ridicule qu'il donne par-là aux Stoiciens, prouve encore ce qu'il a dit au commencement de cette Epître, qu'il n'éousoit les sentimens d'aucune secte . . . *Nullius addictus jurare in verba magistri.*"[12] We can only smile at the clipped rhythm of those last words ("pituita molesta est") and delight in the flash of detachment.

Pope's imitation of this whole conclusion is the climax of his poem. He begins with a fine re-creation of Horace's confession of his inconsistencies, but then transforms Horace's last lines into something very different indeed:

> You laugh, half Beau half Sloven if I stand,
> My Wig all powder, and all snuff my Band;
> You laugh, if Coat and Breeches strangely vary,
> White Gloves, and Linnen worthy Lady Mary!

But when no Prelate's Lawn with Hair-shirt lin'd,
Is half so incoherent as my Mind,
When (each Opinion with the next at strife,
One ebb and flow of follies all my Life)
I plant, root up, I build, and then confound,
Turn round to square, and square again to round;
You never change one muscle of your face,
You think this Madness but a common case,
Nor once to Chanc'ry, nor to Hales apply;
Yet hang your lip, to see a Seam awry!
Careless how ill I with myself agree;
Kind to my dress, my figure, not to Me.
Is this my Guide, Philosopher, and Friend?
This, He who loves me, and who ought to mend?
Who ought to make me (what he can, or none,)
That Man divine whom Wisdom calls her own,
Great without Title, without Fortune bless'd,
Rich ev'n when plunder'd, honour'd while oppress'd,
Lov'd without youth, and follow'd without power,
At home tho' exil'd, free, tho' in the Tower.
In short, that reas'ning, high, immortal Thing,
Just less than Jove, and much above a King,
Nay half in Heav'n—except (what's mighty odd)
A Fit of Vapours clouds this Demi-god.

This is certainly one of Pope's finest passages written in imitation
of Horace: he follows Horace very closely at first, but then Pope
makes the different parts of Horace's ending flow together into
one continuous whole. The key I think lies in the intensity of his
feelings for Bolingbroke and in his desire that Bolingbroke should
make *him* into the Stoic wise man of Horace's poem. Pope's
address to Bolingbroke is clearly based on what Horace says to
Maecenas, but Pope's feelings seem to be much more intense than
Horace's are. Horace is amusing, "Insanire putas solennia me;
neque rides, . . ."; but Pope is emotionally demanding:

> You never change one muscle of your face,
> You think this Madness but a common case . . .

He says that Bolingbroke is not concerned with his true self:
"Kind to my dress, my figure, not to Me". He develops Horace's
short description of the Stoic wise man into an elaborate image of
a great Stoic figure, "That Man divine whom Wisdom calls her

own"; and he insists that if Bolingbroke really loves him he ought to *make* him into such a figure. Indeed he makes a point of saying that only Bolingbroke could achieve this, "(what he can, or none,)". I think this is more than just light raillery: there is irony in this self-characterization but there is also emotional involvement. The ideal figure is a composite image of himself and other men, men he has known and loved, Atterbury, Oxford, and most importantly Bolingbroke himself. The lines are set explicitly in apposition to "me". Pope drives the rhetoric to a climax, but then cuts it short with calculated sarcasm:

> Nay half in Heav'n—except (what's mighty odd)
> A Fit of Vapours clouds this Demi-god.

Pope sees that both he and his ideals have become preposterous, and he ends his poem on a note of scorn for this grand image of himself.[13]

The immediate contrast with Horace here is of course very impressive: Horace's lively joke directed at the Stoics is so different from Pope's sharp ridicule of himself. But the whole ending is so different, really because Pope's relationship with Bolingbroke is much more important in his poem than Horace's relationship with Maecenas in his. Pope forms the final section of his poem around the idea that Bolingbroke as his friend must try to make him into a great person but at the same time recognizes with him the complexity of his nature and the inevitability of his failure.

The subtle demands that Horace makes on Maecenas are justly famous— one thinks particularly of *Epistle I. vii*—but he never makes such demands as Pope is making here, for such intensities are not part of Horace's idea of friendship. Indeed Horace's ultimate need in friendship is freedom from such demands; above all else Horace requires independence, and his expressions of affection are always restrained. Pope's appeal to Bolingbroke greatly extends Horace's delicately controlled "De *te pendentis, te suspicientis*, Amici," and in it Pope bears witness to his very deep admiration for his "Guide, Philosopher, and Friend".

But of course Pope's ending is also striking in that it contains a confession of personal failure which seems extraordinary after the tremendous confidence of the poem's central section. His poem's overall Horatian structure can hardly contain such tensions. But in this we see why the sustained comparison between Pope's poem and Horace's epistle is so meaningful: as whole works these poems are at once profoundly similar and profoundly different. Horace's poem is about his own desire for inner fulfilment, but it shows also what he has in fact achieved: his calm wisdom, his wit, his detachment, and his subtle flexibility. In the free movement of his poem Horace holds together his scepticism and his confidence, his sense of himself and his sense of others, his recognition of moral demands and his acceptance of the limitations of human achievement. Pope's poem is much more paradoxical: it is at once more passionate and more disillusioned, more idealistic and more deeply sceptical, and in Pope's poem the yearning for improvement struggles hard against the threat of failure. This troubled work is less unified than Horace's epistle, and less rounded; but it is in some ways a stronger poem than Horace's. Pope can recreate Horace's rich poetry of the inner self, but he shows also that he recognizes the limitations of Horace's vision. The dark moments of Pope's poem give it a depth Horace's epistle does not have; and its intensities of feeling make it more compelling. Horace's poem is wonderfully open and honest, but Pope's poem has all the aggressive power of truth as well, and it stands as a greater indictment of its age.

The mood of this imitation was very much the mood of Pope in 1738. The attacking, bitter notes struck here were heard in the powerful imitation of Horace's *Epistle I. vi* which preceded it, and were heard again in the two "Dialogues" of the *Epilogue to the Satires* which followed it. It was in this pessimistic mood that Pope turned away from Horace whom he had been imitating on and off for five years. Seen in this light the contrasts between Horace's *Epistle I. i* and Pope's imitation are particularly moving. Horace's *Epistle I. i* is the fresh beginning of a book which suggests throughout that with thought and imagination it is possible to be a sane, whole person, more or less in control of circumstances and oneself. Pope's imitation implies that in 1738 the forces which drive men are greater than the men themselves, and more subtly corrupting. The poet's relationship with his society is strained, and his image of "himself" is disturbed and unsettled. It is no wonder that the *Epistle to Bolingbroke* was Pope's last *Imitation of Horace.*

NOTES

1 See especially R. A. Brower, *Alexander Pope: The Poetry of Allusion* (Oxford, 1959), Chapters vi and ix; G. K. Hunter, "The 'Romanticism' of Pope's Horace", *Essays in Criticism*, x, 1960, pp. 390–404; A. L. Williams, "Pope and Horace: *The Second Epistle of the Second Book*", in *Restoration and Eighteenth-Century Literature, Essays in Honor of Alan Dugald McKillop*, ed. Carroll Camden (Chicago, 1963), pp. 309–21; John M. Aden, *Something Like Horace* (1969); and Howard D. Weinbrot, *The Formal Strain, Studies in Augustan Imitation and Satire* (Chicago, 1969).

2 Maynard Mack comments on the significance of this in *The Garden and the City* (London, 1969), pp. 168–69.

3 See Maresca, *op. cit.*, pp. 151–93, and p. 197.

4 *Oeuvres d'Horace en Latin et en François avec Des Remarques Critiques et Historiques*, ed. A. Dacier, 3rd edition (Paris, 1709), 10 vols. Pope praises this work in a letter to the Duke of Buckingham on 1 September 1718; see *The Correspondence of Alexander Pope*, ed. G. Sherburn (Oxford, 1956), I, p. 492.

5 All quotations from Horace's poem and Pope's imitation are from *Alexander Pope: Imitations of Horace, The Twickenham Edition of the Poems of Alexander Pope*, Vol. IV, ed, John Butt, 2nd ed. (London, 1953), which reproduces Pope's carefully prepared texts of Horace, including the key words and phrases placed in different type. After each passage of Horace I have provided the Loeb translation from *Horace: Satires, Epistles, and Ars Poetica*, ed. and tr. H. Rushton Fairclough (London, 1929), to facilitate reading the Latin. I have once modified this translation to suit Pope's Latin text; and one should note that Pope has omitted lines 49–51 from Horace's epistle in order to make his argument in the imitation at that point flow more smoothly.

6 See TE, IV, p. 297.

7 Maresca comments aptly on the Christian overtones here, *op. cit.*, pp. 175–76.

8 See also Peter Dixon, *The World of Pope's Satires* (London, 1968), p. 189.

9 H. H. Erskine-Hill emphasises the general importance of Pope's flexible treatment of Horace in the introduction to his edition of these poems, Pope, *Horatian Satires and Epistles* (Oxford, 1964).

10 Warburton says that this "fine stroke of satire" was inspired by Dacier's note on "murus aheneus", "an old veteran, armed cap-à-pie in *brass, and placed to cover his Fellow*", *The Works of Alexander Pope*, ed. William Warburton (London, 1753), IV, p. 112.

11 See Paul Gabriner, "Pope's 'Virtue' and the Events of 1738", *Further Studies in English Language and Literature*, ed. A. A. Mendilow, *Publications of the Hebrew University*, XXV, (Jerusalem, 1973), pp. 96–119.

12 Dacier, *op. cit.*, Vol. VIII, p. 122.

13 Interpretations of this important final section vary considerably: Peter Dixon sees it as a passage of light raillery, *op. cit.*, pp. 160–61; while for Maresca it shows Pope's outward confusion but inner spiritual triumph, *op. cit.*, pp. 181–90.

10

The Book of Genesis and the Genesis of Books: The Creation of Pope's *Dunciad*

by J. PHILIP BROCKBANK

It is as if the prophet Isaiah had spent decades of his life in Grub Street, for Pope's progress from *Messiah* to *The Dunciad* is at once cosmic and parochial. "As Prophecy hath ever been one of the chief provinces of Poesy," says a "Scriblerus" note at the end of Book III, "our poet here foretells from what we feel, what we are to fear; and in the style of other Prophets, hath used the future tense for the preterite: since what he says shall be, is already to be seen."[1] The poem reaches from past things to last things, from Genesis to Revelation; and, exercising both the sublime and the bathetic voices of poetry, it keeps tune at once with Milton and Virgil and with the clamorous chorus of the City. A laborious mode of analysis can never arrive at its art, for like the life and literature and language from which it emerges, it is not so much a structure, conforming to or dissenting from theoretical *genres*, as a flux, refusing to stay for methodical inspection. It is designed to confound the blockheads who wait upon every bard, and Pope the annotator is his own blockhead.

Taking the poem in motion, however, we may still hope to keep pace with its verbal and allusory skill, and still glimpse its shaping conceptions and preoccupations. The teeming, wriggling wit that in recent years has been generously and fruitfully annotated, may continue to be random in its effects if we fail to recognize that much of it is composed within the large metaphor which makes the creation of fiction analogous to the creation of the natural world. Since fiction must, in Pope's actual London and in the phantasmagoric territory of the poem, be disseminated and marketed, the Book of Genesis gets itself transposed into a prophecy on the genesis of books.[2] *The Dunciad* is about the material and spiritual conditions under which books are "created" in Augustan England. We discover early in the poem that creation out of chaos is not a grand cosmic idea but a comical parochial one:

> Here she beholds the Chaos dark and deep,
> Where nameless Somethings in their causes sleep,
> 'Till genial Jacob, or a warm Third day,
> Call forth each mass, a Poem, or a Play.
>
> (I, 55–8)

The lines, we find from the Twickenham notes, have their allusive history; the mysterious sleep of forms in their first causes, waiting to be born, solemnly observed in Cowley's *Davideis*, had already been domesticated in Garth's *Dispensary*—turned into vegetables waiting to grow. The cosmic vehicle of Pope's metaphor commemorates the central mystery of creation—the emergence of indentifiable forms from gross and random states; its comic tenor tells us that Grub Street hacks struggle to make a name for themselves by shaping poems and plays out of the "native anarchy" of their minds. If we wonder why Jacob is "genial" and the third day "warm", we may find parochial answers in the circumstance that Jacob Tonson was the publisher of Theobald's *Shakespeare* and that the third night of a play's performance yielded the author's benefit. Pope's cosmic poem, however, is harking back to the description given by Milton's Raphael of the third day of creation:[3]

> over all the face of Earth
> Main Ocean flowd, not idle, but with warm
> Prolific humour soft'ning all her Globe,
> Fermented the great Mother to conceive,
> Satiate with genial moisture.
>
> (*Paradise Lost*, VII, 278–82)

In the early version Pope has Dulness as a "great Mother" (A.I, 33) beholding "Chaos dark and deep", with his annotator referring us to Virgil's Juno; but the blockhead would do better to take us to Milton's "fecund globe", where "genial" relates to "generation" and "warm" to the conditions of incubation.[4] At the same time, Pope keeps in touch with neo-platonic theories of literary creation. We may think, for example, of Shakespeare's Theseus:

> as imagination bodies forth
> The forms of things unknown, the poet's pen
> Turns them to shapes, and gives to aery nothing
> A local habitation and a name.
> (*A Midsummer Night's Dream*, V, i, 14–18)

"Call forth", as Pope uses it, suggests the God of Genesis calling forms into being from a primordial state of matter; but the syntax reminds us that poems and plays are being churned out every morning ("each mass") in hope of fame and profit from bookshop or theatre.

As the process gets under way the embryology of literary creation breeds a new crop of mysteries attended by absurdities:

> How hints, like spawn, scarce quick in embryo lie,
> How new-born nonsense first is taught to cry,
> Maggots half-form'd in rhyme exactly meet,
> And learn to crawl upon poetic feet.
>
> (I, 59–62)

In Milton's creation, "the Waters generate . . . with spawn abundant . . . each Soul living, each that crept"; all is accomplished under the spell of the poet's untroubled awe. Pope, who knows about the misery of getting things written, oscillates between the shock of human genesis (the slap into life) and the pestiferous labour of making "maggots"—the word punning on the sense "literary trifles".

Much of the poem's first book is contained by "creation", from the birth of Pallas from the head of Jove (A. I, 7) to the learned joke about the *uterus* of the Trojan horse (A. I, 212n). The "Great Mother" presides over an empire populated by the intimate collaboration of Curll's "chaste press' and Lintot's "rubic post"; hence the inward genesis of "momentary monsters" and the public traffic in "Journals, Medleys, Merc'ries, Magazines". As Milton's God looks upon his creation through a "dewie mist" on the third day, to find "that it was good" (VII, 333–38), so Dulness looks upon hers "thro' fogs, that magnify the scene" (I, 80). False creation is the ubiquitous skill of the Grub Street race (I, 65–78), but at the climax of the first book the "image" of Dulness is "full-exprest" in "Tibbald's" (then in "Cibber's") "monster-breeding breast". As in Genesis, man is created in God's image and allowed

194

dominion over all creeping things, so the Dunces' hero is allowed to preside over his travesty of creation.

The isolated poet struggling to make a living—singing for his supper—is at once compassionately and cruelly compounded with the vanity and destructive nullity to which literary creation is reduced under the economic pressures of Grub Street. The unfurnished garret, the unfed belly and the hollow head are the emblems of "Music caus'd by Emptiness" (I, 36), and in "The Cave of Poverty and Poetry" we are made obscurely aware that even the very word "poetry" has got itself lost in the word "poverty".[5]

"Sinking from thought to thought", "Tibbald" and Cibber may be said to practise the "Art of Sinking", which is the sub-title of the Peri Bathous published by Pope as "Martinus Scriblerus" in 1727. "The Bathos, or Profund," says Scriblerus, "is the natural Taste of Man, and in particular of the present Age." The cosmic history of man's natural taste may be said to be written in *Paradise Lost*, and his exposure to the profound is best expressed at the point where Sin opens the gates for Satan's voyage through the abyss:

> Before thir eyes in sudden view appear
> The secrets of the hoarie Deep, a dark
> Illimitable Ocean without bound,
> Without dimension, where length, bredth, and highth
> And time and place are lost; where eldest *Night*
> And *Chaos*, Ancestors of Nature, hold
> Eternal Anarchie, amidst the noise
> Of endless Warrs, and by confusion stand.
>
> (II, 890–97)

Pope's Cibber version is the more resonant a sound-board to Milton's effects:

> Now (shame to Fortune!) an ill Run at Play
> Blank'd his bold visage, and a thin Third day:
> Swearing and supperless the Hero sate
> Blasphem'd his Gods, the Dice, and damn'd his Fate.
> Then gnaw'd his pen, then dash'd it on the ground,
> Sinking from thought to thought, a vast profound!
> Plung'd for his sense, but found no bottom there,
> Yet wrote and flounder'd on, in mere despair.
> Round him much Embryo, much Abortion lay,
> Much future Ode, and abdicated Play;

195

Nonsense precipitate, like running Lead,
That slip'd thro' Cracks and Zig-zags of the Head;
All that on Folly Frenzy could beget,
Fruits of dull Heat, and Sooterkins of wit.

(I, 113–26)

The more personal plight of "Tibbald" in the early version ("Where yet unpawn'd, much learned lumber lay") is displaced by a diagnosis of Grub Street consciousness which is both familiar, because it charts the frustrations of inspiration so precisely, and remote, because it covertly sets up, in allusion to *Paradise Lost*, a new set of relationships between blasphemy, fall, and exposure to chaos. The fall of the pen coincides with the catastrophic collapse of the psyche, but heroically (like Satan on the burning marl) Cibber recovers and keeps going. The opening equivocations which turn literary creation into a gamble ("an ill run at Play", "his Gods, the Dice") may remind us that in Milton's "profound"[6]:

Chaos Umpire sits,
And by decision more embroils the fray
By which he Reigns: next him high Arbiter
Chance governs all.

(II, 907–10)

Pope's cosmic embryology is an internalized rendering of the ambiguous fecundity of Milton's chaos:

Into this wilde Abyss,
The womb of nature and perhaps her Grave,
Of neither Sea, nor Shore, nor Air, nor Fire,
But all these in thir pregnant causes mixt
Confus'dly, and which thus must ever fight,
Unless th'Almighty Maker them ordain
His dark materials to create more Worlds.

(II, 910–16)

In Cibber's false consciousness (the Marxian phrase is not inappropriate)[7] the womb and the grave are confused, embryo and abortion co-existing: "things destroy'd", as a later line has it, "are swept to things unborn" (I, 242). From the confusion of elements the Dunces' intelligence has already in the poem created "more Worlds" in which "heavy harvests nod beneath the snow" (I, 78). The febrile activities of Cibber's creative consciousness, elsewhere associated with sleep (the primordial state) and vision (the apocalpytic state) are here, in the wakeful, working poet, a complex of mania (Folly mating with Frenzy) and self-congratulation ("In pleasing memory of all he stole"). Any moral response is diverted, however, by the comedy of genesis. In sober ignorance we might suppose that "Fruits of dull Heat, and Sooterkins of wit" is a metaphor in the tradition of Shakespeare's "quick forge and working-house of thought"—Cibber is hammering the cold iron over a smoky fire. But the notes take us to the old dictionaries which tell us that sooterkins were little mouse-like animals believed to have been bred in the bodies of Dutch women, through their habit of carrying stoves under their petticoats.

In the active figurative field of the poem it is Cibber's labours that establish a connection between the games to come and the aborting creator. Cibber falls into the abyss and sinks into the profound. His skull, precipitating running lead (perhaps a casting metaphor from his Bedlam "brazen brainless brothers" in I, 32) at once symbolizes the "new Saturnian age of Lead" (I, 28) and prefigures the games-trophy which prompts the punning rhyme of "head" and "lead" in Book II:

> Not so bold Arnall; with a weight of skull,
> Furious he dives, precipitately dull.
> Whirlpools and storms his circling arm invest,
> With all the might of gravitation blest.
> No crab more active in the dirty dance,
> Downward to climb, and backward to advance.
> He brings up half the bottom on his head,
> And loudly claims the Journals and the Lead.
>
> (II, 315–22)

My own eagerness to remark that Pope's use of the word "precipitate" in the two passages keeps the root sense of "head-first" and enables him to nullify the energies of dullness, will serve as a reminder that every commentator upon Pope is obliged to join the dunces.

The newly emergent race of professional editors and commentators are actively related to the commerce of Grub Street and deserve the same applause:

> O! ever gracious to perplex'd mankind,
> Still spread a healing mist before the mind;

And lest we err by Wit's wild dancing light,
Secure us kindly in our native night.

(I, 173–76)

The uncreating wit of the dunce-scholar and the dunce-poet are,
in the dancing light of Pope's wit, sunk with a "gravity" which is
distinctly connected in the full version of the poem with the
"gravitation" of Newton's physical world, operating still in the
psyches of Bathos:

As, forc'd from wind-guns, lead itself can fly,
And pond'rous slugs cut swiftly thro the sky;
As clocks to weight their nimble motion owe,
The wheels above urg'd by the load below:
Me Emptiness, and Dulness could inspire,
And were my Elasticity, and Fire.

(I, 181–86)

The "might of gravitation" which carries Arnall's heavy head to
the bottom is the dominant law of Dulness's cosmos, prevailing
both inside and outside the skull. Gravity binds creation together;
and when, in the last phase of the second book, the heavy heads bow
low to the weighty exposition of ponderous books, the movement
of the poem is not only a sinking-to-rest, but also a flowing-into-
stillness and a gathering-into-unity, the congregation composed
into everlasting sleep.

The activity of the poem is, to recall Milton's phrase, a "warm
prolific flow". Its creative operation is a proud, irresistible forward movement, encountering the distracting resistance of dullness and making a perpetual turbulence.[8] Pope compels the
language he has inherited (literary and colloquial) to scavenge as
it flies. The field of metaphor, its allusive range and its directing
insight had flourished earlier, in *Mac Flecknoe*, where Shadwell is
"Born upwards by a subterranean wind" in the proud sail of Dryden's verse; and it was later to find different expression in D. H.
Lawrence:

Sex is a creative flow, the excrementory flow is towards dissolution, de-creation, if we may use such a word. In the really healthy
human being the distinction between the two is instant, our pro-
foundest instincts are perhaps our instincts of opposition between
the two flows.
But in the degraded human being the deep instincts have gone

198

dead, and then the two flows become identical. *This* is the secret
of really vulgar and of pornographical people: the sex flow and
the excrement flow is the same to them.

(*Phoenix*, 1936 [1967], p. 176)

The comic zest of Pope's re-creation of the Grub Street dissolution is carried in the vehicle of a verse that constantly reassures
us of its heroic, elegaic and sublime potential. It is not Pope, but
the hacks of the Empire of Dulness, presided over by George II
("Still Dunce the second reigns like Dunce the first") that, in
Book II particularly, are carried along and away by the excre-
mental flow. The sewage problems associated with the commercial
growth of the City are mirrored in the imaginative aspirations of
the Cits, in, as it were, their "stream of consciousness". Where the
springs of the ancient muses had been fed by the underground
river of Alphæus, the Smithfield muses are inspired by the Fleet:

> Then sung, how shown him by the Nut-brown maids
> A branch of Styx here rises from the Shades,
> That tinctur'd as it runs with Lethe's streams,
> And wafting Vapours from the Land of dreams,
> (As under seas Alphæus' secret sluice
> Bears Pisa's off'rings to his Arethuse)
> Pours into Thames: and hence the mingled wave
> Intoxicates the pert, and lulls the grave:
> Here brisker vapours o'er the Temple creep,
> There, all from Paul's to Aldgate drink and sleep.
>
> (B. II, 337–46)

The Fleet "Rolls the large tribute of dead dogs to Thames" (II,
272) and leaves the more expendable dunces to lie like blind puppies
drowned in the mud (II, 305–10). In a Rabelaisian rendering of
Dulness's anti-creation, the "Nectarous humor" that "issuing
flow'd" from Milton's wounded Satan (itself recalling the bleeding
of Homer's gods) is transmuted into a kind of divine diarrhoea
(A. II, 88n) whose virtues refresh the energies of Curll and Lintot.
In parody of the plenitude and fecundity of Milton's creation, the
uncreating labour of "purgings, pumpings, blankettings, and
blows" lets the "fresh vomit run for ever green" (II, 156).

The figure dominating this province of the Empire of Dulness
is Orator Henley. The "fluent nonsense" that trickles from Henley's tongue, his "strain" that "breaks the benches" and his com-

plexion "embrown'd with native bronze" take their uncreative verbal colour from Philosophy's "rent breeches" in the same pageant scene (III, 197–204). Henley finds his own course through the mysteries of uncreation when talking, drinking and vomiting leave him oblivious; he "lay inspir'd beside a sink / And to mere mortals seem'd a Priest in drink" (II, 425). The many "flows" of the poem admit Bentley's port (bringing him to harbour) and Welsted's ale:

> "Flow Welsted, flow! like thine inspirer, Beer,
> Tho' stale, not ripe, tho' thin, yet never clear:
> So sweetly mawkish, and so smoothly dull;
> Heady, not strong, and foaming tho' not full."
> (A. III,163–166)

Denham's original address to the life-and-poetry-sustaining flow of the Thames is perverted to exquisitely reductive purpose. The satire is comprehensive, taking in the human condition (*inter urinam et faeces nascitur*), the immense waste produce of the London book-market, and the spiritual plight of those who hope to prosper by whatever issues from the body and the labouring brain. The thunder that attends the rhyme of "bog" with "King Log" when Jove's "block" descends from "on high" at the end of Book I, is heard again in Book IV (71) before the sounding of "Fame's posterior Trumpet". Scatological jokes—verbal and graphic—were commonplace in an age that could celebrate the "feast of the golden rump" and depict ambitious statesmen kissing Walpole's buttocks.[9] But the scatology of *The Dunciad* aspires to eschatology.

In a comprehensive trope of the poem, all life reverts to the "native anarchy" from which it emerges. Dryden's fine elegiac pathos ("All humane things are subject to decay, / And when Fate summons, Monarchs must obey") is inherited to comparable purpose and again subverted to satire. Yet the satire never quite extinguishes the pity, the suggestion that Grub Street, from Shadwell's time to Pope's, was, in a range of senses from "contemptible" to "poignant", *pathetic*. But to be at the very nexus of the mutable cosmos is a great honour:

> As man's Maeanders to the vital spring
> Roll all their tides, then back their circles bring;

> Or whirligigs, twirl'd round by skilful swain.
> Suck the thread in, then yield it out again:
> All nonsense thus, of old or modern date,
> Shall in thee centre, from thee circulate.
>
> (III, 55–60)

In the rapturous condition of the visionary, the cycle or whirligig is a consolatory process; we flow on and on, and round and round, and backwards and forwards, and down and down, but we keep the solace of a centre—the ego and the hero still intact. The poem's many flurries yield from time to time specific images of gulfs and whirlpools. The "skull cap Of solid proof, impenetrably dull" plunged in the "oblivious lake" of Book II (25–6) still stirs the circling tides of Book III, and Pope entertains many possibilities of immersion in the interim:

> Next Smedley div'd; slow circles dimpled o'er
> The quaking mud, that clos'd, and op'd no more.

Concanen, in contrast, leaves not a ripple, and his profound assimilation finds expression in a rhythmic commemoration of human transience that could take us back to Bishop King or on to Wordsworth:

> No noise, no stir, no motion can'st thou make,
> Th'unconscious stream sleeps o'er thee like a lake.
>
> (II, 303–4)

The "whirlpools and storms" precipitated by the weighty skulls of Welsted or Arnall are reconciled to depth, stillness and oblivion by the "might of gravitation". And heavy heads again infectiously trouble the "unconscious stream" in the reading that concludes the games:

> Toland and Tindal, prompt at priests to jeer,
> Yet silent bow'd to Christ's No kingdom here.
> Who sate the nearest, by the words o'ercome,
> Slept first; the distant nodded to the hum.
> Then down are roll'd the books; stretch'd o'er 'em lies
> Each gentle clerk, and mutt'ring seals his eyes.
> As what a Dutchman plumps into the lakes,
> One circle first, and then a second makes;
> What Dulness dropt among her sons imprest
> Like motion from one circle to the rest;

So from the mid-most the nutation spreads
Round and more round, o'er all the sea of heads.
(II, 399–410)

The congregation coheres into sleep, profoundly united, but in a kingdom that is still very much of this world, as the wakeful (like Hogarth depicting the "Sleeping Congregation") are in a position to notice.

The Third Book opens with a vision of the world to come. Like the corresponding sequences in the *Aeneid* (VI) and in *Paradise Lost* where Adam is "Sunk down and all his spirits become intranc'd" (XI, 420), it contrives to be both a retrospective and a prospective history of creation's long processional progress into the contemporary theatre. Theobald's *Rape of Proserpine* is made occasion for another excursion into a false cosmos, with another comic feat of genesis, this time on the public stage and not merely in the theatre of the mind:

All sudden, Gorgons hiss, and Dragons glare,
And ten-horn fiends and Giants rush to war.
Hell rises, Heav'n descends, and dance on Earth:
Gods, imps, and monsters, music, rage and mirth,
A fire, a jigg, a battle, and a ball,
'Till one wide conflagration swallows all.
  Thence a new world to Nature's laws unknown,
Breaks out refulgent, with a heav'n its own:
Another Cynthia her new journey runs,
And other planets circle other suns.
The forests dance, the rivers upward rise,
Whales sport in woods, and dolphins in the skies;
And last, to give the whole creation grace,
Lo! one vast Egg produces human race.
(III, 235–48)

The 1729 notes insist that the fantasies are not Pope's, "All the extravagancies in the sixteen lines following were introduced on the Stage, and frequented by persons of the first quality in *England* to the twentieth and thirtieth time," and (of the rising of Hell) "This monstrous absurdity was actually represented." But Pope keeps in touch with the apocalyptic end—"'Till one wide conflagration swallows all", and with creation's beginnings. The figure of John Rich chipping the egg in Theobald's farce and taking his "quick Harlequin trip round the empty shell" waits for the day in

Revelation when fire will consume the kingdom of darkness. The connection between the extravagances of City theatre and the coming down of the final curtain is more confidently made in the early version of the poem, in three books. Cibber as "Lord Chancellor of Plays" presides over the closing movement:

> Lo! the great Anarch's ancient reign restor'd,
> Light dies before her uncreating word.

The uncreating word, however solemnly conceived as an anti-logos (as Cibber in II, 16 is the "Anti-Christ of wit"), does not cease to be the word casually set down on paper. It is words that first made the plays (however much pantomime they prescribed) and words continue to be the poem's covert and occasionally explicit material. In Book IV, a triple pun on the process of writing, on the judiciary and on the role of lackeys, has Morality die "when Dulness gives her Page the word" (IV, 30).

When Pope came to re-make the poem into four books he had accumulated much material once intended for an Essay on Education. Book IV often reads therefore like a mocking response to Scriblerus's disingenuous comment on the conclusion of the original poem, that the poet "conceiveth better hopes from the diligence of our Schools, from the regularity of our Universities, the discernment of our Great men, the encouragement of our Patrons, and the genius of our writers of all kinds" (A.III, 337n). Our educators, as transmitters of literary tradition, have some place in the creation story, and their function, according to Pope, is to subdue all creative art to dullness:

> Turn what they will to Verse, their toil is vain
> Critics like me shall make it Prose again.
>
> (IV, 213–14)

Bentley's enlightened concern with accuracy is deliberately confounded with his Enlightenment arrogance, his inability to allow the dead poet his proper autonomy. It may be that Pope did major injustice to both Bentley and Handel, and minor injustice to the more secondary figures; but they are the peripheral victims of a necessary purge. Throughout the book the deeper perspectives of Genesis and the Apocrypha are kept open, from the spurious Miltonic invocation:

Yet, yet a moment, one dim Ray of Light
Indulge, dread Chaos, and eternal Night!
Of darkness visible so much be lent,
As half to shew, half veil the deep intent.
(IV, 1–4)

to the formidably re-cast coda:

Lo! thy dread Empire, CHAOS! is restor'd;
Light dies before thy uncreating word:
Thy hand, great Anarch! lets the curtain fall;
And Universal Darkness buries All.
(IV, 653–56)

If the B version is less precisely aligned than the A version upon
the state of the theatre, it is partly because Book IV is complicated by metaphysical jokes which should not too hurriedly be set
aside as the work of Warburton. In a noble (and ignoble) passage
about the great unity of the state of Dulness, the poem makes an
impudent raid into the cosmographies of Newton and Descartes:

The young, the old, who feel her inward sway,
One instinct seizes, and transports away.
None need a guide, by sure Attraction led,
And strong impulsive gravity of Head.
(IV, 73–6)

The sinking disposition of the grave and heavy is diverted towards
the centre, becoming a planetary principle, and a fresh metaphoric
impetus is given to the poem's preoccupation with the creative
whirl:

None want a place, for all their Centre found,
Hung to the Goddess, and coher'd around.
Not closer, orb in orb, conglob'd are seen
The buzzing Bees about their dusky Queen.
    The gath'ring number, as it moves along,
Involves a vast involuntary throng,
Who gently drawn, and struggling less and less,
Roll in her Vortex, and her pow'r confess.
Not those alone who passive own her laws,
But who, weak rebels, more advance her cause.
Whate'er of dunce in College or in Town
Sneers at another, in toupee or gown;

Whate'er of mungrel no one class admits,
A wit with dunces, and a dunce with wits.
(IV, 77–90)

The note, attributed to Pope and Warburton, blandly expounds the
text in terms of the creation theories of the time. Three classes
of dunces are said to concur in the harmony of the system; the
first by simple attraction fall directly into Dulness's centre; the
second move about it by planetary motion at varying distances;
and the third are "*eccentrical*, and no constant members of her
state or system" (IV, 76–101n). Pope's interest in astronomy, it
has been observed,[10] extended to Descartes's theory of vortices,
about which he could have learned from William Whiston's lectures, or from a choice of published responses to the *Principia
Philosophiae* (1644). Of these, the most celebrated and most likely
to be known to Pope was Fontenelle's, translated by Glanvill in
1688 as *A Plurality of Worlds*; but there were many others, one
of which, published in 1670, offered to show, "That the systeme
of M. Des Cartes . . . seems to have been taken out of the First
Chapter of Genesis."[11] Pope's Dulness is an imaginative creation
on the same scale as the Gnostic Sophia—another "great Mother"
embodying the ontological and teleological principles of creation.
It is therefore apt, in the comedy of the poem, that the Newtonian
and the Cartesian processes of cosmos should be at her disposal.
The conglobed bees (like the concentric ripples over the sea of
heads) naturalize and externalize the process by which in the
unconscious lake the dullness of some sinking dunces is trans-
mitted to others. The frantic activities of Grub Street are subdued
to a kind of settled order by the irresistible power of the vortex.
The adherents of dullness are a vast *involuntary* throng, and the
dusky Queen is a Queen of Darkness whose motion reverses that
which, in Descarte's account, brought light into being. On the
first day of creation, says the 1670 *Discourse*, with an eye on
Genesis, "Light was made before the sun . . . M. *Des Cartes* hath
supposed, that there were formed divers *Vortexes* or *Whirl-pools*,
of these little round Bodies and that many of them turning round
and about one and the same Center, a part of the matter, which
fills up their Intervalls, was gathered towards the Center, whence
it did propel the *Globules* which surround it; so that this pressure
of the *Globules*, made light in all those places, where was found

a sufficient conflux and heap of subtile matter."[12] "Conglobulation" is a key concept in seventeenth-century accounts of creation—Milton's Raphael, for example, speaks of "drops on dust conglobing from the drie" (*Paradise Lost*, VII, 292). There is therefore no need to suppose Pope directly acquainted with any of the numerous illustrations which appeared in the 1644 *Principia* and in many subsequent discussions. They assist the modern reader, however, to take more confidently the point of Pope's cosmic wit. Figs. 1 and 2 are from the account in Book III of the *Principia*, of stellar, planetary and cometary motions and show the disposition of particles into vortices; the first could suggest cohering orbs of bees, and the second shows the track of a comet, transiently responding to the vortices but essentially independent.

Fig. 1

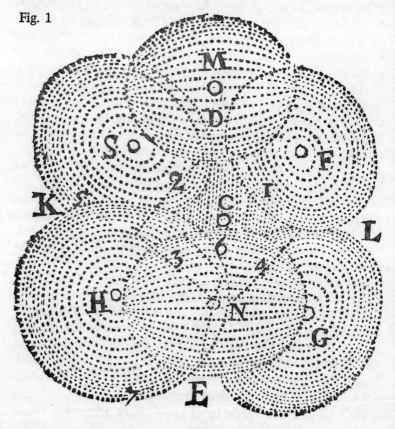

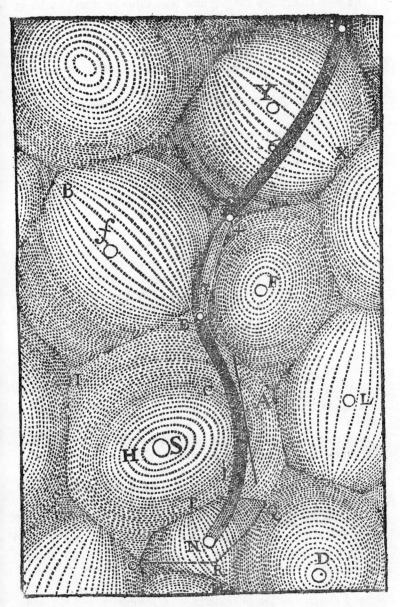

Fig. 2

The note transposes the physical laws into the moral world, in a manner characteristic of much cosmic speculation before and after Leibnitz. It says of the eccentrics that "Their use in their Perihelion, or nearest approach to Dulness, is the same in the moral World, as that of the *Comets* in the natural, namely to refresh and recreate the Dryness and decays of the system" (IV, 76–101n). Back in the poem there are no true comets, for the "weak rebels" do not escape the Grub Street vortex, and even those who come from afar, stay to pay due homage. The metaphor still serves well, however, as a gloss on Pope's own art in relation to the Grub Street scene. The art, as it were, visits the vortex and goes on its way. The energies and insights of literary tradition are not totally circumscribed by the "culture" of the day—either its mode of production or its pervasive ideology—but have their own continuity and momentum. Hence the effect, powerful in Pope's poetry, that the autonomous, self-sustaining activities of Augustan London are exposed to the re-creating power of other times and places. To speak of Hebraic or Classical tradition, of Homer, Virgil, Horace or Milton as "presences" in *The Dunciad*, is not simply to say that imitation in these literary modes was a gentlemanly pastime which other gentlemen were prepared to patronize. It is to recognize that through the arts of imitation the civilization of the time was immensely able to visit itself from a distance and so "refresh and recreate the Dryness and decays of the system". It is a privilege that not all civilizations have, either because the artist lapses into the vortex or because he is expelled from it.

The fourth book of *The Dunciad*, however, finally abstains from offering the kind of comfort that might be derived from reflecting on the Pope-Warburton note. For it leaves the impression that Pope felt himself to be confronting a virulent and implacable historical process. It is usual to represent the process, expressed throughout the poem by images of the Lord Mayor's procession, as the rise of the new mercantile bourgeoisie with its reading and theatre-going public. Pope can then be heard as the reactionary and nostalgic voice of a dying order—that of a court supported by a landed aristocracy and gentry. But Pope himself had proclaimed the civilization of trade in *Windsor Forest*, and his satire in the Essays on the Use of Riches had alighted on "Timon" and Buckingham as well as Hopkins and "Balaam". Pope's allegiance was not to a social class or to a political party (" 'Tis the same rope at several ends they twist") but to a community of wit that included Gay, Garth, Swift and Prior. That community was a cell in a larger and more complex historical growth, taking in Pope's early mentor, Isaiah, and the Roman satirists, and reaching to Clough and to Arnold's "aliens", and to all who disdain class allegiances and seek to transcend them. Pope's is not a patrician art, holding the populace in condescension or contempt, but it is actively hostile to that vulgarity of public taste which made Curll prosperous and Cibber and Welsted "famous", and which still provoked Lawrence's wrath two hundred years later:

> Today the public is tickled into laying the golden egg. With imaginative words and individual meanings it is tricked into giving the great goose-cackle of mob-acquiescence. *Vox populi, vox Dei*. It has always been so, and will always be so. Why? Because the public has not enough wit to distinguish between mob-meaning and individual meaning. The mass is for ever vulgar because it can't distinguish between its own original feelings and feelings which are diddled into existence by the exploiter.
>
> (*Phoenix*, 1936 [1967], p. 176)

The world of *The Dunciad* is still familiar enough: great cities continue to create garbage, hack writers to satisfy our huge appetite for trifles, pedants to traffic in banalities masked as profundities, and scholiasts to "explain a thing till all men doubt it / And write about it, Goddess, and about it". In the dialect of our own protesting dunces, we cart our loads of crap to market, and it is still possible for an advertised English "poet" to piss in a public pot at a city festival under the patronage of the Arts Council: "His rapid waters in their passage burn".

If the comedy still bites, however, the revelation still illuminates. The Lucretian idea of creation, touched occasionally in the poem, makes the great movement from void to void exalting and exhilarating, for we create whatever significance there is in the interim. It was Pope's privilege to create a poem which refreshed the purgative resources of the language, which from one point of view was to hasten what a note calls the Lucretian "Dissolution of the natural world into Night and Chaos". In the same note Pope entertains the Lucretian hope that "a new one should arise", but in the poem the new world brings "saturnian days of

209

Lead and Gold" in which wealth without intelligence ("wit") breeds boredom and inanity and leaves the stage wide open to the antics of Rich and Cibber. In its final movement the poem apparently finds no lasting solace in wit. The elegiac note is orchestrated by despair, the comet of the footnote displaced by a meteorite:

> In vain, in vain,—the all-composing Hour
> Resistless falls: The Muse obeys the Pow'r.
> She comes! she comes! the sable Throne behold
> Of *Night* Primaeval, and of *Chaos* old!
> Before her, *Fancy's* gilded clouds decay,
> And all its varying Rain-bows die away.
> *Wit* shoots in vain its momentary fires,
> The meteor drops, and in a flash expires.
> As one by one, at dread Medea's strain,
> The sick'ning stars fade off th'ethereal plain;
> As Argus' eyes by Hermes' wand opprest,
> Clos'd one by one to everlasting rest;
> Thus at her felt approach, and secret might,
> *Art* after *Art* goes out, and all is Night.
>
> (IV, 627–40)

At precisely the point where Pope dramatizes the pathos of his own expendable art, however, that art is at its most assured. If "Universal Darkness" has not yet buried all it is because the dead wits at least are still alive, reaching us from outside our own vortex. Creativity is a condition of life; without it, at the end of an exhausting cosmic day in Grub Street, we are composed (indeed composted) to everlasting rest.

NOTES

1 References are to the Twickenham Edition to which I am much indebted; all are to the B text except when prefixed by "A".

2 In what follows I am conscious of indebtedness to much valuable work on *The Dunciad*, and in particular to essays by F. R. Leavis, Hugo M. Reichard, Alvin B. Kernan and H. H. Erskine-Hill, reprinted in Maynard Mack, *Essential Articles: Alexander Pope* (London, 1964, 1967), to Aubrey L. Williams, *Pope's Dunciad* (London, 1955), and to Reuben Brower, *Alexander Pope: The Poetry of Allusion* (Oxford, 1959).

3 Quotations from Milton are from B. A. Wright's edition (1962).

4 Arthur Sherbo also connects the word with "generation" and compares "genial spring" (*Windsor Forest*, 135) and "Genial Ray" (*The Temple of Fame*, 4); see, "No Single Scholiast", *MLR* 65, 1970, pp. 503–16.

5 Compare Hogarth's "The Distressed Poet" in which Theobald's misery is sympathetically depicted yet glossed from *The Dunciad*.

6 Milton uses the word, for example, in Bk. II, 80.

7 Cibber's self-delusion assists him in creating in the patrons of the city press and theatre a false sense of their own function and importance.

8 Kernan observes, "Dulness in the many forms and shapes it assumes, pours, spreads, sluices, creeps, drawls on, stretches, spawns, crawls, meanders, ekes out, flounders on, slips, rolls, extends, waddles, involves, gushes, swells, loiters, decays, slides, wafts, lumbers, blots o'erflows, trickles." (*Essential Articles* [1964], p. 729).

9 See Maynard Mack, *The Gardens and the City: Retirement and Politics in the Later Poetry of Pope, 1713–43* (Oxford, 1969), pp. 143–49.

10 See Marjorie Nicolson and G. S. Rousseau, *"This Long Disease, My Life": Alexander Pope and the Sciences* (Princeton, 1968), especially pp. 199–206. In a long discussion of Pope and the vortices the authors draw attention to Pope's more precise use of "gravitation" (as distinct from "gravity") in Book Four, and to the apparent disparity between the poem and the note in its treatment of "eccentrics". Warburton may indeed have been reading the Cartesian documents more attentively than the poem, but Pope could have welcomed the idea (if only in a footnote) that true wits, like comets, refreshed the system in passing.

11 M. Des Fourneillis, *A Discourse etc.*, "By Francis Bayle" (1670).

12 *Des Fourneillis, A Discourse*, p. 12.

11

Pope's Bestiary: The Iconography of Deviance

by CLIVE T. PROBYN

> I am his Highness' Dog at *Kew*;
> Pray tell me Sir, whose Dog are you?
> Pope, *Epigram* (1738)

> But who would have expected that both Tennyson and Pope should mention the Amphisbaena?
> T. H. White, *The Book of Beasts* (1954)

Tennyson's sleeping Kraken and W. B. Yeats's "rough beast" in *Second Coming* ("A shape with lion body and the head of a man / A gaze blank and pitiless as the sun") indicate that the symbolic appeal of mysterious animals has never quite disappeared either from the poetic consciousness or from imaginative currency. The bestiary as such began in oral tradition long before it was taken up by Pliny, Physiologus, Isidore of Seville (*c.* 630), the medieval bestiaries of the twelfth century, and the sixteenth-century naturalists (Gesner and Aldrovandus). Though it was conceived as a serious work of natural history the bestiary provided occasions for sharply sceptical attacks on human credulity: Lucretius ridiculed the belief in centaurs and chimaera in *De Rerum Natura* (on strictly physiological grounds), as did Sir Thomas Browne in *Pseudodoxia Epidemica* (1646).[1] Yet elements of the traditional bestiary flourish in Ariosto, in Du Bartas, in Spenser, in Milton, and in Dryden (one thinks immediately of *The Hind and the Panther*). But what of Pope's position? His is the voice of a city-, if not court- or country-orientated poet, its accents moulded by the unmysterious post-Renaissance dialect of Newton, of Locke, of the Royal Society (whose Robert Hooke revealed in *Micrographia*, 1665, a miniature insect world under every leaf, astonishing but nonetheless intelligible). Pope's well-known epitaph for Newton expressed a comprehensive acceptance of the scientific enlightenment: "Nature, and Nature's Laws lay hid in Night. / God said, *Let Newton be!* and All was Light." Swift had mercilessly pilloried the scientists of the Royal Society for speculative inanities in Gulliver's third voyage, and used a beast fable in the fourth voyage in order to shock man into a sense of his rational limitations. Pope shared Swift's contempt for those who neglected moral philosophy in favour of natural philosophy and on one particular occasion demonstrated the limits of his tolerance of zoological dissectors. Stephen Hales was a neighbour of Pope and a distinguished animal physiologist, but some of his experiments were a moral affront to Pope's view of the animal creation and of man's stewardship of it. Spence exclaimed: "What, he cuts up rats?", and Pope replied,

"Aye and dogs too!" (and with what emphasis and concern he spoke it.) "Indeed, he commits most of these barbarities with the thought of its being of use to men. But how do we know that we have the right to kill creatures that we are so little above as dogs, for our curiosity, or even for some use to us?"[2]

Taking the lead from Pope, critics have observed Pope on dogs, and Pope's use of insect imagery; but with very few exceptions Pope's extraordinarily rich manipulation of the broader context of animal imagery has been ignored.[3] There have been some curious near-misses, however.

In her study of Pope's poetry Edith Sitwell found "a kind of smoky and appalling beauty . . . a kind of hell-born inspiration" in these two lines from *The Dunciad*: "So watchful Bruin forms, with plastic care, / Each growing Lump, and brings it to a Bear."[4] It is hard to say what Sitwell believed she discerned in these lines, but certain that she completely overlooked their reference. And neither is the allusion here to "folklore", as one recent and more percipient commentator puts it.[5] Pope's allusion is not a smoky horror dredged from his subconscious mind but a bright literary topos of maternal solicitude. The bestiary describes how the bear "sculptures her brood with her mouth . . . For they say that these creatures produce a formless foetus, giving birth to something like a bit of pulp, and this the mother-bear arranges into the proper legs and arms by licking it."[6] It was not required by Pope that his

213

readers should carry in their minds the particular twelfth-century bestiary from which this passage is taken: it had developed an independent life. Gloucester had used the analogy ("Like to a chaos, or an unlick'd bear-whelp": *Henry VI, Part 3*, III, 2, 161–62) to depict his deformed body and to convey his self-loathing. John Donne deployed the image in Elegie XVIII, "Loves Progress":

> Love is a bear-whelp born, if we o're lick
> Our love, and force it new strange shapes to take,
> We erre, and of a lump a monster make.

But for Pope the most recent previous usage was in the final, sumptuous product of Dryden's last years, *Fables Ancient and Modern* (1700). In his translation of Book XV of Ovid's *Metamorphoses*, "Of the Pythagorean Philosophy", Dryden observes:

> The cubs of bears, a living lump appear,
> When whelp'd, and no determin'd Figure wear.
> Their Mother licks 'em into Shape, and gives
> As much of Form, as she herself receives.

The particular inflection which Dryden gives to the figure may have provided Pope with a hint for the *Dunciad*. The creation and lineage of the Dunces generates a mirror image of decent order, a complex paradigm of formlessness, an increasingly attenuated tradition of effete plagiarists, nerveless imitators, illustrated in terms of biological mutants, animal fictions and beasts of a surrealist generation not less but more fantastic than anything in the bestiaries.

Just as the term "lick into shape" has passed into the language of ordinary discourse, so the language of Pope's commentators occasionally poaches from Pope's animal language in order to feed a subjective critical response. Sitwell again aptly remarks of the line in *An Essay on Criticism* about Camilla (who "Flies o'er th'unbending Corn, and skims along the Main") that "The dipping and bending of that line is miraculous. No swallow ever flew more lightly."[7] Another study refers to the swelling tide of Dulness in Book IV of *The Dunciad* as "that hydra-headed monster that infests Parnassus in a thousand disguises and undermines the fair temple of true literature".[8] I quote these two examples for a positive reason. Both critics have *felt* the undeniable movement and urgency of Pope's animal imagery, but in both cases they choose a meta-language which is itself already penetrated with animal imagery in order to describe their reactions to Pope. What has happened is that Pope's language, already saturated with either *inferred* or *overt* animal imagery, has been submerged by the success of its evocations. In this respect Pope's poetry is, I hope to show, unusual: animal homologues are a habitual element in its rhetoric of satiric contempt, vital realizations of Pope's imagination, a feature of both style and subject, at times an inseparable amalgam of tenor and vehicle, a way of looking at the world and of man's part in it.

Beast analogies of human society were commonplace in Pope's time, if not for ours, and certain parallels came to hand almost by instinct. Apart from traditional bestiary lore the most obvious source was the animal fable. One example will have to suffice. The first book of *The Dunciad* closes with what Aubrey Williams calls "a prophetic statement about the extension of Dulness' reign over Britain".[9] But the Book actually ends with the words "God save King Log!" Pope's note refers us to John Ogilby's paraphrase of Aesop's *Fables* (1651), but satire of the relatively obscure Ogilby is the least important function of the allusion. In Aesop's fable the discontented frogs petition Jupiter for a strong ruler. Jupiter sends a log instead, which the frogs proceed to worship. After more discontent and a further petition they are sent a predatory stork, with obvious consequences. Moralized as a sermon against popular discontent in the better-known translation of Sir Roger L'Estrange, the *significatio* is given thus:

> The Mobile are uneasie without a Ruler: They are as Restless with one; and the oftner they shift, the Worse they Are; So that Government, or No Government; a King of God's Making, or of the Peoples, or none at all; the Multitude are never to be satisfied.[10]

Pope's assembled dunces are "the Hoarse nation" of frogs: their acclamation "God save King Log" is an assertion of their idiocy, an admission (Pope implies) that they too are prepared for empty totemic worship. They need the pomp and circumstance of an *empty* kingship in order to provide the form and coherence which their anarchic natures seek. But by brilliant semantic suggestion Pope has also insinuated another meaning into this tag from the beast fable: *Log* is a suitably abbreviated form, a travesty, of

Logos, the creating word which is at once Pope's ideal and the scourge of the Dunces. It evokes the paradigm of *Genesis* in which they are to be conjugated before they are condemned. Apart from demonstrating the conciseness of Pope's satiric wit this single locution also demonstrates what Pope could do with such commonplaces as the fable and the *Genesis* story. In fact Pope's use of conventional or hand-me-down beast analogies such as the two I have discussed is comparatively rare. As we can see in the later portrait of Sporus Pope develops his own complex, allusive approach to the beast image which generates a new grammar of contempt in which theological imagery is only one item, but hybridization the dominating idea.

1

The central metaphoric vehicles of Pope's cultural satire are animate in a particular sense. The intellectual disaster of *Grub* Street begins with embryonic, foetus-like growths and develops into finished abortions. Goddess Dulness observes:

> How hints, like spawn, scarce quick in embryo lie,
> How new-born nonsense first is taught to cry,
> Maggots half-formed in rhyme exactly meet,
> And learn to crawl upon poetic feet.
> Here one poor word an hundred clenches makes,
> And ductile dulness new meanders takes;
> There motley Images her fancy strike,
> Figures ill pair'd, and Similies unlike.
> She sees a Mob of Metaphors advance,
> Pleas'd with the Madness of the mazy dance.[11]

Here the brain-pattern of a disordered intelligence is given free rein to turn its cerebral chaos into animated fictions. Pope's language fuses real simile ("like spawn") with actualized metaphor ("new-born nonsense"), and breathes into the animal imagery the rhythmic heart-beat of a prosodic and semantic progress ("And ductile dulness new meanders takes"). This example combines the two central types of beast or insect imagery in Pope: the (initial) overt comparison and the (consequential) inferred or suppressed metaphor which is often characterized by an ambivalent motive power. It is to this distinction I now turn, for the essential and most interesting feature of Pope's poetic bestiary is change, metamorphosis, mutation, the merging of species into fantastic forms of what Pope called "equivocal generation".

At its simplest level Pope's avoidance of specificity is a technique of poetic elevation: "a thousand winged wonders", "Aerial Audience", and "the green myriads in the peopled grass" (respectively from *The Temple of Fame*, *Spring* and *An Essay on Man*, I) are liberating formulae which allow Pope to suggest pertinent didactic homologues between the human and animal worlds. A generic noun is often qualified by a specific and usually mobilizing adjective: thus "rising game", "whirring pheasant", "mounting lark", and in *An Essay on Man* Pope classifies all non-human animals by the habitat in which they move: "all that roam the wood, / Or wing the sky, or roll along the flood". Elsewhere in the *Essay* (III, 184) the anthropomorphic intention determines the nature of the analogue: man may learn a lesson in social organization from the "Ant's republic, and the realm of Bees", or the "towns aerial on the waving tree" (l. 182). Learning from the beasts by an intelligent act of the understanding and will is, Pope suggests, the route to the discovery of a planned cosmic harmony; but when the distinctive and special ethical imperatives in man are ignored his nature is literally downgraded in the scale of being. He becomes an animal. The prelapsarian man "walk'd with beast, joint tenant of the shade" (III, l. 152), but postlapsarian man "Murders their species, and betrays their own" (l. 164). The Dunces provide a standing indictment, their intellectual degradation constantly at odds with the obligations of their humanity. Modern huntsmen are metamorphosed like the Homeric sailors were by Circe:

> The vulgar herd turn off to roll with Hogs,
> To run with Horses, or to hunt with Dogs;
> But, sad example! never to escape
> Their Infamy, still keep the human shape.
> (*The Dunciad*, IV, ll. 525–28)

Even the reductive similes which satirize by overt analogy are well on the way to a moral metamorphosis, indicating that moral health for Pope is an energy and a resource, not a fixed state. Thus Sappho in *Epistle II. To a Lady*, "at her toilet's greasy task", is encompassed by the image of evanescent insect-life: "So morning Insects that in muck begun, / Shine, buzz, and fly-blow in the

217

setting-sun!" (ll. 27–8). A further stage of inferential animal metaphor is indicated in the well-known line from *An Essay on Criticism*, "And ten low words oft creep in one dull line," where the unstated decapodic creature is deftly motivated by the loco-motion of syntax and rhythm. Pope's interest in this kind of in-ferred metaphor re-shapes his use of more conventional "surface" metaphors, such as the well-known comparison of the medieval scholastic theologians to spiders spinning insubstantial frame-works in the air from their own guts. With little modifications the image was used, among others, by Bacon, Milton, Cowley, and Swift in *The Battle of the Books*.[12] Pope firmly classifies them by genre to a dusty and motion-*less* purlieu both topographically and satirically appropriate; "*Scotists* and *Thomists*, now, in Peace re-main, / Amidst their kindred *Cobwebs* in *Duck-Lane*" (*Essay on Criticism*, ll. 444–45).[13] Even a dead metaphor can be given a new half-life.

The more one analyzes Pope's animal imagery the more one realizes that this particular taxonomic motif involved almost the entire range of his poetic resources. There are synecdochic images such as "the Finny Prey" (*Windsor Forest*); the "Tortoise [shell] and Elephant [ivory] unite" their natural disparities to form the expensive and ingenious combs on the pampered Belinda's dress-ing table in *The Rape of the Lock*; zeugma silently humiliates the proud or indicates mental and ethical disarray in the *Rape* ("Men, Monkies, Lap-Dogs, Parrots, perish all"); the list flattens all zoological hierarchy to the same moral level of self-enclosed conceit. Pope's contribution to the levelling wisdom of the King of Brobdingnag concludes:

> When Pride in such contemptuous Beings lies,
> In Beetles, Britons, Bugs and Butterflies
> Shall we, like Reptiles, glory in Conceit?
> Humility's the Virtue of the Great.[14]

Depending on the specific context the same animal image may be incipiently symbolic or overtly metaphoric: thus Aaron Hill escapes contamination in the Dunces' mud-diving contest (Book II of *The Dunciad*), "And mounts far off, among the swans of Thames" (l. 286). Pope spares Hill's poetry this time, but the verdict on the man is "not proven". On the other hand John Taylor, the Water poet, is "sweet bird of Thames" in the *Dunciad*

Variorum and in the 1743 version becomes "Once swan of Thames, tho' now he sings no more" (Book III, l. 20). There are also conventional beast associations such as "Morning Cock", "cow-like udders", "ox-like eyes", and periphrastic formulae such as (Cibber's) "gray-goose weapon" (pen), and what Pope called "A Simile with a long tail, in the manner of Homer" (*Dunciad Variorum*, II, 237n.), in this case an animal image attenuated to the point of absurdity: "As when the long-ear'd milky mothers wait / At some sick miser's triple-bolted gate". Serious analogical transferences from human social hierarchy to those in the animal world do not come easily to Pope, and when they do occur they seem inchoate, weak echoes of the Elizabethan Renaissance system of interlocking and inter-dependent hierarchies (most familiar perhaps from Ulysses' speech on degree in *Troilus and Cressida*). In Pope the hint of such hierarchical cross-reference is soon submerged in a keener sense of their limited validity in a new world governed not by ideals of Renaissance kingship but by merchant capitalism and a money economy: "Well, if a King's a Lion, at the least / The People are a many-headed Beast: / Can they direct what measures to pursue, / Who know themselves so little what to do?" (*First Epistle of the First Book of Horace Imitated*, ll. 120–23). Conversely, Pope's imagination is quickened by the prospect of dis-order: the new world of Dulness, "to Nature's laws unknown", lets loose from the recesses of the cultural memory the medieval and mythological creatures of superstition (Book III, ll. 235–38):

> All sudden, Gorgons hiss, and Dragons glare,
> And ten-horn'd fiends and Giants rush to war.
> Hell rises, Heav'n descends, and dance on Earth,
> Gods, imps, and monsters . . .[15]

whilst in the animal creation "The forests dance, the rivers upward rise, / Whales sport in woods, and dolphins in the skies" (245–46). Amorphousness and ambivalence as subject matter are represented in style by one metaphoric class merging with another, and sometimes without the first becoming fully developed: thus the poets without Wit "Still humming on, their drowzy Course they keep, / And *lash'd* so long, like *Tops*, are lash'd *asleep*" (*Essay on Criticism*, ll. 600–1), are implicitly animate (drones?) on one side of *humming*, inanimate children's playthings (which

219

Johnson exquisitely defined as "an inverted conoid which children set to turn on the point, continuing its motion with a whip") on the other side of the verb.

By comparison with such subtle effects in Pope's poetic bestiary, deeply embedded in the very rhythm and grammar, his prose bestiary in chapter VI of *Peri Bathous: Or, Of the Art of Sinking in Poetry* is almost mechanically unsubtle. Pope here lists thirty sets of initials under nine classifications, each identified with an animal: Flying Fishes, Swallows, Ostriches, Parrots, Didappers, Porpoises, Frogs, Eels, and Tortoises. The list of writers thus attacked is predictable (Gildon, Theobald, Rochester, Hervey, Eusden, Cibber, Dennis, Oldmixon, among others).[16] Even so, there is a rationale behind their animal identifications which closely relates to the theme of metamorphosis and mutation in the poetry. Eight out of the nine creatures exist in more than one element, more or less amphibious in the case of the flying fish, didappers, porpoise, frog, eel, and perhaps the swallow—whose migratory habits were a total mystery at the time, as any reader of Johnson or even Gilbert White will recall[17]—whereas the ostrich is a winged but flightless bird, the parrot a talker without understanding, the tortoise a creature with an elegant shell conjoined with ponderous body (as Pope points out). In a fixed system of habitats and elements each of these animals suggests an untidiness or a confusion of purpose, a natural aberration cross-referred to examples of artistic disorder. In the same way Welsted is described as a crab (a shellfish with legs) in the *Dunciad*. Artimesia in Pope's imitation of the Earl of Dorset is likened to the parti-coloured magpie. ("A stately, worthless Animal, / That plies the Tongue, and wags the Tail, / All Flutter, Pride, and Talk", ll. 21–3). The wit-turned-critic-turned-poet in *An Essay on Criticism* (ll. 36–43) is the sterile product of breeding between two species, "neither *Horse* nor *Ass* . . . as half form'd Insects on the Bank of *Nile*; / Unfinish'd things, one knows not what to call, / Their Generation's so *equivocal*." Sterile hybrids are thus generated from the confusion of purposes mis-applied talents, and otherwise discrete literary genres. The class of Duncely graduands in the last book of *The Dunciad* is made up of "Whate'er of mungril no one class admits, / A wit with dunces, and a dunce with wits" (ll. 89–90), and in the Cave of Poverty and Poetry (Book I, ll. 33–8), "Hence Bards, like Proteus long in vain ty'd down, / Escape in Monsters,

and amaze the town." The symbolic beast of this chaotic aristocracy is a genetic freak, only imaginable by accepting the appalling
comic bestiality of a Swiss theatre manager and a nocturnal bird:
"And lo! her bird (a monster of a fowl, / Something betwixt a
Heideggre and owl)" (I, ll. 289–90).

2

Sinking into beast categories is, in Pope's satire, a zoological
analogue for the betrayal of moral and cultural standards by failure in intelligence, in scholarship, in taste, in morality. It has
been said that what interests Pope "is less the similarity of species
in being all expressive of the divine delight in sheer plenitude than
the fixity of the distinguishing lines which separate them. An "in-
superable line" has been drawn as a boundary between species,
and the coherence of the whole Chain of being depends upon
distinctions and subordination—that is, almost upon the divine
principle of genre."[18] This is perfectly accurate in terms of what
Pope believed as doctrine: the *Essay on Man* is an extended contemplation on the notion of hierarchical order as heaven's first law.
But, like Ulysses' speech in *Troilus and Cressida*, the *Essay on Man*
sets out doctrine which the rest of Pope's poetry illustrates only
by negative images. Pope's sense of chaos and disorder was, like
Swift's, the energizing force of his satire, exercising a fatal attraction for the positive celebrant of cosmic harmony. Pope's most
subtle artistry went into the cogent, imaginative re-creation of
ambivalent, hybrid imagery of man's weakness in the actual
world, where mutability is the essence, not the accident of his
being. The animal imagery in Pope's poetry is designed to enforce
a positive moral standard in human affairs by means of a negative
satiric method. A conviction of the reality of distinct boundaries
between species provided Pope with the confidence to create
imaginative transgressors of those boundaries. Pope's greatest
fear was that the hybrids and deviants would prevail and become
the norms of a new species. It is in this sense that ethics and
anthropology become intertwined. Not even the theologian, perhaps, has supreme confidence in their separate identities. Lady
Philosophy's instructions to Boethius in *The Consolation of Philosophy* include the precept that "wicked men cease to be what
they were; but the appearance of their human bodies, which they

221

keep, shows that once they were men. To give oneself to evil, therefore, is to lose one's human nature." She then provides a system of animal analogues for moral decline:

> . . . you cannot adjudge him for a man whom you see trans-formed by vices. The violent plunderer of others' wealth burns with avarice: you would say he was like a wolf. The wild and restless man exercises his tongue in disputes: you will compare him to a dog. The secret trickster rejoices that he succeeds in his frauds: let him be on a level with the little foxes. He that cannot govern his anger roars: let him be thought to have the spirit of a lion. The timorous and fugitive is afraid of things not fearful: let him be reckoned like a deer. The stupid sluggard is numb: he lives an ass's life. The fickle and inconstant changes his pursuits: he is no different from the birds. A man is drowned in foul and unclean lusts: he is gripped by the pleasure of a filthy sow. So he who having left goodness aside has ceased to be a man, since he cannot pass over into the divine state, turns into a beast.[19]

What we have here is a moral bestiary, providing a counterpoint to human failings by a separate scheme of animal characteristics from which similes may be drawn. Sin is a consequence of the merging of animal attributes with a failing moral will. Similarly, what Pope does may be geometrically impossible but morally effective: he brings the parallels together, so that a man can be brought down to the level of the beasts not only by the external act of the theologian's imagination grasping for a convenient analogy, but by the result of an *inner* failure of individual moral intelligence, a betrayal in himself of what Boethius called *goodness*. There is no obvious equivalent in Pope's work for this single concept of *goodness* (except perhaps the slippery notion of *Taste*), but we can be sure that above everything else Pope's good man possesses a sense of genre and an awareness of his own separated position in the chain of moral and physical creation, together with a recognition of reciprocal responsibilities which are distinct and ascertainable. There is no single individual like this in Pope, but certain individuals possess some of these virtues: Pope comple-mented Swift on his sense of appropriate style and place and dedicated the *Dunciad* to him ("Dean, Drapier, Bickerstaff, Gulli-ver", I, l. 20); there is Burlington's good (architectural) sense, "your just, your noble rules" (*Epistle to Burlington*, l. 25), which

"Jones and Palladio to themselves restore" (l. 193); and there is the economic paternalism of the Man of Ross ("Him portion'd maids, apprentic'd orphans blest, / The young who labour, and the old who rest," *Epistle to Bathurst*, ll. 267–68). There is, however, no need to speculate on the obverse: Pope provided a complete iconography of deviance in his portrait of Sporus, wherein every conceivable genre is violated:

> Let *Sporus* tremble—'What? that thing of silk,
> *Sporus*, that mere white curd of Ass's milk?
> Satire or Sense alas! can *Sporus* feel?
> Who breaks a Butterfly upon a Wheel?
> Yet let me flap this Bug with gilded wings,
> This painted Child of Dirt that stinks and stings;
> Whose Buzz the Witty and the Fair annoys,
> Yet wit ne'er tastes, and Beauty ne'er enjoys,
> So well-bred Spaniels civilly delight
> In mumbling of the Game they dare not bite.
> Eternal Smiles his Emptiness betray,
> As shallow streams run dimpling all the way.
> Whether in florid Impotence he speaks,
> And, as the Prompter beathes, the Puppet squeaks;
> Or at the Ear of *Eve*, familiar Toad,
> Half Froth, half Venom, spits himself abroad,
> In Puns, or Politicks, or Tales, or Lyes,
> Or Spite, or Smut, or Rymes, or Blasphemies.
> His Wit all see-saw between *that* and *this*,
> Now high, now low, now Master up, now Miss,
> And he himself one vile Antithesis.
> Amphibious Thing! that acting either Part,
> The trifling Head, or the corrupted Heart!
> Fop at the Toilet, Flatt'rer at the Board,
> Now trips a Lady, and now struts a Lord.
> *Eve's* Tempter thus the Rabbins have exprest,
> A Cherub's face, a Reptile all the rest;
> Beauty that shocks you, Parts that none will trust,
> Wit that can creep, and Pride that licks the dust.[20]

The shocking validity of this famous piece of character-assassination arises from a paradox. The character of Sporus, as an image in the mind, is never allowed to come into sharp focus. Pope has, it could be argued, conveyed more than he has contained: the rapid transmogrification of Sporus into a flimsy entomological fiction is somehow at odds with the depth of violent hatred and the resonant theological implications which accompany it. As Arbuthnot says, What is the point of breaking a butterfly on a wheel? Whatever the reasons, Pope proceeds to do just that. Yet for all its swarming profusion of detail there remains an arm's length condescension, even a kind of fastidiousness in Pope's insect imagery. Sporus does not simply annoy "the Witty and the Fair", as Pope claims: he violates Pope's notion of decent order as well, and the result is a complete paradigm of transgressed genres, a crazy and pernicious anti-grammar of sexuality, literary art, social manners and physical appearance. Content and style, tenor and vehicle are inseparable: the Sporus portrait is Pope's most studied essay in metaphoric ambivalence. By comparison, Swift's image of the Yahoo is the result of a deep, vertical slice into man's fallen nature and into the irredeemable legacies of his animal parentage. Pope's imagination is more concerned with surfaces: the Satanic image of Sporus may well reflect Pope's sense of the real evil and consequent social infection represented by Sporus, but it is significant that the analogy is not primarily to *Paradise Lost* but to medieval biblical exegesis ("thus the Rabbins have exprest"[21]), i.e. to iconography. If Sporus's gutless androgyny is not memorable in the same manner as Swift's visceral Yahoos it is because Pope is primarily concerned with a social phenomenon and not with an image of general psychic collapse. The genres remain intact because Sporus is only Lord Hervey, not Everyman. Whereas Swift dissects, Pope amputates away the disease, and can therefore maintain his belief in the chain of being and in its system of linked but discrete entities: "On superior pow'rs / Were we to press, inferior might on ours" (*Essay on Man*, I, 241–42). From a firmly hierarchical system Pope ventures out with confidence to create its imaginative antithesis, i.e. a surrealist vision of genetic anarchy.

Few of Pope's readers would claim, I think, that the strident philosophical confidence of the *Essay on Man* has made better poetry than the upside-down world of *The Dunciad*. Even so, the equivocal forms in the latter arose as perversions of Pope's serious convictions, and he was not alone in the period. There were others who looked at the contiguity of animal species with alarmed fascination. The cosmic toryism of Soame Jenyns's *Free Inquiry into the Nature and Origin of Evil* (1757) was, to Johnson, a meditation to which humanity was unequal. At the bottom of the chain,

> Between the lowest positive existence and nothing, wherever we suppose positive existence to cease, is another chasm infinitely deep; where there is room again for endless orders of subordinate nature, continued for ever and ever, and yet infinitely superior to non-existence.[22]

and likewise at the top, where Jenyns imagines "some beings above us, *who may deceive, torment, or destroy us for the ends only of their own pleasure or utility*", Johnson gleefully remarks:

> I cannot resist the temptation of contemplating this analogy, which I think he might have carried further very much to the advantage of his argument. He might have shown that these *hunters whose game is man* have many sports analogous to our own. As we drown whelps and kittens, they amuse themselves now and then with sinking a ship, and stand round the fields of *Blenheim* or the walls of *Prague*, as we encircle a cock-pit. As we shoot a bird flying, they take a man in the midst of his business or pleasure, and knock him down with an apoplexy.[23]

One wonders whether Johnson had entirely forgotten the celestial interference in human affairs of Greek tragedy or even Gloucester's "As flies to wanton boys, are we to the gods; / They kill us for their sport" (*King Lear*, IV, i, 36). Presumably any attempt to explain evil, in the sense of justifying it, makes self-evident nonsense of something as terrifying as Gloucester's anguish, thus Johnson's reaction to Jenyns's argument was to deny it the dignity of serious consideration. But nevertheless Pope and Jenyns's concept of the ladder of creation provided comparative anthropologists with the opportunity to suggest in all seriousness the kind of transferences which Pope's imagination created only for satiric effect. By far the most unnerving was the comparison to be drawn between man and the apes. Lucretius had categorically denied that there ever could be "creatures with a double nature, combining organs of different origin in a single body", and went on to assert that "each species develops according to its own kind, and they all guard their specific characters in obedience to the laws of nature."[24] But others were less sure about the impossibility of the merging of species. Within twenty years of the *Essay on Man* Buffon was suggesting both biological hypotheses and anatomical homologies for the community of descent which would not only have outraged Pope's conviction of definable boundaries, but also have suggested an unwelcome confirmation of the moral descent explicit in his satire of contemporary cultural disorders:

> Not only the ass and the horse, but also man, the apes, the quadrupeds, and all the animals, might be regarded as constituting a single family . . . If it were admitted that the ass is of the family of the horse, and differs from the horse only because it has varied from the original form, one could equally well say that the ape is of the family of man, and he is a degenerate (dégénéré) man, that man and ape have a common origin; that, in fact, all the families, among plants as well as animals, have come from a single stock, and that all animals are descended from a single animal, from which have sprung in the course of time, as a result of progress or of degeneration, all the other races of animals.[25]

But in 1752 the evolutionary implications of this were far too heterodox and Buffon enters an immediate retraction:

> But no! It is certain from revelation that all animals have participated equally in the grace of direct creation, and that the first pair of every species issued fully formed from the hands of the creator.[26]

James Burnett, Lord Monboddo, thought that the orang-utang was "altogether man, both outside and inside, excepting some small variations, such as cannot make a specific difference between the two animals", but hastily added:

> Though I hold the Orang Utang to be of our species, it must not be supposed that I think the monkey or ape . . . participates of our nature . . .[27]

Pope's theriomorphic imagery worked in the same way. If the Dunces, or anyone else for that matter, fall beneath the required standards in intelligence, taste, or moral behaviour, the simian species can be elevated into the space on the chain of being thereby vacated. Pope thus makes negative and positive ventures into comparative anthropology: his satire distributes contempt on the one side and intellectual humility on the other—the Dunces are "Monkey-mimicks" and, when a race of superior beings lately saw the publication of Newton's works, they observed "A mortal Man unfold all Nature's law, / Admir'd such wisdom in an

earthly shape, / And shew'd a NEWTON as we shew an Ape"
(*Essay on Man*, II, ll. 32–4), i.e. as an exceptional and amusing example of a creature groping towards a fundamental intelligence,
but no more than that. The *Principia* is thus, comparatively speaking, only a primer of basic mathematical physics.

Pope's bestiary therefore expands and contracts its rationale
according to the demands of his moral satire. He does not find
a world in Blake's grain of sand, but he does interpret man's
actions in terms of the animal creation. The symmetry of the
world remains a mystery to Pope as much as it was to do for
Blake in *The Tyger*, however, but for Pope the very existence and
perception of that symmetry provided man with the finest opportunity to appreciate the harmony of a providential world:

> Who taught the nations of the fields and wood
> To shun their poison, and to chuse their food?
> Prescient, the tides or tempests to withstand,
> Build on the wave, or arch beneath the sand?
> Who made the spider parallels design,
> Sure as De-moivre, without rule or line?
> Who bid the stork, Columbus-like, explore
> Heav'ns not his own, and worlds unknown before?
> Who calls the council, states the certain day,
> Who forms the phalanx, and who points the way?
> *Essay on Man*, III, 99–108.

Pope's relentless pursuit of human failings by emblematic animal
and insect analogues complements a humanitarianism which is
expressed for the animal creation as such. Pope's *Guardian* paper
61 (21 May 1713) is an impassioned plea, buttressed by classical
and biblical authorities, for man to accept the responsibilities of
his stewardship, and in particular the reciprocal duties conferred
on his pivotal position in the chain of being:

> Mankind are no less, in Proportion, accountable for the ill Use
> of their Dominion over Creatures of the lower Rank of Beings,
> than for the Exercise of Tyranny over their own Species. The more
> entirely the Inferior Creation is submitted to our Power, the more
> answerable we should seem for our mismanagement of it.

It is in this context that Pope's poetic bestiary should be regarded, as the nervous system of his ethical concerns and, perhaps,
as the supreme moral achievement of his imagination. When man

abrogates this stewardship he makes way not only for the automatic elevation of the rough beast from within but also wilfully brings into focus the ultimate apocalypse when "Universal Darkness" will bury all degrees and render the act of moral discrimination a faint memory.

NOTES

1 For a brief, illustrated account of the bestiary tradition, see T. H. White, *The Book of Beasts* (London, 1954), pp. 230–68. This is a prose translation of a Latin bestiary of the twelfth century. Some of my points in this paragraph are condensed from White. The amphisbaena (see White, *op. cit.*, pp. 176–78) was a serpent with two heads. Pope wrote an epigram, *On Burnet and Ducket* (1729–39) which contains the reference: "Thus *Amphisboena* (I have read) / At either end assails; / None knows which leads, or which is lead, / For both Heads are but Tails." For Tennyson's usage, see *Queen Mary*, III, iv, l. 26. In passing, Yeats's "rough beast" seems very like a manticore – a suggestion I owe to my medievalist colleague Mrs. M. A. Twycross (see also White, *op. cit.*, pp. 51–2, and, for other possibilities, A. Norman Jeffares, *A Commentary on the Collected Poems of W. B. Yeats* (London, 1968), pp. 243–44). The manticore also appears in Act V of Gay's *Three Hours after Marriage*, in which Pope collaborated with Arbuthnot. See also *Essay on Man*, I, 215, for the lynx.

2 James M. Osborn, ed. (Spence's) *Observations, Anecdotes, and Characters of Books and Men*, 2 vols. (Oxford, 1966), I, 148.

3 See Norman Ault, *New Light on Pope* (London, 1949), pp. 337–50. Paul Fussell, *The Rhetorical World of Augustan Humanism* (Oxford, 1965), pp. 233–61. For Pope's own "Discourse of Dogs", see the letter to Cromwell, *Correspondence of Alexander Pope*, ed. George Sherburn, 5 vols. (Oxford, 1956), I, 73–5.

4 Edith Sitwell, *Alexander Pope* (London, 1930), p. 276.

5 John E. Sitter, *The Poetry of Pope's Dunciad* (Minneapolis, 1971), p. 14. Sitter notes the bear image in Shakespeare and Donne.

6 White, *op. cit.*, p. 45. Tact prevented White from identifying Sitwell's slip, but he shows clearly enough how crical guesswork results in artificial mystery-making.

7 Sitwell, *op. cit.*, p. 271.

8 E. W. Edmunds, *Pope and his Poetry* (London, 1921), p. 83.

9 Aubrey Williams, *Pope's Dunciad: A Study of its Meaning* (London, 1955), p. 23. There are other sources for Pope's beast analogues: for and adaptation of *Proverbs* 23, 5, see *The Epistle to Bathurst*, ll. 171–72.

10 Sir Roger L'Estrange, *Fables of Aesop and other Eminent Mythologists with Morals and Reflections*, Part I, third edition (London, 1699), p. 20. Aesop becomes one of the two "Antient Chiefs" in Swift's *Battle*

of the Books (1710), as a direct result of Sir William Temple's remark in *An Essay upon Ancient and Modern Learning* (1690) that Aesop, for his *Fables*, has been agreed "by all ages since for the greatest master of his kind, and all others have been but imitations of his original" (see *Five Miscellaneous Essays by Sir William Temple*, ed. Samuel H. Monk [Ann Arbor, 1963], p. 64).

Ogilby's *Morall* (p. 36), like that of L'Estrange, is political also: "No government can th'unsettled vulgar please, / Whom change delights think quiet a disease, / Now Anarchie and Armies they maintain, / And wearied, are for Kings and Lords again." The lines to which Pope refers are: "Then all the bog / Proclame their King, and cry *Jove* save King Log."

11 *Dunciad*, Book I, ll. 58–68. All quotations from Pope's poetry are from *The Twickenham Edition of the Poems of Alexander Pope*, general editor John Butt, 11 vols. (London, 1939–69), and all quotations from *The Dunciad* are from the four-book version of 1743.

12 See Bacon, *Novum Organum*, I. CXV; Milton, *Of Education*; Cowley's poem "Life and Fame", and Swift's spider in *The Battle of the Books*, among many other examples.

13 The argument here is in the form of a suppressed topographical syllogism. The books written by the medieval scholastics are like flimsy intellectual cobwebs; second-hand bookshops are dusty and full of cobwebs; therefore the place for Scotus and Thomas Aquinas is in Duck Lane. Pope's animal imagery works in a similar way, combining the logic of argument with the associations of imagery.

14 *The Words of the King of Brobdingnag*, ll. 31–4. It will be recalled that the King of Brobdingnag's contemptuous estimate of humanity (*Gulliver's Travels*, II, vi) ends with the words, "I cannot but conclude the Bulk of your Natives, to be the most pernicious Race of little odious Vermin that Nature ever suffered to crawl upon the Surface of the Earth."

15 Pope's image of the amphisbaena works in this way: see above, note 1. The subjects of Pope's cultural bestiary in *The Dunciad* retorted in kind, of course, and with cruel accuracy. Curll's *Farmer Pope and his Son* (1728) attacked Pope as "A little scurvy, purblind-Elf; / Scarce like a Toad, much less himself. / Deform'd in Shape, of Pigmy Stature; / A proud conceited, peevish Creature". Ned Ward's *Apollo's Maggots in his Cups* (1729) included such details as "A frightful indigested Lump, / With here a Hollow, there a Hump". See J. V. Guerinot, *Pamphlet Attacks on Alexander Pope 1711–1744* (London, 1969), pp. 155, 177–78 *et passim*. My point is that Pope, unlike his detractors, generally employs such beast metaphors not only for purposes of abuse but also as indicators of moral collapse, in the sense that Pope's notion of a public cultural disorder is a consequence of an individual confusion of genres, standards and motives.

16 For the correlation of animals and writers, see Edna L. Steeves, ed., *The Art of Sinking in Poetry* (New York, 1952), pp. 111 and ff. It has been recently suggested that "A. P." may not only apply to Ambrose

Philips, but also to Pope himself. In which case *"a heavy Lump"* may allude to Pope's spinal disorder. See Pat Rogers, "Of Torts and Tortoises", *The Scriblerian*, VI, 2 (1974), 104–5.

17 Johnson informed Boswell that swallows "conglobulate together" and hibernate in the beds of rivers (*Boswell's Life of Johnson*, ed. R. W. Chapman [London, 1904], p. 393); Gilbert White's entry for 4 November, 1767 suggest that there could be truth in this "strange" opinion (*The Natural History of Selborne*, 1788); Defoe believed that they migrated to warmer climates, but his tutor, Charles Morton, suggested in 1703 that swallows migrated to the moon in winter; White's twelfth-century Latin bestiary stated all along that swallows in fact migrate "overseas".

18 Fussell, *op. cit.*, p. 241.

19 *The Consolation of Philosophy*, translated by S. J. Tester, Loeb Classical Library (London and Cambridge, Mass., 1973), p. 335.

20 For the relationship between Pope's Sporus and the real Lord Hervey, see Robert Halsband, "Sporus, or Lord Hervey," *TLS*, 15 September, 1972, pp. 1069–70. Sporus's hermaphroditism, and most of his other attributes, have no exact correspondence with the historical truth, it would seem: a fact which does not detract in any way from the moral force of Pope's portrait.

21 See J. M. Evans, *Paradise Lost and the Genesis Tradition* (Oxford, 1968), pp. 46–8, and Howard Erskine-Hill, *The Social Milieu of Alexander Pope* (New Haven and London, 1975), pp. 257–59)

22 *The Works of Samuel Johnson*, ed. Arthur Murphy, 12 vols. (London, 1806), VIII, 42.

23 *Ibid.*, p. 42.

24 Lucretius, *The Nature of the Universe*, translated by R. E. Latham (London, 1951), pp. 188, 189.

25 *Histoire Naturelle*, vol. 4 (1753), p. 383: cited in and translated by A. O. Lovejoy, "Buffon and the Problem of Species", *Forerunners of Darwin: 1745–1859*, ed. Bentley Glass and others (Baltimore, 1959), reprinted in the Bobbs-Merrill Reprint series HS-46, p. 97.

26 *Ibid.*, p. 98.

27 James Burnett, Lord Monboddo, *Origin and Progress of Language* (1773), I, 271, 311: quoted Lovejoy, *op. cit.*, p. 47.

Notes on Contributors

J. PHILIP BROCKBANK is a graduate of Trinity College, Cambridge, and Professor of English at the University of York. He has previously held posts at the Universities of Saarbrücken, Cambridge and Reading. His published work includes a commentary on Marlowe's *Dr. Faustus*, a number of articles on Shakespeare and other Renaissance poets, editions of Jonson's *Volpone* and Shakespeare's *Coriolanus*, and an anthology of Pope's poems. He is general editor of the forthcoming New Cambridge Shakespeare.

HOWARD ERSKINE-HILL is editor of Pope, Horatian *Satires and Epistles* (1964), and author of *Pope: The Dunciad* (1972), *The Social Milieu of Alexander Pope* (1975) and numerous articles on seventeenth- and eighteenth-century subjects. He is a graduate of Nottingham University, and taught English at University College Swansea from 1960 to 1969, when he became University Lecturer in English at Cambridge and Fellow of Jesus College.

ROBIN GROVE is a Senior Lecturer in English at the University of Melbourne. First trained as a musician, he was awarded the A.B.C. Orchestral Composition Prize in 1957 before entering Melbourne University to study English and Philosophy. Since 1963 he has been a frequent contributor to *The Critical Review* and other periodicals on subjects as diverse as Greek drama, Romantic poetry, opera, and ballet. His work in theatre and music continues, and he is a Director of the State company, Ballet Victoria.

I. D. MacKILLOP is a lecturer in English Literature at the University of Sheffield. Worked on neo-classic literary criticism in France and England in the seventeenth century. Edited *Delta, a Literary Review* 1960–72 in which and elsewhere he has published on varied non-Augustan subjects. Currently writing on the "ethical movement" in Edwardian England.

231

DAVID B. MORRIS is a graduate of Hamilton College and the University of Minnesota, and is currently Professor of English and Director of Doctoral Programs in English at the University of Iowa. He has held a NEH Younger Humanist Fellowship (1972) and a Guggenheim Fellowship (1976), and has published *The Religious Sublime: Christian Poetry and Critical Tradition in 18th Century England*, as well as numerous articles on seventeenth- and eighteenth-century literature.

CLIVE T. PROBYN is a lecturer in English and Chairman of the School of English at Lancaster University. He is British Editor of *The Scriblerian*, contributing editor of a companion volume in the Vision Critical Studies series on Jonathan Swift (1978), author of several articles on Swift, Pope, the Earl of Burlington, Johnson, and of the Introduction to the Everyman *Gulliver's Travels* (1975), and of *Jonathan Swift: the Contemporary Background* (Manchester University Press, 1978). He has recently been appointed Professor of English in a new university in Nigeria.

PAT ROGERS has taught at the Universities of Cambridge, London, and Wales, and is now Professor of English at the University of Bristol. His books include *Grub Street* (1972); *Defoe: The Critical Heritage* (1972); *The Augustan Vision* (1974), and *An Introduction to Pope* (1976). He has published essays on Pope in *Literary English Since Shakespeare* (1970); *Writers and Their Background: Alexander Pope* (1972), and *Augustan Worlds* (1978). He is now editing Swift for the Penguin English Poets and completing a life of Fielding. He is also engaged on a study of Pope's subscription public.

FELICITY ROSSLYN is engaged in research work at Newnham College, Cambridge, on the making of Pope's *Iliad* translation. From 1972–1974 she was a Frank Knox Fellow at Harvard.

FRANK STACK is a graduate of the universities of Durham and York, and now lectures in English at the University of Southampton.

SIMON VAREY is a graduate of St. Catherine's College, Cambridge, where he wrote his dissertation on "*The Craftsman* 1726–1752: An Historical and Critical Account," and now lectures in English in the University of Utrecht.

JAMES A. WINN is the author of *A Window in the Bosom: The Letters of Alexander Pope* and of articles on Milton and Faulkner. He is Assistant Professor in English at Yale University, which has awarded him a Morse Junior Faculty Fellowship in support of his current project, a book on music and literature.

Index

Restriction of space precludes a full index of literary names. Only the more significant have been included; and none has been included which is referred to only in the notes.